ENDORSEMENT

Finally, an in-depth look at biblical prophecy in relation to the Bahá'í Writings by a well-informed Bahá'í author! While Mirza Abu'l-Faḍl Gulpáygání (1844-1914) covered this range of literature in his talks, and was largely responsible for the conversion of many Persian Jews to the Faith of Bahá'u'lláh, he did not commit to writing most of what he knew, at least that we have access to in English translation. After him, Haj Mehri Arjmand (1870-1941) was known for his immense learning success in convincing Persian Jews to embrace the Bahá'í Faith. He was a prolific author, but his writings have not yet been translated into English. Most of what English-speaking Bahá'ís knew about the prophetic literature of the Bible as referred to in the Bahá'í Writings was communicated in fragmentary fashion by some early American authors whose books are no longer in print. Then, in a systematic work that was responsible for many people becoming Bahá'ís, William Sears wrote *Thief in the Night*. However, Sears did not intend to provide an in-depth look at all of the prophecies found in the Old Testament.

Ms. Maddocks may well be the first Bahá'í author to attempt a comprehensive survey of the Old Testament. She has wisely separated her narrative into manageable volumes, as the topic can be quite overwhelming, especially for the uninitiated. Her sources are clearly cited, and her correlations between academic literature including accounts of archaeological discoveries and the Bahá'í teachings are well reasoned. Any Bahá'í with an interest in how the books of the Hebrew Bible are cited and explained in the Bahá'í writings should begin here. And any Jew or Christian with an interest in exploring an alternative approach both to contemporary academic and traditional interpretations could also fruitfully read this third as well as the first and second volumes of *The Coming of the Glory: How the Hebrew Scriptures Reveal the Plan of God.*

Peter Terry
https://independent.academia.edu/PeterTerry
https://bahai-library.com/author/Peter+Terry

BOOKS
BY EILEEN MADDOCKS

1844: Convergence in Prophecy for Judaism, Christianity, Islam and the Bahá'í Faith (2018)

The Coming of the Glory: How the Hebrew Scriptures Reveal the Plan of God, Vol. I, Göbekli Tepe to Elijah (2020)

The Coming of the Glory: How the Hebrew Scriptures Reveal the Plan of God, Vol. II, The Preexilic Years: Amos to Jeremiah (2022)

The Coming of the Glory: How the Hebrew Scriptures Reveal the Plan of God, Vol. III, The Exilic and Postexilic Years: Ezekiel to Malachi (2024)

Printed in the United States of America
First Printing: 2024

ISBN (paperback): 978-1-954102-17-0
ISBN (ebook): 978-1-954102-21-7
Library of Congress Control Number: 2020935114

Edited by Beth Rule
Cover design by Dragan Bilic
Interior design by Amit Dey

Published by:
SOMETHING OR OTHER PUBLISHING LLC
Brooklyn, Wisconsin 53521
For general inquiries: Info@SOOPLLC.com
For bulk orders: Orders@SOOPLLC.com

The
COMING
— of the —
GLORY

How the Hebrew Scriptures Reveal the Plan of God

VOLUME III
THE EXILIC AND POSTEXILIC YEARS:
EZEKIEL TO MALACHI

EILEEN MADDOCKS

DEDICATION

Writing four books during a ten-year stretch has been comforting and inspiring, exhilarating and soul-satisfying. It has also been a lonely road. Unless an author has a co-writer or ghostwriter, they work alone. They face the blank screen in solitary silence and wonder if a career change might be in order.

Being an independent researcher and writer has meant working solo. However, I've had the love, help, and emotional support of my sister Geraldine Maddocks Whitfield during this lengthy journey. Although we live three thousand miles apart, we've together been through computer breakdowns and illnesses as well as the highs and lows of life. She's seen me through four books, reviewed my work, and called out some embarrassing mistakes with priceless comments like, "What are you trying to say?" She's been more supportive and steadfast than any muse.

I dedicate this book to Geraldine.

CONTENTS

FOREWORD

With pleasure I write this foreword for *The Coming of the Glory: How the Hebrew Scriptures Reveal the Plan of God* trilogy by Eileen Maddocks, concluding with Volume III. This trilogy of hers is a remarkable achievement in biblical scholarship.

Shared interest in biblical prophecies has brought Eileen and me together. Her interest is prophecies in the Hebrew Bible. My interest is prophecies in the Apocalypse (book of Revelation). My Anglican schooling made the Old Testament required reading for study of the New Testament. It focused from Adam to David in the Torah and their monotheism. Its riveting stories were spiced with juicy reports of high-level deceit, betrayal, assassination, retribution, adultery, and incest! No surprise, then, that interest in other Old Testament books faded. They were mere background material. Apart from sporadic memorable prophetic wording or prediction, all they seemed to report was less than holy tribes fighting or being soothed and scolded by their prophets.

The trilogy by Eileen has changed all this! Her systematic work draws on extensive research into the Hebrew Bible prophets and prophecies from Genesis to Malachi. Each prophet she intimately fleshes out as a real-life person, as meticulously as possible. She determines when he lived, where he came from, and whom his prophecies calmed or alarmed. Her rich mosaic of historical and religious research combines comprehensive geographic, archaeological, military, linguistic, economic, and mythological inputs. It leaves no stone unturned or narrative thread unexplained. It explores how prophecies unveiled divine plans that for millennia guided and comforted Hebrews, Israelites, and Jews. They foresaw events up to twenty-five centuries ahead. Eileen's profound work deepens understanding of particular prophecies that predict the advents of Jesus, Muḥammad, the Báb, and Bahá'u'lláh and their Faiths. It complements similar prophecies examined by my own *Apocalypse Secrets: Baha'i Interpretation of the Book of Revelation*.

Eileen rightly prefers the term *Hebrew Bible* instead of *Old Testament*. After all, Hebrew is the prime language in which it was written. And, as the *Hebrew Bible*, it does more than augur the New Testament of Jesus. It further foretells the Revelations of Muḥammad, the Báb, and Bahá'u'lláh. At the same time, it involves not just Hebrews. Its religious story involves a whole tribal continuum comprising Hebrews, Israelites, and Jews. Serially they evolved the Faiths of Adam, Noah, and Abraham through to the Torah Faith of Moses and Judaism. Although some biblical texts muddle these tribal names, each did exist in a sequential span of time.

Except for one, Eileen presents 'her' prophets chronologically. Volume I discusses Hebrew and Israelite prophets in the Torah up to Elijah in the Books of Kings. Volume II examines Israelite and Jewish prophets facing Assyrian and Babylonian invasions as divine punishments. Volume III deals with Jews and prophets exiled in Babylon and their return to Jerusalem through Malachi, and concludes with Daniel.

Eileen's dedicated scholarship shows Hebrew Bible prophecies as quite significant for today's world. Her insightful explanatory apparatus sheds fascinating new light on the Hebrew Bible's extensive imagery and symbolism. It reveals ancient prophecies as spiritual treasures and mysteries relevant to our lives. The web she weaves braids clarity and prescience into prophecies from a time of idolatry through to a time of exile. Her material is enjoyable to read and easy to understand. Anecdotes bring it to life. Her clear engaging style connects the dots between complex ideas with impressive ease. Every page testifies to her meticulous attention to detail. Her commitment to truth shines throughout. Nor does she shy away from exploring alternative interpretations or from challenging conventional wisdom or dogma.

Eileen's list of Hebrew Bible prophets has a dramatic finale. It ends with noble Daniel, as an exception out of exact chronological sequence. Daniel is unique in that five of his many prophetic visions are special time-prophecies. Each prophesies both an event and also codifies a specific year for the fulfillment of the event. Time-specific prophecies also serve as litmus tests. Their very precision enhances the scriptures that contain them. This, in turn, validates other prophecies in the same scriptures, in particular those in the books of Daniel and Revelation. While many prophecies in the Hebrew Bible foretell the advents of Jesus, Muḥammad, the Báb, and Bahá'u'lláh, only the time-prophecies of Daniel say when.

In conclusion, I wholeheartedly recommend Eileen Maddocks' trilogy and her Volume III. Her profound and comprehensive trilogy assiduously endorses religious Revelators as messengers who connect us humans with the unknowable Infinite Force we call God. Her work will prove an invaluable resource of guidance and inspiration for all to know the Hebrew Bible better.

John Able
Author, *Apocalypse Secrets*

INTRODUCTION

W elcome back, readers of Volumes I and II of *The Coming of the Glory: How the Hebrew Scriptures Reveal the Plan of God.* This third volume can be read as a standalone; however, you are urged to read the first two because they give explanations of many concepts that will not be repeated here. Instead, references will be given to the volume, chapter, and page for previously written discourses on various subjects.

This trilogy started with exploring the post-Ice Age evolution of human spiritual consciousness suggested by excavations of the Paleolithic hunter-gatherer site Göbekli Tepe, in today's southeastern Turkey, and the Neolithic site Çatalhöyük, located in south-central Turkey. Most probably, the swift advances in human consciousness and civilization indicated by these archeological sites in the ancient Near East were triggered by divine Messengers whose names have been lost to history. The rapid advancement of the culture and civilization of the Mesopotamian city-states along the Tigris and Euphrates Rivers seems to have been triggered by the advent of the Prophet Adam.[1] Progress continued with the missions and legacies of Noah, Abraham, and Moses. According to Bahá'í understanding, these were Prophets of God sent to educate humanity. The days of the judges, with the emergence of the schools of the prophets, were the first phase of Israelite settlement in Canaan. Then came the rise of the united kingdom of Israel with its first three kings—Saul, David, and Solomon—and the subsequent split into two kingdoms, the northern Kingdom of Israel and the southern

Kingdom of Judah. The early Israelite prophets warned the Israelite kings of the errors of their ways, usually to no avail.

The first volume also covered the three Central Figures of the Bahá'í Faith—the Báb, Bahá'u'lláh, and 'Abdu'l-Bahá—as well as Shoghi Effendi, the Guardian of the Bahá'í Faith. The concepts of the divine seasons and cycles were also clarified.

The first volume ended with the *still small voice* heard by the prophet Elijah on Mount Sinai. The Israelite perception of God as a "storm god" in the Mesopotamian tradition was evidenced by Mount Sinai covered with billowing smoke while the mountain trembled violently, with the sound of a trumpet for further effect (Exodus 19:18-19), when Moses ascended the mount to receive the Ten Commandments. Elijah had rather noisily summoned God to light his altar when he confronted the priests of Baal. But towards the end of his ministry, Elijah heard the voice of God within himself, as did the Hebrew prophets who followed him.

The second volume reviewed the split of the united kingdom into the two kingdoms of Israel and Judah. As recipients of the most recent dispensation from God, the Israelites of the united kingdom had the most spiritually advanced civilization in the Near East. They experienced the spring and summer of the Mosaic Dispensation.

The emergence of the writing prophets, that is, those prophets who have their own books in the Hebrew Bible, was a unique phenomenon in religious history. The Hebrew prophets emerged for many reasons, the foremost one being an attempt to counter the decline of the Mosaic teachings. Most Israelites had not fully embraced monotheism and showed signs of sliding into the spiritual fall and winter seasons common to religious movements. These prophets worked tirelessly to steer the Israelites from monolatry and idolatry to monotheism. The core aspect of their missions was to renew the spiritual essence of the Mosaic Dispensation.

Individual sensitivity to the divine voice developed within the Mosaic Dispensation, partly because only three methods of prophecy and divination were endorsed—the use of the Urim and Thummim by the high priest, who kept them in his breast piece over his heart, and through dreams and visions, neither of which came on demand. It was an extraordinary occurrence that the voice of the Divine flowed through those souls known as the Hebrew prophets for over three hundred years and that their words were preserved throughout the centuries.

Volume II includes an exposition on the unique aspects of the canonical Hebrew prophets. Prophethood was hardly a career choice for them. Unlike those prophets who were trained in schools for the prophets to serve the royal court or the Temple priesthood, the canonical prophets were chosen by God and could only utter or write what He gave them. Most of the prophets seem to have arisen to their missions immediately after receiving their call. A few first protested before obeying their call.

Amos and Hosea, who were both active in the northern kingdom of Israel, and First Isaiah and Micah in the southern kingdom of Judah, warned the people in no uncertain terms about the consequences of their idolatry and unfaithfulness to the Revelation of Moses. They warned of the divine punishment that would fall upon them. Punishment was indeed inflicted upon them in the form of the Assyrian conquest of the northern kingdom in 722 BCE. This catastrophe left the southern kingdom of Judah on its own with only two of the original twelve tribes of Israel, but also with the city of Jerusalem, the Temple of Solomon, and the Davidic kings.

The other preexilic prophets—Zephaniah, Nahum, Habakkuk, and Jeremiah—counseled and warned their kings, priests, and people of defeat at the hands of the Babylonian empire as divine retribution for disobedience to the spiritual laws of the Mosaic Covenant. This happened in 586 BCE.

This third volume covers the exilic, apocalyptic prophets Daniel and Ezekiel, and the prophets Second and Third Isaiah, Obadiah, First and Second Zechariah, Haggai, Joel, and Malachi, as well as the return to Jerusalem. A basic history of ancient Israel continues to be woven throughout the saga of the prophets, aided by timeline charts. The prophets' missions were so entwined with Israelite history that they must first be understood within that context before following the leaps into the far future. The prophets' missions and Israelite history are presented chronologically and systematically. The common thread running through all the prophets' missions is that they all foresaw the coming of the Báb and Bahá'u'lláh and the days we are now in.

BIBLE AUTHENTICITY

It's wise to ask when embarking on a study of the Bible, "How authentic is the Bible?" One hint is the inscription made by 'Abdu'l-Bahá in a Bible in a London church. Abdu'l-Bahá visited London in 1911 and gave his first public address at the City Temple to a Western audience of about two thousand individuals. Upon leaving the church, He inscribed in a Bible that had been used by generations of preachers the following words in His native Persian, as translated: *THIS book is the Holy Book of God, of celestial Inspiration. It is the Bible of Salvation, the Noble Gospel. It is the mystery of the Kingdom and its light. It is the Divine Bounty, the sign of the guidance of God. 'Abdu'l-Bahá 'Abbás."* [2]

'Abdu'l-Bahá also wrote, *"The Bible and the Gospels are most honored in the estimation of all Baha'is. One of the spiritual utterances of His Holiness Christ in his Sermon on the Mount is preferable to me to all the writings of the philosophers. It is the religious duty of every Baha'i to read and comprehend the meanings of the Old and New Testament."* [3] We need to take to heart His admonishment, *"You must know the Old and New Testaments as the Word of God."* [4]

'Abdu'l-Bahá clarified the authenticity of the Torah, the first five books of the Hebrew Bible, when He wrote, *"Know ye that the Torah is that which was revealed in the Tablets to Moses, may peace be upon Him, or that to which He was bidden. But the stories are historical narratives and were written after Moses, may peace be upon Him."* [5] He also said, *"The only true Explainer of the Book of God is the Holy Spirit, for no two minds are alike, no two can comprehend alike, no two can speak alike. That is to say, from the mere human standpoint of interpretation there could be neither truth nor agreement."* [6]

Validation and caution are rolled together when perusing 'Abdu'l-Bahá's statement, *"The Words of God have innumerable significances and mysteries of meanings—each one a thousand and more."*[7] This is a warning not to argue about the meanings of biblical verses but to keep an open mind and investigate more deeply. Shoghi Effendi noted, "Except for what has been explained by Bahá'u'lláh and 'Abdu'l-Bahá, we have no way of knowing what various symbolic allusions in the Bible mean." [8] The Universal House of Justice (see Appendix C) reinforced trust in the Bible by providing assurance about the divine care and protection it had been given:

> The Bahá'ís believe that God's Revelation is under His care and protection and that the essence, or essential elements, of what His Manifestations intended to convey has been recorded and preserved in Their Holy Books. However, as the sayings of the ancient Prophets were written down sometime later, we cannot categorically state, as we do in the case of the Writings of Bahá'u'lláh, that the words and phrases attributed to Them are Their exact words.[9]

This care and protection may have included the legacies of the Hebrew prophets who spoke for God and whose divinely inspired words have spoken to hearts and minds for thousands of years. They not only labored to renew the Mosaic Revelation, but they also foretold future Revelations.

The scholar Michael Sours commented on Bahá'u'lláh's admonition to reflect on scriptural words. The background was that Bahá'u'lláh was commenting on the denial of Christianity by the Arabs of Muḥammad's day by claiming that the Bible had been corrupted. Sours wrote:

> In defending the Pentateuch and the Gospel, Bahá'u'lláh writes: "Reflect: the words of the verses themselves eloquently testify to the truth that they are of God." [*The Kitáb-i-Íqán*, no. 91, 84v] This statement need not be misunderstood as simply meaning that the scriptures make claims, but rather, the intrinsic spiritual authority of the verses is self-evident. There is something about the verses which indicate that they

are "of God." They are not verses originating from people seeking self-interest or trying to enhance their material prosperity. The verses are not from some evil source intending to mislead people. The verses are "of God" by their very nature. They reveal the nature and will of God, God's redemptive activity in the world. They tell us how to draw close to God. In such ways, the verses eloquently testify that they are of God. The more a person seeks to know God's will and to commune with God, the more that person will be able to discern that the verses are of God.[10]

In the final analysis, solid ground for the authenticity of biblical interpretations from a Bahá'í perspective can only be found in the Bahá'í scriptures. That is why this trilogy is "heavy" with scriptural quotations. A certain level of deduction, that is, the deriving of a conclusion by reasoning, can sometimes lead to valid interpretations. But the slippery slope of syllogism awaits, that is, a crafty or subtle argument that leads to a specious conclusion.

DIVINE TIME

An aid to understanding the prophetic verities in the Bible is an understanding of divine time, God's time. In short, our concept of time is severely limited. The legitimacy of biblical prophecies can best be understood within the sphere of divine time, which 'Abdu'l-Bahá described as follows:

In the world of God, there is no past, present, or future: All of these are one. So when Christ said, "In the beginning was the Word,"[a] *He meant that it was, is, and shall be; for in the world of God there is no time. Time holds sway over the creatures but not over God.*

---

[a] John 1:1

So in the prayer where Christ says, "Hallowed be Thy name",[b] *the meaning is that Thy name was, is, and shall be hallowed. Again, morning, noon, and evening exist in relation to the earth, but in the sun there is neither morning, nor noon, nor evening.*[11]

We depend on linear time to understand our material world and to live our lives. However, linear time does not apply to the mind of God. 'Abdu'l-Bahá sympathized with our problem of understanding the idea of no past, present, or future. *"Know that it is one of the most abstruse questions of divinity that the world of existence—that is, this endless universe—has no beginning."*[12] He elaborated on this concept when He wrote:

For God the beginning and the end are one and the same. Similarly, the reckoning of days, weeks, months, and years—of yesterday and today—is made with respect to the earth; but in the sun such things are unknown: There is neither yesterday, nor today, nor tomorrow, neither months nor years—all are equal. Likewise, the Word of God is sanctified above all these conditions and exalted beyond every law, constraint, or limitation that may exist in the contingent world.[13]

Does prophecy of an event cause its fulfillment? 'Abdu'l-Bahá said it does not. *"The knowledge of a thing is not the cause of its occurrence; for the essential knowledge of God encompasses the realities of all things both before and after they come to exist, but it is not the cause of their existence. This is an expression of the perfection of God."*[14]

People often ask, how can anyone know the future? Yet, to one extent or another, each of us taps into the future while dreaming. Bahá'u'lláh wrote that when our spirits transcend *"the limitations of sleep"* and detach from *"all earth attachment,"* we are free to travel throughout *"a realm*

---

[b] Matthew 6:9, Luke 11:2

which lieth hidden in the innermost reality of this world." We may have puzzling experiences in that realm and wake up confused and disregard the fragmentary memories, but Bahá'u'lláh advised, *"Do thou meditate on that which We have revealed unto thee, that thou mayest discover the purpose of God, thy Lord, and the Lord of all worlds. In these words the mysteries of Divine Wisdom have been treasured."* [15]

'Abdu'l-Bahá summarized the dream state quite succinctly: *"Awake, the eye sees only a short distance, but in the realm of dreams one who is in the East may see the West. Awake, he sees only the present; in sleep he beholds the future."* [16]

WRITING AND EDITING CONSIDERATIONS

Every effort was made to provide the context for all cited verses within their sources, within the continuity of the Hebrew experience and the socioeconomic conditions of the times. Excerpts from Bahá'í texts are provided to enhance understanding of various prophetic utterances. My own opinions are noted as such.

Unless mentioned otherwise, the New International Version (NIV) of the Bible is used throughout. The title Hebrew Bible is used instead of the Old Testament because it is more accurate and respectful. The Old Testament is only *old* when it is paired with the New Testament and when its relevance is considered secondary to the coming of Jesus. As you progress through the volumes, you will discover how relevant the Hebrew Bible is to our times.

The acronyms BCE (before the Common Era) and CE (Common Era) are used instead of BC and AD.

Quotations from the Sacred Scriptures of all faiths are given in italics, including those from the three Central Figures of the Bahá'í Faith—the Báb, Bahá'u'lláh, and 'Abdu'l-Bahá. For Bahá'ís, the writings of the Central Figures are considered authoritative, as are those of Shoghi Effendi and the Universal House of Justice. All other interpretations of Scripture presented here are matters of opinion, offered as contributions to discussion, thought, and understanding.

The book of Exodus introduces the term Yahweh (YHWH) for God, which was used for several centuries. I've used Yahweh in a few places, especially in the chapter on monolatry. Otherwise, I've used God for consistency, with the understanding that God and Yahweh are interchangeable.

The ancient people whose history the Hebrew Bible tells are called Israelites; Israelis, in contrast, are citizens of the modern state of Israel. The term *Jews* did not come into use until postexilic times when the former kingdom of Judah became the Persian province of Yehud.

The Prophets of God are also called Manifestations and Mirrors. The Prophets of God are referred to as Prophets with a capital "P." A small "p" indicates the classical prophets. Pronouns referring to the Prophets and the central figures of the Bahá'í Faith are also capitalized.

Concerning the dates of the prophets, it is immensely helpful that many of their books contain time markers, such as Daniel serving the Babylonian rulers Nebuchadnezzar II and Belshazzar. The days of the prophet Haggai were definitively given: *"In the second year of King Darius, on the first day of the sixth month, the word of the Lord came through the prophet Haggai to Zerubbabel"* (Haggai 1:1). Most conveniently for biblical scholars, Haggai continued to state exactly, to the day, when he received the word of the Lord. The prophet of Second Isaiah acknowledged the Persian King Cyrus II as God's *anointed* (Isaiah 45:1) who would enable the Jews to return to Jerusalem, thus indicating that he was a prophet of exilic times. Others have few or no historical markers by which to date them, such as Joel and Malachi.

Unfamiliarity with the Hebrew Bible is not a barrier to understanding this trilogy. Readers are encouraged to keep a Bible handy or to refer to Bible Gateway online (www.biblegateway.com). I also encourage the use of The Bible Project website (https://bibleproject.com) which has over one hundred and fifty visual presentations with dialogues about the books of the Bible and a variety of biblical subjects. Each of the Hebrew prophets has a separate presentation.

CHART OF THE EXILIC
AND POSTEXILIC
HEBREW PROPHETS

Exilic	Prophets	Approximate Dates
	Daniel	606-534 BCE
	Ezekiel	596-574 BCE
Babylonian	Second Isaiah	No dates available, lived in the exile
	Obadiah	Early sixth century, soon after the fall of Jerusalem in 586 BCE

Postexilic	Prophets	Approximate Dates
	Haggai	Late sixth century
	First Zechariah	520-518 BCE, the second year of the reign of Darius through his fourth year
	Third Isaiah	About 520 to 500 BCE, or later
Persian	Second Zechariah	Fifth century BCE, perhaps a century after First Zechariah
	Joel	Late fifth century BCE or possibly early fourth
	Third Zechariah	Fourth century BCE, perhaps a century after Second Zechariah
	Malachi	Mid-fifth century BCE or possibly later

MAP OF
THE BABYLONIAN EXILE

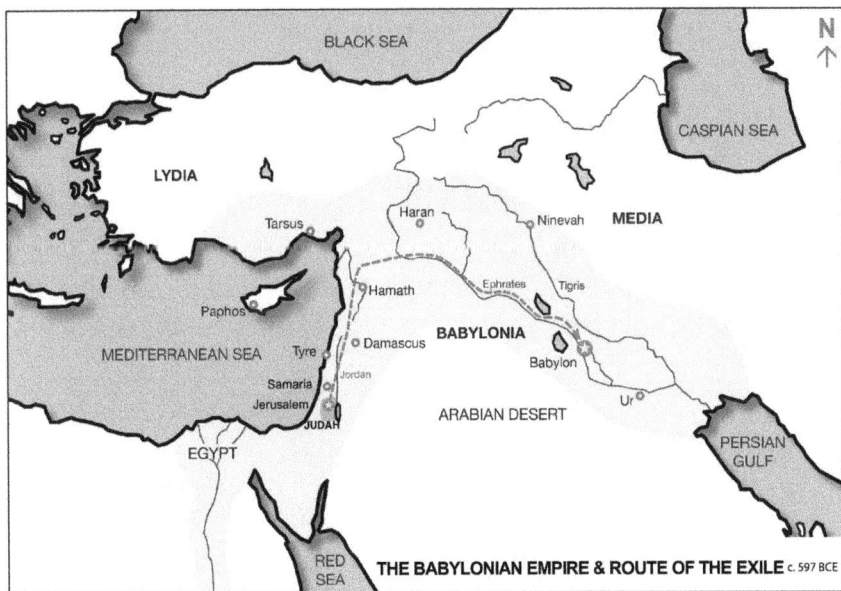

BLACK SEA

CASPIAN SEA

LYDIA

Tarsus

Haran

Ninevah

MEDIA

Hamath

Ephrates

Tigris

Paphos

MEDITERRANEAN SEA

Tyre

Damascus

BABYLONIA

Babylon

Samaria

Jordan

Jerusalem

JUDAH

ARABIAN DESERT

Ur

EGYPT

PERSIAN GULF

RED SEA

THE BABYLONIAN EMPIRE & ROUTE OF THE EXILE c. 597 BCE

Chapter 1

BIBLICAL CRITICISM AND ARCHAEOLOGY

"Ask and it will be given to you; seek and you will find;
knock and the door will be opened to you."

Matthew 7:7

B ackground and context are vital to understanding the spiritual journey of the Israelites. Therefore, before discussing those fascinating exilic prophets Ezekiel and Daniel, we will examine the intriguing contributions of biblical criticism and archaeology, the land of Canaan and Canaanite religious culture, and the complicated tension between monotheism and monolatry. Yes, it sounds like a history lesson is coming—but it's a captivating one.

The Bible has been the foundation of Western civilization. It was the accepted authority and basis for belief in the West since the early days of conversion of the European pagan tribes to Christianity. Christian monks and missionaries spread their faith throughout Europe. In time, the Catholic Church attained power and wealth that made monarchs tremble. In turn, the Protestant Reformation gave the Catholic

Church reasons to tremble. But the Hebrew Bible and the New Testament remained foremost in Western consciousness.

The Enlightenment, or the Age of Reason, was an intellectual and philosophical movement of the seventeenth and eighteenth centuries that developed in Europe and spread to North America. This movement broke with the tradition of total, literal reliance on the Bible and dependence on ecclesiastical authority. It promoted the pursuit of knowledge on an individual basis through rational thought and the evidence of the physical senses rather than faith. The Enlightenment promoted the happiness of the individual and progressive concepts such as liberty, progress, human fraternity, constitutional government, and the lessening of ecclesiastical influence on society. This movement opened the door to skepticism about the Bible, and in the nineteenth century an area of study called biblical criticism emerged. It reflected a search for truth based on reason and new knowledge rather than tradition, and on a scholarly approach to studying, evaluating, and critically assessing the Bible to better understand it.

BIBLICAL CRITICISM

The term "biblical criticism" is misleading. It does not mean a focus on finding errors in the Bible. Instead, biblical criticism indicates the effort to use scientific criteria such as the physical sciences, historical and literary knowledge, and human reasoning to understand and explain as objectively as possible the intent of the biblical writers. A whole spectrum of critical methods could be used to evaluate the Bible texts. Even mathematics.

There are two divisions of biblical criticism called lower and higher. "Lower criticism, also called Textual criticism, generally asks questions having to do with the preservation and transmission of the biblical text, including in what manuscripts the text has been preserved, their dates, settings, and relationship to each other, and therefore what is the most reliable form of the text." [17] Lower criticism is generally concerned with the literary and historical aspects of biblical texts. Higher biblical criticism differs as follows:

> Higher criticism, arising from 19th century European rationalism, generally takes a secular approach asking questions regarding the origin and composition of the text, including when and where it originated, how, why, by whom, for whom, and in what circumstances it was produced, what influences were at work in its production, and what original oral or written sources may have been used in its composition; and the message of the text as expressed in its language, including the meaning of the words as well as the way in which they are arranged in meaningful forms of expression. The principles of higher criticism are based on reason rather than revelation and are also speculative by nature.[18]

Higher criticism also extends the search into disciplines such as studies in ancient Near Eastern history, linguistics, religions, and mythology. This field of study has used philology, the study of language and relationships within language families, to investigate when the books of the Hebrew Bible were committed to writing and what sources they might have been drawn upon.

There has been stress between the traditional, fundamentalist approach to the Bible and that of biblical criticism. By the early twentieth century, universities and seminaries started to teach biblical criticism, and Protestantism in general became more liberal, nontraditional, or modernist regarding the Bible. The conservative response was to take drastic action to reaffirm what they believed to be biblical and Christian truth.

The line of demarcation between the modernist approach to Protestantism and the conservative one was drawn by publication of the twelve-volume series *The Fundamentals: A Testimony to the Truth*.[19] This statement of theological belief in four volumes was issued from 1910 to 1915. Its purpose was to reinforce traditional Protestant theology with literal interpretation of the Bible, stressing its infallibility, and to issue the call for fundamentalist evangelicalism. *The Fundamentals* also endorsed the literal, imminent return of Jesus Christ, thereby joining with the Adventist churches in this doctrinal belief.

Despite this renewal of fundamentalist Protestantism, the Bible has been put on the defensive as western society and institutions crumble. Bible literacy has plunged and verses are too often derided instead of understood within their historical or social context. How often has the verse *eye for eye* (Exodus 21:24) been used to criticize Mosaic criminal law without understanding its vast improvement over its predecessor, the Hammurabi Code? [20]

ARCHAEOLOGY

There are two histories of ancient Israel, the textual and the material. These two run on parallel tracks as equal witnesses. Simply put, archaeology is the scientific study of the human past through examination of material remains. This approach is conducted through the recovery and analysis of material culture ranging from the walls and rooms of a city to the discovery of a coin or piece of jewelry.

Archaeology had initially been welcomed by fundamentalists as a method to prove the literal truth of the Bible, thus countering the scholarly findings of biblical criticism. The conservative approach to archaeology in the Holy Land has been called the "prove-the-Bible" faction. The first wave of archeologists in the Holy Land started arriving in the nineteenth century and was motivated to prove the Bible as literal truth. These early explorers and diggers tended to be Christian ministers and biblical enthusiasts, but amateurs in the field of archaeology, who often damaged their dig sites in ways that later impeded the work of trained archeologists. For example, the stratification of soils in a dig indicates the time frame in which artifacts are found, but this stratification was often ignored or, worse, destroyed. Field notes for discovered artifacts were inadequate and many artifacts were taken out of Palestine and are now mostly in museums without proper provenance.[c] Fortunately, this wave of primitive archaeology largely died out by the mid-twentieth century. The respected archeologist William G. Dever summarized this movement, and its demise, as follows:

> In the first place, the portraits of archaeology by some biblicists are caricatures, especially those of the "revisionists." This is largely because their target is an old-fashioned kind of prove-the-Bible "biblical archaeology" that was long ago discredited in *archaeological* circles.... [I]n the end, few mourned the passing of an amateur enterprise that had really been a branch of biblical studies. The term "biblical archaeology" now designated only the dialogue *between* archaeology and biblical studies, documenting the "coming of age" of archaeology, and biblical scholars cannot be excused for being unaware of the evolution of what is still a related discipline.[21]

Dever stated that archaeologists are sensitive to the many aspects of ancient life such as political events, socio-economic movements, development of technology, changes in culture, and so forth. He wrote, "It is clear that archaeologists *are* historians, simply students of human culture over long time spans, basing themselves mostly on material culture remains (although not excluding texts when they find them, since these are also artifacts)."[22]

Some of these early amateurs did make major contributions, though. In 1838, an American scholar of ancient languages named Edwin Robinson identified many biblical sites including Robinson's Arch, a monumental staircase carried by an unusually wide stone arch, which once stood at the southwestern corner of the Temple

---

[c] The term provenance means the chronology of ownership, custody, or location of an object.

Mount in Jerusalem. It supported a flight of stairs from a first century CE street to the Temple Mount at the southern end of the western retaining wall. Robinson was an expert in ancient languages and a professor of sacred literature at Andover Theological Seminary. He was accompanied by Eli Smith, an American Protestant missionary and scholar.

But ineptitude was widespread. Robinson also discovered King Hezekiah's tunnel, an engineering marvel, in 1838 but he didn't know what it was. In 1865, Charles Warren rediscovered the tunnel, noting the Siloam Pool at the south end, and realized that it was Hezekiah's tunnel. A few years later, a young boy found an inscription on the tunnel wall twenty feet from the southern end that came to be called the Siloam Inscription. This inscription confirmed the biblical account of Hezekiah's tunnel that was built to bring water into Jerusalem in case of an Assyrian siege. This 2,700-year-old-artifact was then stolen and sold to the Ottoman Empire. This priceless artifact was badly damaged when it was chiseled out of the tunnel wall, and it ended up in in the National Museum in Constantinople (Istanbul). In 2022, the Turkish government agreed to return the inscription to Israel in a reciprocal exchange.[23]

The Ottoman Empire recognized the value of Holy Land antiquities as taxable items and passed a law in 1884 that established national ownership over all artifacts in its empire. All artifacts discovered during excavations were to be Turkish property. Enforcing this law, though, was impossible. Early archaeologists became busy digging up artifacts and easily smuggling them out of Ottoman territory. Travelers and pilgrims did the same. An extensive criminal enterprise developed among the local people who stole objects from graves and excavations and sold them to smugglers, as well as the production of fakes for sale to gullible tourists.

After the defeat of the Ottomans at the end of World War I, the British enacted the Antiquities Proclamation of 1918 that endeavored to recognize and protect the cultural and religious heritage of the Holy Land. The British Mandate was established in 1922 and its oversight stressed legal factors rather than religious significance, policies that spurred archaeological excavations.

Untrained searchers and diggers were gradually replaced by university-educated, scientifically trained archaeologists, especially after the state of Israel was established in 1948. The state of Israel continued the Mandate's policies until the Antiquities Law of the State of Israel of 1978 was enacted and the Israel Antiquities Authority (IAA) was established with oversight from the Archaeological Council. Since then, applicants for excavation licenses in Israel have been required to possess solid credentials and to move through several government layers to obtain permission to conduct archaeological excavations. Strict, new standards for professional, responsible archaeology smoothed the way for a secular approach that combined biblical criticism with physical science and other objective evidence. Some archeological data supported biblical texts and other data did not.

There is still stress between Bible students and archaeologists. Secular archaeologists tend to see the Bible as a "closed book" but see their own discipline as "dynamic, making revolutionary, new discoveries daily" using scientific technologies for dating such as Carbon 14 and analyzing patina, the thin layer that forms on the surfaces of copper, brass, bronze, and other metals. As Dever states, the Bible is seen as "theocratic history" and archaeology as "secular history" of ancient Israel, with archaeology often "more realistic, more comprehensive, better balanced, and ultimately more satisfying." [24]

The prove-the-Bible faction is active online. The various sites offer conjecture of how supposed material evidence supports this or that in the Bible. Noah's ark is a favorite subject with its remains allegedly sighted on Mount Ararat. Scientific evidence is usually lacking to support these claims.

Over time, however, the relationship between biblical students and archaeologists has improved with respect for what each discipline can do best. Archaeology has provided much evidence for certain aspects of biblical historicity and has also refuted others. We will look at one example of each.

VALIDATION

The background to the first example is that some scholars have questioned whether King David was a historical figure. In 1993-94, archaeologists excavating at the site of the ancient city of Dan, located at the headwaters of the River Jordan, discovered a broken stone, approximately 32 cm high by 22 cm wide, with an Aramaic inscription on it. Dated to the ninth century BCE, well over a hundred years after David's reign, this stele fragment bore the inscription "bytdwd" (Beit David, or House of David). It records the victory of the King of Aram over the king of Israel and his ally, the king of the "House of David."

The Madain Project, whose purpose is to locate and identify the sites associated with Abrahamic faiths and conduct multidisciplinary and systematic study of these historical sites, posted an article on this stele that is excerpted as follows:

> Hazael (or more accurately, the unnamed king) boasts of his victories over the king of Israel and his ally the king of the "House of David" (bytdwd). It is considered the earliest widely accepted reference to the name David as the founder of a Judahite polity outside of the Hebrew Bible. Archaeologists and epigraphers put the earliest possible date at about 870 BCE, whilst the latest possible date is "less clear", although according to Lawrence J. Mykytiuk it could "hardly have been much later than 750." [25]

REFUTATION

It can be difficult for archaeology to refute biblical historicity because an apparent lack of evidence doesn't negate the possibility of such evidence being found later. Usually, a lack of evidence does not get the interest that revealed evidence does. However, in a few cases, a lack of evidence can constitute a major refutation. The archaeologist Lawrence E. Stager noted that some archaeologists had believed that excavations at sites thought to be identified with biblical Heshbon, Jericho,

Bethel, Ai, Lachish, Eglon, Debir, and Hazor supported the conquest of Canaan as reported in the book of Joshua, chapters 6-12, and the book of Judges, chapter 1. Stager addressed this viewpoint that widespread and synchronous destruction at many of these key cities buttressed the traditional belief that Israel swept into Canaan from the eastern desert and swiftly conquered city after city.[26] While acknowledging the dramatic cultural change that affected Canaan at the end of the Late Bronze Age (c. 1200 BCE), Stager set three criteria to make a persuasive archaeological case for the mass migration of peoples from one homeland to another, as follows:

1. The implanted culture must be distinguishable from the indigenous cultures in the new zones of settlement. If the intrusive group launches an invasion (as proponents of the Israelite "conquest" postulate), then there should be synchronous discontinuities, such as destruction layers, separating the previous "Canaanite" cultures from the newly established "Israelite" cultures in the zone of contention.

2. The homeland of the migrating/invading groups should be located, its material culture depicted, and temporal precedence established in its place of origin. In the case of invading Israel, this should be in Transjordan or in Egypt.

3. The route of migration/invasion should be traceable and examined for its archaeological, historical, and geographical plausibility. If the new immigrants took an overland route, the spatial and temporal distribution of the material culture should indicate the path and direction of large-scale migrations.[27]

Stager identified 31 sites that were named in the book of Joshua as having been conquered by the Israelites and presented his conclusions:

At Heshbon and Dibon, extensive excavations have uncovered no Late Bronze Age occupation, and only meager remains from Iron Age I. ...most of Transjordan was unoccupied when the Israelite invaders are said to have moved through these territories in the late thirteenth century BCE.

This miracle [fall of the walls of Jericho] has no archaeological reflex; in fact, there is little or no occupation at Jericho in the thirteenth century.

When Joshua and his troops moved farther west, up the wadi to Ai (Joshua 7:2-8:29), they ultimately scored a great victory over the king of Ai and the inhabitants of the city. But here again archaeology demonstrates that a tall tale is being told. Ai, whose name means the "ruin," had not been occupied during the second millennium. Its "ruins" dated from the latter part of the third millennium.[28]

Stager made two concessions to the conquest belief. He agreed that nearby Bethel had been put to the sword (Judges 1:22), confirmed by archaeology to have happened in the thirteenth century. Also, Hazor was burned to the ground (Joshua 11:10-13). Hazor was the largest city of Canaan, its inhabitants numbering twenty thousand or more. Since the only agents who claimed responsibility for destroying this Canaanite city were the Israelites, Stager saw no reason to deny them their claim.[29]

Stager believes that of the 31 cities said to be taken by the Israelites, only Bethel and Hazor meet criterion 1, and even there, it is debated whether their destruction occurred at the time of Joshua and the judges. "Thus, by the most generous interpretation of the archaeological data, the 'unified conquest' hypothesis fails to meet the minimal standards of criterion 1."[30] He finds that the biblical account of the Israelites being an outside force that conquers Canaan lacks evidence. "Perhaps, then, there is something to be said for a migration, if not an actual invasion, of Israelites into Canaan toward the end of the Bronze Age. For this more general explanation of culture change, variants of criteria 1 through 3 are still valid. They pertain to the other hypotheses concerning the emergence of early Israel as well." [31] After acknowledging the need to summarize new data in the archaeology of the Late Bronze Age and Early Iron Age that have emerged from later excavations, he adds a "zinger": "The evidence from language, costume, coiffure, and material remains suggest that the early Israelites were a rural subset of Canaanite culture and largely indistinguishable from Transjordanian rural cultures as well." [32] With just one sentence, he suggests that the early Israelites *emerged* from the land of Canaan.

YES/BUT

Sometimes archaeology concludes with a yes/but. An example of a mixed conclusion after exhaustive study is the following situation. In 2019, a Proto-Canaanite inscription was found on two joining pieces of a jug unearthed at Khirbet al-Ra'i, a site located three miles west of the ancient Israelite city of Lachish. The pieces were found in a level dated to the late twelfth or early eleventh century BCE, the time of the judges. The five letters that survived indicate the personal *Yrb'l* (Jerubba'al).[33] The fifth named judge in the book of Judges was Gideon, who had been surnamed Jerubba'al (Jerub-Baal).

By way of background before discussing Gideon's surname, the book of Judges states that after Joshua died, the Israelites served Baal and other gods of the people around them and forsook the Lord, the God of their ancestors. The Lord thereupon turned them over to their enemies. After they lost many battles and reached a point of great distress, the Lord raised up the judges. The succession of judges tried to guide the people from their evil ways, but the people rebelled. The Israelites were living among the Canaanites and *"took their daughters in marriage and gave their own daughters to their sons, and served their gods"* (Judges 3:6), which further reinforced paganism within family and tribe.

The first appointed judge was Othniel, who was followed by Ehud and Shamgar in the warrior-judge tradition. *"After Ehud came Shamgar son of Anath, who struck down six hundred Philistines with an oxgoad. He too saved Israel"* (Judges 3:31). The famous prophet and judge Deborah was next. She is remembered for having foreseen and masterminded the successful battle against Sisera, the army commander for Jabin, a Canaanite king who reigned in Hazor.

Then came Gideon. The Israelites had been oppressed by the Midianites for seven years when an angel of the Lord visited Gideon and told him to save Israel. Gideon protested; the Lord persisted. He was told to tear down his father's altar to Baal and build a proper altar for sacrifice of a bull using the burning wood of the Asherah pole. The next morning the people demanded Gideon's death, but his father intervened and replied to the hostile crowd: *"Are you going to plead Baal's cause? Are you trying to save him? Whoever fights for him shall be put to death by morning! If Baal really is a god, he can defend himself when someone breaks down his altar." So because Gideon broke down Baal's altar, they gave him the name Jerub-Baal that day, saying, "Let Baal contend with him"* (Judges 6:31-32).

Gideon was a successful warrior-judge. He is remembered for his 300 soldiers blowing trumpets to defeat the Midianites, who fled the noise in the middle of the night. Gideon's sword was immortalized. *"The three companies blew the trumpets and smashed the jars. Grasping the torches in their left hands and holding in their right hands the trumpets they were to blow, they shouted, 'A sword for the LORD AND FOR GIDEON!' While each man held his position around the camp, all the Midianites ran, crying out as they fled"* (Judges 7:20-21).

The above-cited article about the Jerub-Baal inscription from Khirbet al-Ra'i states that the personal name Jerub-Baal does not appear after the tenth century and, "It would be tempting to posit that this inscription is that of the biblical figure. After all, the chronological framework for this figure is the period of the judges, and so a time frame for him in the twelfth or eleventh century BCE (the date of the inscription) is entirely plausible." [34] However, for the inscription to be compelling, "the presence of a patronymic, title, or epithet (etc.) is necessary, even when the putative biblical and archeological time frames seem to correspond fairly nicely." [35]

Whether this inscription of Jerub-Baal pertained to Gideon will likely never be known. However, if it did not, this name on a pottery shard did indicate the custom of naming a child after a god, in this case Baal. This archeological discovery indicates monolatry, which is examined in Chapter 3.

A THIRD CONSIDERATION

The two traditional means of biblical research—the textual and the material—have been joined in this trilogy by a third, the Qur'án and the Bahá'í writings. The original, handwritten documents of the Central Figures of the Bahá'í Faith were authenticated either by seal or signature and are available to humanity today. This volume refers sparingly to the Qur'án because an in-depth inclusion would require yet another volume.

The Hebrew Bible is like the proverbial onion that must be peeled layer by layer to find its inner, deeper meanings. Many of the inner layers could not have been understood until after the advents of Jesus, Muḥammad, the Báb, and Bahá'u'lláh, and even after Bahá'í history unfolded in the nineteenth and twentieth centuries, as the prophecies of Daniel aptly demonstrate (see Chapter 18). No longer is the Bible a "closed book" as considered by many archaeologists but a living book that expands with our growing maturity of insight.

Sometimes wide variations of opinion occur between higher biblical criticism and archaeology. Fortunately, the third approach is now available but only if the sacred texts address the issue at hand. Even if they do, the results are not always quick fixes or shortcuts in the research process. For example, when 'Abdu'l-Bahá was asked the truth about Adam and his eating from the tree, He responded:

> If we were to take this account according to the literal meaning of the words, as indicated by their common usage, it would indeed be exceedingly strange, and human minds would be excused from accepting, affirming, or imagining it.... The account of Adam

and Eve, their eating from the tree, and their expulsion from Paradise, are therefore symbols and divine mysteries. They have all-embracing meanings and marvellous interpretations; but only the intimates of the divine mysteries and the well-favoured of the all-sufficing Lord are aware of the true significance of these symbols.[36]

'Abdu'l-Bahá explained that the verses of the Torah about Adam, Eve, and the Garden of Eden have numerous meanings, and He gave one interpretation that filled five pages of *Some Answered Questions*. He ended by stating, *"This is but one of the meanings of the biblical account of Adam. Reflect that you may discover others."*[37] Freedom was given for individual study and investigation that often offer profound insights.

Another subject that has defied literal interpretation is the accounts of extreme longevity for the descendants of Adam as given in Genesis 5. For example, the years of Adam were 930, of Seth 912, of Enosh (Enoch) 905, of Kenan 910, of Mahalalel 895, of Jared 962, of Enoch 365, of Methuselah 969, and of Lamech, the father of Noah 777 (Genesis 5:5–31). *"Noah lived a total of 950 years, and then he died"* (Genesis 9:29). Concerning the 950 years of Noah, a letter written on behalf of Shoghi Effendi stated: "The term year does not refer to a period of time such as our year. It was entirely different."[38] The scholar Sohrab Kourosh wrote:

Moreover, 'Abdu'l-Bahá wrote in a tablet in Persian and Arabic cited in the book *Amr-vas-khalq* (Vol. 1, p. 192) explains that such passages quoted in the ancient scriptures that indicated that Noah lived for nine hundred and fifty years do not signify solar years. Some authors, he explains, have counted each month as a year. Otherwise, he explains that the length of their lives was the same in the past as it is now, but because their lifestyle was simpler, they were stronger.[39]

Another example is the flood story and Noah's ark. Shoghi Effendi relieved biblical scholars of any need to argue for a literal acceptance of this story when he wrote: "The Ark and the Flood we believe are symbolical." [40] For an example of a personal symbolic interpretation, see Appendix A, "Noah and His Numbers," for a summary of Don Dainty's symbolic interpretation of the flood and the ark.

With these tools in hand, let's investigate the prevalence of monolatry, a form of polytheism, among the ancient Israelites and their painful journey of spiritual maturation to understand that there had been only the one true God all along.

Chapter 2

CANAAN AND
THE CANAANITES

"So Abram went, as the LORD *had told him; and Lot
went with him. He took his wife Sarai, his nephew Lot,
all the possessions they had accumulated and the people
they had acquired in Harran, and they set out for the land
of Canaan, and they arrived there."*

Genesis 12:4-5

The Hebrew Bible mentions the land of Canaan and the Canaanite people more than one hundred fifty times. Depictions of the
Canaanites were usually derogatory although their lives, beliefs, and
gods were much the same as those of other Near East peoples of the
time. The writers of the Hebrew Bible cast the Canaanites as idolatrous people with detestable practices who tempted the Israelites away
from the religion of Moses. They were denigrated as foils to righteous
Hebrews observing the laws of Moses, abiding under the terms of the
Mosaic Covenant. The reality was much more complex.

THE LAND

The land of Canaan was the Southern Levant, the bottom third of the Fertile Crescent along the Mediterranean coast.[d] This area is today known as Syria, Lebanon, Israel, Gaza and the West Bank, and Jordan. The land of Canaan was reasonably livable, but it was not *"a land flowing with milk and honey"* (Deuteronomy 6:3). The land ranged from reasonable fertility in the north to poor and rocky in the south, with levels of rainfall decreasing from north to south. Thirty to forty inches of rain fell annually in the upper Galilee, but only four to eight inches in the south. The summer months were hot and dry with the rains falling only from November through March. Insufficient winter rain meant drought and famine.

The geography was varied with fertile valleys, semi-arid deserts, marshes, and hills. The peaks in the central hill country rose to three thousand feet and those in the upper Galilee reached four thousand. The extremes in elevation ranged from Mount Hermon at nine thousand feet above sea level, to the Sea of Galilee at seven hundred feet below sea level, and to the Dead Sea, which was just fifty-four miles south of the Sea of Galilee but more than a thousand feet below sea level. The heartland of the country was Judea, Samaria, and the hills of Galilee, but its terrain was fragmented by hills and ravines that gave young David, the future king of Israel, and his men plenty of hideouts.

The land of Canaan had four primary geographical zones—the coastal plain, the central hill country, the Jordan Valley, and the Trans-jordanian plateau. The coastal plain ran north-south along the Mediterranean Sea. Inland were marshes and fertile land. This coastal plain transitioned south-eastward to the hills and valleys of the Shephelah

---

[d] The Levant is part of the Fertile Crescent and refers to the eastern Mediterranean region that today consists of Cyprus, Israel, Jordan, Lebanon, Gaza and the West Bank, Syria, and part of southern Turkey. The Fertile Crescent is a crescent-shaped area of fertile land that curves around the Arabian Desert that separates the river valley of the Tigris and Euphrates Rivers from the Mediterranean area.

that served as a barrier to invasion from the south. The central hill country ran north-south down the middle of Canaan and included the prime agricultural land. It would become the heart of Canaanite settlements and later the Israelite monarchies. To the east, the Jordan River started north of the Sea of Galilee and eventually ended in the Dead Sea. The Jordan River Valley was hot and dry and, in the south, it became a desert wilderness. The Transjordanian Plateau started with Mount Hermon in the north and stretched 250 miles to the Gulf of Aqaba in the south. The geographic and climatic diversity of this small land was remarkable.

Canaan was a connecting point for many ancient empires. Four international trade routes reached Canaan and then continued to points beyond. Collecting tolls was a financial bonanza that brought a measure of prosperity to an area that otherwise would have been limited to subsistence farming. The western trade route, the Via Maris, followed the coast from Egypt, cut through the Jezreel Valley, and went north to Damascus. The King's Highway ran south-north along the fertile plain east of the Jordan River. These two routes met in Damascus where one continued north to Antioch and the other east to Mesopotamia. The Ridge Route went through the hills of Judea and Samaria and passed Jerusalem. Merchants arrived by camel with frankincense, myrrh, and spices from the Arabian Peninsula along the Incense Route and sometimes transferred their wares onto boats for travel to lands accessible by the Mediterranean Sea. Each major route had several minor routes branching off. The land of Canaan served as a nerve center for international trade in the known world.

THE CANAANITE PEOPLE

Who were these Canaanites who were so maligned in the Hebrew Bible? Canaanite history has mostly been reconstructed from ancient Egyptian and Greek records and archaeological excavations because Canaanite history, as portrayed in the Hebrew Bible, was often biased to fit the perceived narrative of Israelite history. The historical part of the Hebrew Bible was put in final form by persons who were not only members of the educated elite but also monotheists who could read available records of the teachings of Moses. To them, Canaanite beliefs were an abomination.

The Canaanites were descended from Neolithic farmers who left the foothills of the Zagros Mountains (which ranged through Iran, northern Iraq, and southeastern Turkey), and the Caucasus (a region between the Black Sea and the Caspian Sea). Archaeological data shows that the southern Levant was continuously populated for several millennia BCE. The Canaanites lived in the eastern Mediterranean region during the Bronze Age (c. 3300 to 1200 BCE) and into the Iron Age (c. 1150-586). The large-scale, thirteenth-century, civilizational collapse is the dividing point for these two Ages, but the collapse did not happen suddenly in 1177, the year generally assigned to it,[41] although this collapse was somewhat complete by 1177. Eric H. Cline wrote an excellent book about this disintegration, *1177 B.C.: The Year Civilization Collapsed*. In short, Cline wrote that the events of the years between 1250 and 1175 BCE were a perfect storm of calamities, a rolling process whereby the interconnectedness between cultures and empires was devastated by a domino effect of disasters that ultimately destroyed the world as it had been known. The land of Canaan had reached a high level of prosperity when one hundred fifty years of climate change brought a long drought and colder temperatures, which led to famine and mass migrations. Earthquakes and volcanoes wrought devastation. The Sea Peoples, a seafaring confederation coming from the west, invaded the coastal areas and not only disrupted but cut international trade routes, thereby severing the cohesion and codependence that had promoted and sustained the Near Eastern empires. Twice the Sea Peoples invaded Egypt, destroying and burning as they went. Egypt defeated them but was left much weakened and had to withdraw from Canaan, which it had ruled for about three hundred years. The Hittite empire to the north also suffered from several invasions, greatly contracted in size, and never recovered. The Sea Peoples moved into Canaan and became known as the Philistines.

The origin and relationship of other ethnic groups of the ancient Near East[e] to today's population remained unclear until recently when DNA investigations started giving some answers. The DNA from the bones of five individuals from 1600 BCE that were found in Sidon, Lebanon, was compared with DNA from the bones of individuals who lived about 1,500 years earlier in Jordan. The scientific team found that the genetic similarity was striking. A paper written about this project that was published in *The American Journal of Human Genetics* stated:

> This suggests that people from the highly differentiated urban culture on the Levant coast and inland people with different modes of subsistence were nevertheless genetically similar, supporting previous reports that the different cultural groups who inhabited the Levant during the Bronze Age, such as the Ammonites, Moabites, Israelites, and Phoenicians, each achieved their own cultural identities, but all shared a common genetic and ethnic root with Canaanites.[42]

This team also gave the Canaanites a wider territory extending to Anatolia in the north, Mesopotamia to the east, and Egypt to the southwest, with access to Cypress and the Aegean lands via the Mediterranean. "Thus the Canaanites were at the center of emerging Bronze Age civilizations and became politically and culturally influential." [43]

Another DNA research study shed light on the extent to which the Hebrews and Canaanites intermarried. A paper published in *Cell* in

---

[e] "While the use of the term Near East has declined significantly and, in its place, the Middle East is used instead, archaeologists and historians often refer to the Near East and the ancient Near East in their scholarly studies and research. Ancient Near East encompassed modern-day Iraq, southeast Turkey, southwest and north-western Iran, north-eastern Syria, Asia Minor, the Armenian highlands, Syria, Lebanon, Palestine, Israel, Jordan, Cyprus, and the Arabian Peninsula. The modern use of the term Near East in archaeology, however, does not affect the fact that the ancient Near East represents regions of the Fertile Crescent." *World Atlas*, https://www.worldatlas.com/articles/what-is-the-near-east.html.

2021 reports that the DNA of 62 Canaanite skeletons recovered from archaeological sites in Lebanon and Israel was compared with a DNA database of 1,663 modern individuals.

> In the study, published in *Cell*, the researchers explain that they used existing DNA analysis of 20 individuals, from sites in Israel and Lebanon, and then added 73 more, taking DNA from the bones of individuals found at Tel Megiddo, Tel Abel Beth Maacah and Tel Hazor (Northern Israel), Yehud (central Israel) and Baq'ah (central Jordan). By first eliminating individuals closely related to other individuals in the sample, then comparing the remaining 62 DNA samples against a dataset of 1,663 modern individuals, they were able to establish the genetic link to the modern populations. The ethnic groups either still living where Canaan once dominated, or from that area before moving elsewhere, are largely descended from the Canaanites.
>
> Most modern Jewish groups and the Arabic-speaking groups from the region show at least half of their ancestry as Canaanite.
>
> The study in *Cell* not only establishes that the ancient Israelites were descended from the Canaanites, but also establishes that the Canaanite people across the separate city-states of the southern Levant, and over a period of 1,500 years, were a genetically cohesive people.[44]

The biblical stories of the conquests of Joshua and the supposed commands from God to annihilate the Canaanites fade in plausibility. If true, how could the Canaanites have so greatly contributed genetically to present-day populations? Archaeological evidence supports peaceful immigration of the Israelites into the land of Canaan. The exploits of Joshua were not written down for several hundred years, and I personally believe that they were quite disremembered.

It's more plausible that God had urged the Israelites to teach the religion of Moses to the Canaanites, thus annihilating their polytheistic beliefs.

And what of the Philistines of Goliath fame? They were not Canaanite. They were part of the wave of Sea Peoples who invaded Canaan from southern Europe during the interlude of the collapse of Near East empires and settled on the southern coast. The genome from ten Bronze and Iron Age individuals from the coastal Philistine city of Ashkelon proved to be genetically distinct from Canaanite because of a European mixture. This genetic signature was not long-lasting, probably because of integration with the local people.[45]

Canaanite city-states evolved from about 1800 to 1550 BCE that featured massive construction for walls, palaces, and temples. This growth indicated a thriving economy supported by trade routes. Whoever controlled them collected the tributes, tolls, taxes, and tariffs. Canaan also prospered by trading its oil, copper, wine, and grain on the routes. During these years, the land of Canaan had relative autonomy with few foreign threats. However, there was little internal stability. A plethora of warrior kings, more likely along the order of war lords, ruled the city-states and small areas around them, alternately fighting the other kings and then making alliances with them to fight outsider threats such as the Ugarits (in today's Syria), the Hittites (in today's Turkey), and the Egyptians. Mary Ellen Buck, an expert on Canaan, wrote:

> While other major empires such as the Ugarit, Babylon, Mitanni, and Egypt all referred to the populations of the land of Canaan as "Canaanites," this term was never adopted by the Canaanite rulers themselves. Rather, they represented themselves as independent monarchs who ruled over semi-autonomous kingdoms and whose affiliation was to their local tribe or location, as opposed to some larger concept of Canaan. Indeed, relations between these local Canaanite rulers were often fraught with tension.[46]

By the time of the Israelites, the Canaanites included the Moabites, Edomites, and Ammonites living east of the Jordan River and the Amalekites and Jebusites living west of the river. Those Canaanites who lived in biblical Canaan at the center of the trade-route crossings were influenced by many cultures. The downside was that Canaan was the battleground of various empires that sought control of the trade routes, especially the Egyptian and the Hittite.

Canaanite life was family- and tribe-based. Life was primarily agricultural and subject to the vagaries of the weather. Textile production was a cottage industry as was the production of olive oil and wine. Canaan was prosperous according to the standards of the time, but life expectancy was short, as it was everywhere. Longevity charts for ancient Middle Eastern populations generally show an average of 30 to 35 years if one survived his first year.

THE CANAANITE LANGUAGE FAMILY

The *lingua franca* of early Canaan was an East Semitic dialect known as Babylonian that was written in cuneiform script. This common language facilitated communication between the empires and their traders. Buck believes that the Canaanite language may have emerged as a separate language by about 1500 BCE and subsequently expanded into dialects. In time, the languages of Hebrew, Phoenician/Punic, Edomite, Moabite, Amana Canaanite, and Ammonite emerged as distinct languages within the Canaanite language family.[47]

Few Canaanite textual materials survived, probably because they were mostly inscribed on papyrus rather than clay tablets. But enough survived for William M. Schniedewind, an expert on northwest Semitic languages, to write: "These small Canaanite city-states developed scribal schools that left ample evidence of writing, albeit largely in the form of administrative texts. Even a tiny city-state like Jerusalem, which numbered no more than two thousand people in the Late Bronze Age, had royal scribes."[48] At this point, writing served the needs of royal administration and merchants. There was continuity from Canaanite to Israelite culture in many ways, and writing was part of it. A literary use of written language would develop later.

Because Hebrew has been identified as originally a Canaanite dialect, one school of biblical scholarship contends that the Hebrews were an indigenous Canaanite population that established itself as a separate identity in the last years of the Bronze Age. Adherents of this hypothesis note that these ethnic groups' languages, including Hebrew, retained elements of the original Canaanite language.

The more widely held belief among biblical scholars is that the Hebrews entered Canaan from outside as recipients of the Mosaic Dispensation to claim the land they believed was theirs through God's promise to Abraham. When the Hebrews settled in Canaan and assimilated with those indigenous people, their languages would have merged to a certain extent and the Hebrew language emerged. Hebrew is the only Canaanite language still spoken today, although it was dead as a spoken language until the nineteenth century when it was resurrected as part of the Zionist movement. Hebrew is the only example of a dead language revived.

According to the Hebrew Bible, the Hebrew slaves who followed Moses were the descendants of Jacob (Israel), and their retainers. Probably non-Hebraic slaves joined the group escaping from Egypt. Then succeeding generations intermarried with the Canaanites, altering the racial and cultural mix accordingly.

My studies often find "yes/but" and "both/and" situations, and the origin of the Hebrews is one of them. The matter of the Exodus is a classic example. On the one hand, the eminent archaeologists Israel Finkelstein and Neil Asher Silberman are adamant that no archaeological evidence has been found to validate the biblical Exodus. "And it has not been for lack of trying. Repeated archeological surveys in all regions of the peninsula, including the mountainous area around the traditional site of Mount Sinai…have yielded only negative evidence: not a single sherd, no structure, not a single house, no trace of an ancient encampment." [49]

On the other hand, something of great magnitude did happen. Moses, a Prophet of God, came! Memories of that experience may have become cloudy, but they were too strong for the Exodus narrative to be dismissed. Most biblical scholars do accept that something monumental happened to generate this national epic. Carol Redmount, an archaeologist, is one of them. She wrote:

> To some, the lack of a secure historical grounding for the biblical Exodus narrative merely reflects its nonhistorical nature. According to this view, there was no historical Exodus, and the story is to be interpreted as a legend or myth of origins. To others, still in the majority among scholars, the ultimate historicity of the Exodus narrative is indisputable. The details of the story may have become clouded or obscured through the transmission process, but a historical core is mandated by that major tenet of faith that permeates the Bible: God acts in history.[50]

There is the linguistic evidence that the Hebrew language has roots in the Canaanite language family, which suggests the possibility that the Hebrews were originally indigenous Canaanites. However, as 'Abdu'l-Bahá was quoted in the previous chapter, the Exodus was both a physical and spiritual journey. Therefore, Moses did lead a group of Hebrew slaves from Egypt to the Promised Land, whereafter the Hebrew immigrants may have adopted the language of their new home, or developed a hybrid language of both. The narrative of the forty years wandering in the Sinai Desert is so overflowing with spiritual teachings, symbolism, and metaphors that it's "true" in the most important sense.[51]

THE CANAANITE RELIGION

The Canaanites in the Holy Land were not isolated culturally or religiously. Because of the trade routes that crossed Canaan, the Canaanites were exposed to people from all over the Near East, to their deities and religious rites, and to the cross currents of culture and communication as well as trade. Canaanite religion was strongly influenced by the beliefs and rituals of Mesopotamia and Egypt.

Polytheism was the norm in the ancient Middle East. The gods and goddesses were anthropomorphic with human-type whims and personalities, sometimes to extremes. They were closely connected with, and in charge of, the various forces of nature. The deities were not only powerful but capricious. People saw their well-being as strongly dependent upon the gods of rain, fertility, and so forth. The deities were honored and supplicated for basics and favors, but they were not loved. They were worshipped at home altars, at hilltop altars in the countryside, and in temples built in their honor. Polytheism developed to an extreme in Mesopotamia with two thousand three hundred gods and goddesses identified in a published list.[52]

Aside from the Mesopotamian influence, though, little was specifically known about Canaanite religion except for what was stated in the Hebrew Bible until a farmer digging in northwest Syria in 1928 stumbled upon an ancient tomb and cemetery in the area of the ancient Canaanite city of Ugarit. Ugarit was a prosperous maritime trading city from about 1450 to 1180 BCE. Archaeologists immediately started excavating with permission of the French Protectorate. A treasure trove was found of two temples dedicated to the gods Baal and Dagan, civic buildings, palaces, and private homes. Most significant was the discovery of a library with clay tablets inscribed in several Near Eastern languages, including alphabetic Ugaritic, the major language of Ugarit. This language was new to Near East scholars, who quickly deciphered it.

The Ugaritic tablets describe the activities of the main gods and goddesses of the Canaanite pantheon. The supreme deity was El, an elder god who was the creator of the lesser gods and humanity and was also the god of wisdom. He was a "storm god" who was pictured as riding on the clouds to bring the rain and fertilize the land. He was seen as somewhat benign despite his power that was associated with the bull. He co-ruled with Baal, who was a warrior god and especially responsible for agriculture. El and Baal served on the divine council called the Elohim (plural for gods) with El's wife, the mother goddess Athirat, called Asherah in the Bible. There were gods for every aspect of life and nature—Molech (Moloch, Molek), the god of fire; Anat, the virgin goddess of war and strife; Qadeshtu, the goddess of love; Resheph, the god of plague and healing; Yamesh, the sun god; Yamm, the sea god; Dagan, the god of crop fertility; and so forth. The number of deities documented from the Ugaritic texts was 234.[53] In addition, every clan, town, and city had its own god whose image was often carried into battle. It was believed that if you could steal a god's image carried by the enemy, that god would lose his power and his people would be defeated.

Like other ancient cultures, Canaanite society was largely concerned with the fertility of the land, domesticated animals, and women. Insufficient rain and drought were major problems. Incessant skirmishes, coupled with low age expectancy and high child mortality, made a high birth rate a vital necessity. The folk religion of the people embraced many gods, each of whom served a purpose. When life was lived on a basic level of striving for survival, all avenues of help were sought, a certain deity for this and another for that. It was inconceivable at that time that one god could handle everything.

There are about ninety references to Baal in the Hebrew Bible, and over forty to Asherah and her cult pole, called the Asherah. The Asherah poles were representations of Asherah as a goddess of fertility and, in some aspects of the Asherah cult, a co-creator with El of seventy minor gods. These wooden poles often symbolized trees and had carvings on them that represented Asherah. Sometimes stylized images of trees were used to depict Asherah. This goddess was also represented by figurines, hundreds of which have been found by archaeologists and dated from the sixteenth through the sixth centuries. They were probably used in family-centered home worship. Her prominence in the deity hierarchy gave women a certain level of empowerment and social status because of the reverence for Asherah as the consort of El and the mother of the gods.

According to 1 Kings 18:19, there were four hundred and fifty prophets of Baal and four hundred prophets of Asherah, all of whom ate at Jezebel's table. Jezebel was the wife of King Ahab, who called the prophet Elijah *"the troubler of Israel"* (1 Kings 18:17) for his denunciation of the gods. Asherah worship was widespread, and Asherah poles were even found in the Temple. However, the reformist King Josiah targeted Baal and Asherah: *"The king ordered Hilkiah the high priest, the priests next in rank and the doorkeepers to remove from the temple of the Lord all the articles made for Baal and Asherah and all the starry hosts"* (2 Kings 23:4). Archaeologists have found fewer Asherah figurines dated to the period after Josiah than before.[54]

Deity worship permeated Canaanite life. James L. Kugel, Professor Emeritus in the Bible Department at Bar Ilan University in Israel, commented on how entrenched polytheism was among the Canaanites:

> They [the deities] were "up there," existing on a kind of upper shelf, while we humans were "down here," on earth. They controlled almost all the things that were vital to our existence—the grain, the wine, and the oil, in fact, how long we live, how many children we have, and what our lives are actually like: prosperity or hardship, peace or war, feast or famine. All these things were in the hands of those mysterious beings on the upper shelf. By the time ancient Israel came along, people had been perceiving reality in terms of these beings for so many millennia that they were simply an irrefutable fact of life. The ones "up there" were as real as the "down here" things that they controlled, as real as the fruit in the trees or the rainwater in the cisterns.[55]

As the immigrants and natives intermingled, they adopted aspects of each other's religion. The Canaanite folk religion remained, and many Israelites adopted parts of it and assigned Yahweh the position of one of the gods. It would be a long, agonizing process from monolatry to the monotheism of Abraham and Moses.

Chapter 3

MONOLATRY AND MONOTHEISM

"The Founder of monotheism was Abraham; it is to Him that this concept can be traced, and the belief was current among the Children of Israel, even in the days of Socrates." [56]

'Abdu'l-Bahá

Ancient Egypt had a pantheon of over two thousand gods and goddesses. Within this culture, the descendants of Jacob (Israel) who had been reduced to slavery in Egypt had probably forgotten the teachings of the Prophet Abraham and the legacies of Isaac, Jacob, and Joseph. Shoghi Effendi described the condition of the Israelites when Moses undertook His mission:

How often have the Prophets of God, not excepting Bahá'u'lláh Himself, chosen to appear, and deliver their Message in countries and amidst peoples and races, at a time when they were either fast declining, or had already touched the lowest depths of moral and spiritual degradation. The appalling misery and wretchedness to which the Israelites had sunk, under the debasing and tyrannical rule of the Pharaohs, in the days preceding their exodus from Egypt under the leadership of Moses; the decline that had set in in the religious, the spiritual, the cultural, and the moral life of the Jewish people, at the time of the appearance of Jesus Christ; ....[57]

Considering the above, it is not a point of pride that a certain country or locality was chosen for the appearance of a Prophet of God,

but rather as a direct consequence of its crying needs, its lamentable degeneracy, and irremediable perversity, has the Prophet of God chosen to appear in its midst, and with it as a lever has lifted the entire human race to a higher and nobler plane of life and conduct.

For it is precisely under such circumstances, and by such means that the Prophets have, from time immemorial, chosen and were able to demonstrate their redemptive power to raise from the depths of abasement and of misery, the people of their own race and nation, empowering them to transmit in turn to other races and nations the saving grace and the energizing influence of their Revelation.[58]

The book of Exodus recounts many incidents of the peoples' lack of faith in Moses and His Revelation and their propensity for backsliding into polytheism. It was a short fall because they had not really left their multiple deities behind.

The incident of the golden calf is one of the best-known examples of recidivism in the Hebrew Bible. And Moses's own brother had not only been involved in the making of the golden calf but had dissimulated and blamed the people for asking him to make gods who would go before them. *"So I told them, 'Whoever has any gold jewelry, take it off.' Then they gave me the gold, and I threw it into the fire, and out came this calf!"* (Exodus 32:24) Aaron—brother of Moses and the future first high priest! The lure of the gods was strong, as was the reluctance of the Hebrews to forsake them. Many of the Hebrews would live for several centuries in the land of Canaan immersed in polytheism.

Pure monotheism recognizes the one true God and denies the existence of other deities. The conventional belief is that the Israelites were monotheists despite the many biblical references to their polytheistic worship. Upon close examination, monolatry[f] and henotheism[g] strongly vied with monotheism from the years of the judges from about 1200 to 1030 BCE, through the centuries of monarchies, the Exile, the restoration to Jerusalem in the sixth century, and even beyond. According to Third Isaiah, who is believed to have been active during the time frame of 520 to 500 BCE, idolatry was still an issue (see Chapter 14). Since the difference between monolatry and henotheism is slight, I use the term monolatry to cover both. Monolatry gives primary worship to a particular god but recognizes the existence of other gods and honors them. The Hebrew Bible records multiple instances of the worship of Canaanite deities and the prophets' condemnation of the practice. It would be a long struggle for the Israelites to truly convert to the monotheistic beliefs brought by Abraham and reinforced by Moses. Most of the Israelites seemed to have had only a partial understanding of this momentous concept. The song of Moses after the Israelites crossed the Red Sea praised the Lord in reference to other gods: *"Who among the gods is like you, Lord? Who is like you— majestic in holiness, awesome in glory, working wonders?"* (Exodus 15:11)

The Lord had said to Abraham: *"I will establish my covenant as an everlasting covenant between me and you and your descendants after you for the generations to come, **to be your God and the God of your descendants***

---

[f] Monolatry (also called monolatrism) is the worship of only one god without denying the existence of other gods.

[g] Henotheism is related to monolatry in that it recognizes many gods yet chooses to focus exclusively on one—usually considered the god of one's family or clan. A monolater or a henotheist is committed to one god, but he leaves room for other deities as well. Many cultures in ancient times believed in more than one god but paid homage to one god above the others.

after you" (Genesis 17:7, emphasis added). No claim was made for Him being a universal God. Currently He was tribal. His people would be the descendants of Abraham.

The Ten Commandments are prefaced by the statement, *"I am the LORD your God, who brought you out of Egypt, out of the land of slavery"* (Exodus 20:2). The First Commandment, as preserved through the ages, states, *"You shall have no other gods **before** me"* (Exodus 20:3, emphasis added). The footnote in the New International Version of the Bible states that *before* could mean *besides*. Would the word substitution *besides* have made the First Commandment unequivocal for monotheism beyond scholarly dispute?

DIALOGS ABOUT MONOTHEISM AND EXODUS 20:3-5

As discussed, archaeological evidence indicates that worship of other deities was prevalent in ancient Israel up through the sixth century BCE. An article in the Jewish Virtual Library states:

> The Mosaic religion was initially a **monolatrous** religion; while the Hebrews are enjoined to worship no deity but Yahweh, there is no evidence that the earliest Mosaic religion denied the existence of other gods. In fact, the account of the migration contains numerous references by the historical characters to other gods, and the first law of the Decalogue is, after all, that no gods be put *before* Yahweh, not that no other gods exist. While controversial among many people, most scholars have concluded that the initial Mosaic religion for about two hundred years was a monolatrous religion.[59]

A major shift came with the Hebrew prophets.

> Whatever the character of Mosaic religion during the occupation and the early monarchy, the prophets unambiguously

made Yahweh the one and only one god of the universe. Earlier Hebrews acknowledged and even worshipped foreign gods; the prophets, however, asserted that Yahweh ruled the entire universe and all the peoples in it, whether or not they recognized and worshipped Yahweh. The Yahweh religion as a *monotheistic* religion can really be dated no earlier than the prophetic revolution.[60]

The Exile marked another point of profound shift.

A small group of religious reformers believed that the calamities suffered by the Jews were due to the corruption of their religion and ethics. These religious reformers reoriented Jewish religion around the Mosaic books; in other words, they believed that the Jews should return to their foundational religion. ...the central character of post-Exilic Jewish religion is **reform**...accelerated by the return to Judaea itself.[61]

An evangelical Protestant commentary on Exodus 20:3 is found in the book *Inspiration and Incarnation: Evangelicals and the Problem of the Old Testament*, written by Peter Enns, an evangelical Protestant and scholar of the Hebrew Bible. He believed that evidence of monolatry is found in Exodus 20:3 and wrote: "The first commandment says not 'there are no other gods' but 'you shall have no other gods.' Yahweh is saying, 'You saw what I did in bringing you up from Egypt. Now, I am the one you are to worship, not the gods of Egypt you are leaving behind nor the gods of Canaan you are about to encounter.'" [62] Enns continued to Exodus 20:4-5: *"You shall not make for yourself an image in the form of anything in heaven above or on the earth beneath or in the waters below. You shall not bow down to them or worship them; ...."*

Enns urged Christians to understand the ancient Israelites and their literature by developing an affinity, as best we can, with their ancient world in which biblical texts were given.

THE STATIONS OF PURE ABSTRACTION AND DISTINCTION

Abraham and Moses were both Manifestations of God. It is, therefore, crucial to understand their nature, their power, and the limitations under which They brought their dispensations. The Bahá'í Scriptures state that all the Manifestations of God have a twofold station: *"One is the station of pure abstraction and essential unity. For they one and all summon the people of the earth to acknowledge the Unity of God, and herald unto them the Kawthar*[h] *of an infinite grace and bounty. They are all invested with the robe of Prophethood and honoured with the mantle of glory."* [63]

If the Manifestations of God shared the station of oneness, why did Abraham, Moses, and Jesus seem to differ substantially from each other in their lives and missions? And why does it appear to some scholars that Moses, the author of the spiritual teachings in the Pentateuch, condoned His people's polytheism as long as the worship of Yahweh came first? The reasons are found in their second station, *"the station of distinction, and pertaineth to the world of creation and to the limitations thereof. In this respect, each Manifestation of God hath a distinct individuality, a definitely prescribed mission, a predestined Revelation, and specially designated limitations. Each one of them is known by a different name, is characterized by a special attribute, fulfils a definite Mission, and is entrusted with a particular Revelation."* [64] The *station of pure abstraction and essential unity* describes their essential oneness, but their *station of distinction* within *specially designated limitations* explains the differences in their missions.

It would certainly have been a *limitation* for Moses that polytheism pervaded the Egyptian and Canaanite cultures. Speaking again of the Manifestations of God, Bahá'u'lláh wrote: *"Know of a certainty that in every Dispensation the light of Divine Revelation hath been vouchsafed*

---

[h] The term *Kawthar* is from the Qur'án, 2:285. The scholar Sohrab Kourosh wrote: "The word *Kawthar* in Arabic means abundance, and a generous person, but in Islamic terminology it is the name of a fountain in Paradise from which all the rivers in Paradise initiate. In the Bahá'í sacred Writings it is translated as 'fountain,' but more frequently as 'the living waters.'"

unto men in direct proportion to their spiritual capacity." [65] And accordingly, "*they have invariably summoned its peoples to embrace the light of God through such means as best befitted the exigencies of the age in which they appeared. They were thus able to scatter the darkness of ignorance, and to shed upon the world the glory of their own knowledge.*" [66]

Jesus referred to the limitations of His time when He told His disciple, "*I have much more to say to you, more than you can now bear. But when he, the Spirit of truth, comes, he will guide you into all the truth. He will not speak on his own; he will speak only what he hears, and he will tell you what is yet to come*" (John 16:12-13).

Bahá'u'lláh wrote of Himself: "*Verily, He Who is the Spirit of Truth is come to guide you unto all truth. He speaketh not as prompted by His own self, but as bidden by Him Who is the All-Knowing, the All-Wise.*" [67]

In other words, kindergarten children are not taught astronomy, second graders are not taught algebra or calculus, and fifth graders are not taught biochemistry. Those subjects are to be learned in higher grades. For example, consider a teacher who mentors a high school student who is preparing a science project to be entered in a science fair. A few years later, that student earns a college degree and proceeds to graduate studies. At this higher level, he might perform science experiments that make his high school science project simplistic. Had his high school mentor insufficiently helped him? Not at all. The mentor had guided that student to the extent of his capacity at that time.

MOVING FORWARD

Moses categorically and emphatically forbade idol worship when He proclaimed on behalf of the Lord: "*They must no longer offer any of their sacrifices to the goat idols* [demons] *to whom they prostitute themselves. This is to be a lasting ordinance for them and for the generations to come*" (Leviticus 17:7). Further, "*Do not turn to idols or make metals gods for yourself. I am the LORD YOUR GOD*" (Leviticus 19:4). And for good measure, "*Do not make idols or set up an image or a sacred stone for yourselves, and do not place a carved stone in your land to bow down before it. I am the LORD YOUR GOD*" (Leviticus 26:1).

The Lord gave the Israelites what must have been the ultimate mandate: *"Speak to the entire assembly of Israel and say to them: 'Be holy because I, the LORD YOUR GOD, AM HOLY'"* (Leviticus 19:2). This directive is from the Holiness Code.[68] This was probably the highest spiritual commandment ever given. Be holy! The deities of polytheism were never considered holy or even honorable, only powerful. They weren't concerned with moral values.

When Moses was approaching the end of His life, He reviewed with His people the terms of their covenant with the Lord. He warned again of idol worship:

> *You yourselves know how we lived in Egypt and how we passed through the countries on the way here. You saw among them their detestable images and idols of wood and stone, of silver and gold. Make sure there is no man or woman, clan or tribe among you today whose heart turns away from the LORD our God to go and worship the gods of those nations; make sure there is no root among you that produces such bitter poison.* (Deuteronomy 29:16-18)

As noted above, the prophetic movement was a major factor in the final embrace of monotheism by the Hebrews. Those selfless souls who served as communicators from God were Moses's helpers working within His dispensation to bring the people fully into His covenant. For the first time in Near Eastern history, a people were raised out of polytheism and into monotheism.

It was during the Babylonian Exile and with the return to Jerusalem that Judaism made major strides towards monotheism. Monolatry would at least not be one of the *limitations* or *exigencies* with which Jesus would have to contend.

Chapter 4

EZEKIEL –
A SPECTACULAR CALL

"This was the appearance of the likeness of the glory of the Lord."

Ezekiel 1:28

The Hebrew Bible is a study in eschatology and a landscape of fleeting images beckoning us forward in time. From a theological perspective, eschatology is defined as "a branch of theology concerned with the final events in the history of the world or of humankind" and "a belief concerning death, the end of the world, or the ultimate destiny of humankind." [69] The word eschatology is based on the Greek word *eschaton*, which means the end. The books of Ezekiel and Daniel are especially eschatological.

Contrary to this doctrinal viewpoint of theological eschatology, divine time has no beginning or end. No complete stop. Not even stasis. Mentions of the Day of God and the Day of the Lord are eschatological clues referring to the end of current religious tradition and the future comings of Prophets of God, especially to the coming of the Báb and Bahá'u'lláh. Shoghi Effendi was referring to Bahá'u'lláh when he wrote, "His Day Ezekiel and Daniel had, moreover, both acclaimed as 'the day of the LORD.'" [70]

The biblical scholar Donald E. Gowan categorized the nature of eschatology in the Hebrew Bible according to four criteria. He described it first as worldly hope that does not scorn, ignore, or abandon the lives humans live in favor of something better, whether after death or in this life. Secondly, the future is totally in the hands of God. In this regard, Gowan wrote: "The basis for hope in the OT [Old Testament] is not faith in human progress, but the assurance of a coming of a divine intervention that will introduce a new thing that people have failed and will fail to accomplish." [71] This does not call for human passivity, though, but for repentance and active responsibility participating in a radical transformation that can only be accomplished by God. Gowan's third category of eschatology is its greater emphasis on human society than on personal salvation. This is contrary to traditional Christian teaching and today's individualism.

Lastly, Gowan sees biblical eschatology as a "comprehensive hope. The OT neither focuses on an improved social structure inhabited by the same kind of people who created the mess we are now in; nor does it promise that personal salvation will somehow make social problems go away; neither does it imagine that a healthy human society can exist without a wholesale interaction with the natural world." [72]

Beginnings are inherent in endings. For example, innocent life in the Garden of Eden ended for Adam and Eve, but humanity made a new beginning by living with awareness of the Tree of the Knowledge of Good and Evil. The Exodus ended Hebrew slavery that was not only physical but spiritual, and the Hebrews were gifted a new beginning under the Mosaic Dispensation.

Each Hebrew prophet spoke at times in eschatological terms, whether through hints or graphic warnings. Their comments were usually three-pronged—indictment of spiritual corruption; a warning of a disaster that would upend conventional religious thought and bring an end to the known world; and a promise of divine forgiveness and future redemption. An end would foreshadow a beginning, but the time of that beginning was often given in indefinite terms.

Westerners are familiar with Christian understanding of the end times, which involve divine judgment and life after death. Before the advent of Jesus, though, the Hebrews had little concept of life after death, the life everlasting. They shared the Mesopotamian belief in Sheol, the abode of the dead, a murky place of semi-consciousness where everyone went whether righteous or evil. Sheol was seen as devoid of love and hate, punishment and reward, work and thought. Sheol was not linked to judgment and justice. Rather, it was a bleak, shadowy destination that no one could avoid. When Jacob was faced with releasing his son Benjamin to go to Egypt under Reuben's care, he wailed, *"If harm should come to him on the journey that you are to make, you would bring down my gray hairs with sorrow to Sheol"* (Genesis 42:38). Gloomy Sheol was seen as an abode of no light or sound, let alone of any praise of deities or of the one true God. The common denominator seemed to be weakness and hopelessness. Job tried to reclaim a few brief moments of joy *"before I go to the place of no return, to the land of gloom and utter darkness, to the land of deepest night, of utter darkness and disorder, where even the light is like darkness"* (Job 10:21-22).

This lack of belief in meaningful life after death explains why the Israelites believed that the good life had to be lived in the here and now. If divine justice was only applicable to life on earth, but little evidence was seen of it, energy was best put into placating the gods to avoid as much misfortune as possible. Since life was short and there was no belief in a meaningful future beyond the grave, there would be little comfort with the prophets' promises of the Lord's redemption sometime vaguely in the future. There was also a disconnect in understanding that obedience to the divine laws of Moses would foster a society with meaningful judgment and justice.

A major part of Jesus's Dispensation was the teaching of eternal life on a much higher level than Sheol. For example, one day when Jesus was drinking water from Jacob's well, He talked with a Samaritan woman and told her: *"Everyone who drinks this water will be thirsty again, but whoever drinks the water I give them will never thirst. Indeed, the water I give them will become in them a spring of water welling up to eternal life"* (John 4:13-14).

First cousin to eschatology is apocalyptic visions, which are often marked by symbolic imagery and the expectation of an imminent cosmic cataclysm, and sometimes reveal secrets of future knowledge. Eschatological and apocalyptic metaphors were effective devices to get peoples' attention, and Ezekiel was especially masterful in their use.

Ezekiel was born into a priestly lineage in Jerusalem where possibly he knew and was influenced by Jeremiah, his contemporary in that city. He was deported to Babylon in 597 BCE after an Israelite uprising against Babylon. Jehoiachin, the penultimate King of Judah, and members of the nobility, the army, and the priesthood—*"the prominent people of the land"* (2 Kings 24:15)—were included in this first deportation. Jehoiachin had only reigned for three months in 597 when he was exiled by Nebuchadnezzar to Babylon. However, Ezekiel always recognized Jehoiachin as the rightful monarch of Judah and dated his visions and experiences according to the years of his reign, which probably were accurate. Ezekiel was active during both the preexilic and exilic periods.

The book of Ezekiel has a clear structure with divisions—the call (Ezekiel 1:1-3:15); oracles[i] of destruction (Ezekiel 3:16-24:27) and against foreign nations (Ezekiel 25:1-32:32); and the promises of restoration (Ezekiel 33:1-48:35). His prophecies can be divided into the categories of the near future of the defeat of Judah by the Babylonians and the far future twenty-five hundred years later and still unfolding today.

THE CALL TO PROPHETHOOD

Ezekiel's divine call came in 592 BCE, and he is documented as active until 585, when it seems he went silent until his last utterances that are

---

[i] The term "oracle" is often used by biblical scholars to describe a denunciation of a person or a nation, usually by a prophet.

dated from 572 to 570. Ezekiel was living with other exiled Israelites who were faced with adjusting to a new land and life. They tended to cling to the hope given by the false prophets living among them, as well as in Jerusalem, who were prophesying that the Israelites would soon be allowed to return and that Jerusalem would never be destroyed. Jeremiah, who lived in Jerusalem, had counseled the deportees to settle down for an extended stay of seventy years (Jeremiah 29:4-10), but that was not well received. Jeremiah was adamant that the Babylonians would conquer Jerusalem if the people didn't submit to them first.[73] Ezekiel was also unwavering in his belief that Jerusalem would be destroyed.

The call to prophethood came while Ezekiel was sitting on the shore of the Kebar (Chebar) River, which was either a canal or tributary to the Euphrates River in southern Mesopotamia. He was living in a Jewish settlement called Tel Abib (Tel Aviv), located south of Babylon. Ezekiel dated this event to the fifth year of King Jehoiachin's reign. *"In my thirtieth year, in the fourth month on the fifth day, while I was among the exiles by the Kebar River, the heavens were opened and I saw visions of God. On the fifth of the month—it was the fifth year of the exile of King Jehoiachin—the word of the LORD came to Ezekiel the priest, the son of Buzi, by the Kebar River in the land of the Babylonians. There the hand of the LORD was on him"* (Ezekiel 1:1-2).

Ezekiel's call narrative was long and vivid (Ezekiel 1:1-3:15). Briefly summarized, he saw an immense cloud of brilliant light inside of which were four living creatures in human form. Each had four faces, six wings, human hands, and legs with feet like those of a calf. The four faces were a lion, an ox, an eagle, and a human. Fire moved among the creatures, who sped back and forth like flashes of lightning. The four creatures sped back and forth on wheels that sparkled like topaz and had rims that were full of eyes. Above the creatures was a vault sparkling like crystal. Then came a voice from above the vault, from a throne of lapis lazuli. High above the throne was a figure of a man who from the waist down was like fire and from his waist up was like glowing metal, with a radiance about him similar to a rainbow.

*Then there came a voice from above the vault over their heads as they stood with lowered wings. Above the vault over their heads was what looked like a throne of lapis lazuli, and high above on the throne was a figure like that of a man. I saw that from what appeared to be his waist up he looked like glowing metal, as if full of fire, and that from there down he looked like **fire**; and brilliant **light** surrounded him. Like the appearance of a rainbow in the clouds on a rainy day, so was the radiance around him.*

*This was the appearance of the likeness of the **glory of the** L*ORD*. When I saw it, I fell facedown, and I heard the voice of one speaking."* (Ezekiel 1:25-28, emphasis added)

The *glory of the* L*ORD* is the translation of Bahá'u'lláh from Arabic. The biblical scholar Hushidar (Hugh) Motlagh noted: "The words 'light' and 'fire' both characterize Bahá'u'lláh. First, one of the meanings of bahá is light; and second...Bahá'u'lláh sometimes identified Himself with the fire in the Burning Bush." [74] One example of Bahá'u'lláh's identification of Himself with the Burning Bush is: *"Say: This, verily, is the heaven in which the Mother Book is treasured, could ye but comprehend it. He it is Who hath caused the Rock to shout, and the Burning Bush to lift up its voice, upon the Mount rising above the Holy Land, and proclaim: 'The Kingdom is God's, the sovereign Lord of all, the All-Powerful, the Loving!'"* [75]

The call narratives of Isaiah, Jeremiah, and Ezekiel had similarities concerning the deafness and denialism they would encounter. Ezekiel was warned of the *rebellious* nature of the Israelites, who would be like briars, thorns, and scorpions.

*"Son of man, I am sending you to the Israelites, to **a rebellious nation** that has rebelled against me; they and their ancestors have been in revolt against me to this very day. The people to whom I am sending you are obstinate and stubborn. Say to them, 'This is what the Sovereign L*ORD *says.' And whether they listen or fail to listen—for they are **a rebellious people**—they will know that*

a prophet has been among them. And you, son of man, do not be afraid of them or their words. Do not be afraid, though briers and thorns are all around you and you live among scorpions. Do not be afraid of what they say or be terrified by them, though they are **a rebellious people**. *You must speak my words to them, whether they listen or fail to listen, for* **they are rebellious**. *But you, son of man, listen to what I say to you. Do not rebel like* **that rebellious people**; *open your mouth and eat what I give you."* (Ezekiel 2:3-8, emphasis added)

The Lord labelled His people *rebellious* sixteen times throughout the book of Ezekiel.

Ezekiel was commanded to eat a scroll that the Lord gave him. *"On both sides of it were written words of lament and mourning and woe"* (Ezekiel 2:10). Ezekiel thus internalized and accepted the sorrows of his ministry that were to come.

Because Ezekiel's fellow Hebrews in exile would not be willing to listen, he was told: *"I will make your forehead like the hardest stone, harder than flint. Do not be afraid of them or terrified by them, though they are a rebellious people. And he said to me, "Son of man, listen carefully and take to heart all the words I speak to you. Go now to your people in exile and speak to them. Say to them, 'This is what the Sovereign Lord says,' whether they listen or fail to listen"* (Ezekiel 3:9-11). The preface, *This is what the sovereign Lord says,* was used over 120 times and would be like a signet ring for Ezekiel.

The vision was ending. *"Then the spirit took me up, and I heard behind me a voice of a great rushing, saying, Blessed be* **the glory of the Lord** *from his place…. So the spirit lifted me up, and took me away, and I went in bitterness, in the heat of my spirit; but the hand of the Lord was strong upon me"* (Ezekiel 3:12-14, KJV, emphasis added).

Ezekiel was shocked, frightened, and disheartened as he sat among the exiles in Tel Abib for seven days. After this anguished week, the word of the Lord came to him. *"Son of man, I have made you a watchman for the people of Israel; so hear the word I speak and give them warning from me"* (Ezekiel 3:17). Watchmen patrolled a city's walls and warned of approaching danger; failure to sound the alarm meant the watchman was responsible for the fate of the city. Likewise, if Ezekiel failed to warn the people of their peril, he would be responsible for their sins. It would be an onerous duty to warn the righteous and the unrighteous alike not to sin lest he be held accountable for their blood and punishment. Next the Lord told him to go forth into the plain where He would talk further. *"So I got up and went out to the plain. And **the glory of the** **LORD** was standing there, like the glory I had seen by the Kebar River, and I fell facedown"* (Ezekiel 3:23, emphasis added).

One significance of beholding *the glory of the* LORD by the Kebar River is described in *The Chosen Highway* by Lady Sarah Blomfield. This book is a chronicle of early Bahá'í history that was obtained by the author verbally from the sister of 'Abdu'l-Bahá, Bahíyyih Khánum, and other members of the holy family. Blomfield recorded a recollection from Bahíyyih Khánum, who said that her mother, Ásíyih Khánum, wife of Bahá'u'lláh, had made a coat for Him out of pieces of precious Persian red cloth call *tirmih*, which she had carefully kept for this purpose out of the remains of her marriage treasures.[76]

Blomfield recalled a tradition called "the red robe." It was the account of an eighth-century Muslim who, when speaking of the Great Day of the Lord, said: "In that day the Holy One will be found abiding in a land called Karkh. He will walk beside the river, wearing the dervish turban, and wrapped in a red robe. He will be teaching His followers on the banks of the river. Would that I might be privileged to enter His Presence, and to shed my lifeblood in His Path." [77] Blomfield further explained: "The red robe which Bahá'u'lláh wore when He was teaching His followers on the banks of the River Tigris was made of some pieces of Persian Tirmih. The wife and daughter of Bahá'u'lláh fashioned this 'Aba in readiness for His return from the mountain land of Sulaymaniyyih. Karkh is the name of the district of Baghdad in which the Holy One dwelt." [78]

The final condition of Ezekiel's mission would be the muting of his own speech. Ezekiel would only be able to speak the Word of the Lord, not his own words.

I will make your tongue stick to the roof of your mouth so that you will be silent and unable to rebuke them, for they are a rebellious people. But when I speak to you, I will open your mouth and you shall say to them, 'This is what the Sovereign LORD says.' Whoever will listen let them listen, and whoever will refuse let them refuse; for they are a rebellious people. (Ezekiel 3:26–27)

In other words, Ezekiel would be bereft of speech except when speaking for God. Yet the elders of Israel came to him and heard admonitions such as:

Some of the elders of Israel came to me and sat down in front of me. Then the word of the Lord came to me: "Son of man, these men have set up idols in their hearts and put wicked stumbling blocks before their faces. Should I let them inquire of me at all? Therefore speak to them and tell them, 'This is what the Sovereign Lord says: When any of the Israelites set up idols in their hearts and put a wicked stumbling block before their faces and then go to a prophet, I the Lord will answer them myself in keeping with their great idolatry. I will do this to recapture the hearts of the people of Israel, who have all deserted me for their idols.'

"Therefore say to the people of Israel, 'This is what the Sovereign Lord says: Repent! Turn from your idols and renounce all your detestable practices!" (Ezekiel 14:1-6)

As a mute, Ezekiel would supplement the Lord's words with pantomime, drama, and street theater. These enacted, visual prophecies were designed to cause people to think through what he was "saying." Even simple, easily understood drama had profound meanings, as we shall see in the next chapter.

Chapter 5

EZEKIEL – JUDGMENT AND REDEMPTION

"Then you will live in the land I gave your ancestors;
you will be my people, and I will be your God."

Ezekiel 36:28

E zekiel and Jeremiah may have known each other in Jerusalem and there were parallels between their respective ministries in Jerusalem and Babylon. Jeremiah had exhorted the people in Jerusalem for many years to accept the yoke of the Babylonians, to surrender to them so that they could live. Next to being known as the weeping prophet, perhaps Jeremiah is best known for the many times he lamented that the people would not listen.[79] The Lord had told him, *"I will bring on them and those living in Jerusalem and the people of Judah every disaster I pronounced against them, because they have not listened"* (Jeremiah 36:31). Ezekiel's message was the same, that is, Jerusalem would fall. Ezekiel first used pantomime to warn the exiles that Jerusalem would fall.

PANTOMIMING JUDGMENT

The pantomiming was an early phase of Ezekiel's ministry. He was instructed by God to draw the city of Jerusalem on a block of clay and then lay siege to it with tiny ramps, enemy camps, and battering rams. *"Then take an iron pan, place it as an iron wall between you and the city and turn your face toward it. It will be under siege, and you shall besiege it. This will be a sign to the people of Israel"* (Ezekiel 4:3).

The second act of this drama was for Ezekiel to lie upon his side *"and put the sin of the people of Israel upon yourself. You are to bear their sin for the number of days you lie on your side. I have assigned you the same number of days as the years of their sin. So for 390 days you will bear the sin of the people of Israel"* (Ezekiel 4:4-5). There are many conjectures about the meaning of the 390 days/years. The traditional interpretation is that the 390 years meant the years of sin, starting in King Solomon's reign and ending with the fall of Jerusalem.

Jeroboam was the first king of the northern kingdom of Israel, and he discouraged his people from going to the Temple in Jerusalem to worship by promoting idolatry in Israel. He made two golden calves and placed one at an altar in Bethel and the other at an altar in Dan. *"And this thing became a sin; the people went even as far as Dan to worship the one there"* (1 Kings 12:30). Jeroboam became a symbol of royal sin for promoting many idolatrous activities, thus earning many denunciations in the obituaries of several kings, such as King Baasha's (c. 909-886): *"And he did evil in the sight of the LORD, and walked in the way of Jeroboam, and in his sin wherewith he made Israel to sin"* (1 Kings 15:34). Jeroboam promoted idolatry early in his reign. Subtracting Ezekiel's 390 from 929, the second year of Jeroboam's reign, results in 539, the year Cyrus the Persian conquered the Babylon empire. Within a year Cyrus issued a decree that ended the Babylonian Exile for the Jews and permitted them to return to Jerusalem.

Then Ezekiel was to lie on his right side in order to bear the iniquity of the house of Judah for forty days. *"I have appointed thee each day for a year"* (Ezekiel 4:6). He would eat only one loaf of bread a day that was cooked over cow dung in front of the people. *"He then said to me: 'Son of man, I am about to cut off the food supply in Jerusalem. The people will eat rationed food in anxiety and drink rationed water in despair, for food and water will be scarce. They will be appalled at the sight of each other and will waste away because of their sin'"* (Ezekiel 4:16-17). Forty years is used symbolically many times in the Bible, often to portend change, preparation, beginnings, and endings.

Next came the drama depicting the fall of Jerusalem and its aftermath. Ezekiel was told to take a barber's razor and shave his head and beard. Then he was to divide the hair on a set of scales.

> *"Now, son of man, take a sharp sword and use it as a barber's razor to shave your head and your beard. Then take a set of scales and divide up the hair. When the days of your siege come to an end, burn a third of the hair inside the city. Take a third and strike it with the sword all around the city. And scatter a third to the wind. For I will pursue them with drawn sword. But take a few hairs and tuck them away in the folds of your garment. Again, take a few of these and throw them into the fire and burn them up. A fire will spread from there to all Israel."* (Ezekiel 5:2-4)

A shaved head was symbolic of humility, and humility was coming to the Lord's people. The few hairs saved would be the remnant that would survive. The Lord's condemnation of Jerusalem was unequivocal.

> *"Therefore this is what the Sovereign LORD says: I myself am against you, Jerusalem, and I will inflict punishment on you in the sight of the nations. Because of all your detestable idols, I will do to you what I have never done before and will never do again."* (Ezekiel 5:8-9)

> *"A third of your people will die of the plague or perish by famine inside you; a third will fall by the sword outside your walls; and a third I will scatter to the winds and pursue with drawn sword."* (Ezekiel 5:12)

"I will make you a ruin and a reproach among the nations around you, in the sight of all who pass by. (Ezekiel. 5:14)

"I will send famine and wild beasts against you, and they will leave you childless. Plague and bloodshed will sweep through you, and I will bring the sword against you. I the LORD have spoken." (Ezekiel 5:17)

Instructions for the next dramatic enactment were given when the word of the Lord came to Ezekiel. He was told to pack his belongings for exile and at dusk to leave with them through a hole in the back wall of his home. People would watch and ask what he was doing.

"Say to them, 'This is what the Sovereign LORD says: This prophecy concerns the prince in Jerusalem and all the Israelites who are there.' Say to them, 'I am a sign to you.'

"As I have done, so it will be done to them. They will go into exile as captives.

"The prince among them will put his things on his shoulder at dusk and leave, and a hole will be dug in the wall for him to go through. He will cover his face so that he cannot see the land. I will spread my net for him, and he will be caught in my snare; I will bring him to Babylonia, the land of the Chaldeans, but he will not see it, and there he will die. I will scatter to the winds all those around him—his staff and all his troops—and I will pursue them with drawn sword." (Ezekiel 12:10-14)

The prince was Zedekiah, the last king of Judah, who had not listened to Jeremiah's warnings even after several personal meetings with him. Jerusalem had been under siege for eighteen months when Zedekiah escaped Jerusalem at night through a hole in the city wall but he was soon caught. He was blinded after witnessing the executions of his three sons and then taken to Babylonia where he lived out his life.

A VISION OF THE TEMPLE

On the fifth day of the sixth month of the sixth year, which would have been September of 591 BCE, a year after his call, Ezekiel again saw the brilliant image of the man he had seen in his call, a figure as bright as glowing metal and fire. He also saw the cherubim just as they had been with four faces and wings full of eyes and the likeness of the throne of lapis lazuli above the vault over the heads of the cherubim. *"And there before me was the glory of the God of Israel, as in the vision I had seen in the plain"* (Ezekiel 8:4).

Ezekiel was taken to the Jerusalem Temple and told to look to the north, where he saw an idol of jealousy in the gate entrance to the altar. *"And he said to me, 'Son of man, do you see what they are doing—the utterly detestable things the Israelites are doing here, things that will drive me far from my sanctuary? But you will see things that are even more detestable'"* (Ezekiel 8:6). Inside the Temple, Ezekiel saw images on the walls of crawling things, unclean animals, and idols. Even worse, seventy elders of Israel were standing at the walls and worshipping with incense. Ezekiel was next shown a group of women sitting and mourning the god Tammuz.[j] Then Ezekiel was shown the inner court of the Temple where he saw twenty-five men at the Temple entrance bowing to the sun in the east.

> *He said to me, "Have you seen this, son of man? Is it a trivial matter for the people of Judah to do the detestable things they are doing here? Must they also fill the land with violence and continually arouse my anger? Look at them **putting the branch to their nose!** Therefore I will deal with them in anger; I will not look on them with pity or spare them. Although they shout in my ears, I will not listen to them."* (Ezekiel 8:17-18, emphasis added)

---

[j] Tammuz (Dumuzi) was a shepherd god. According to mythology, he was condemned to spend six months of every year in the underworld with only six months spent above. An annual mourning was held for him when he disappeared into the underworld and would not reappear for six months.

The ritual of *putting the branch to their nose* refers to the worship of the goddess Asherah, a fertility goddess who was symbolized by a sacred tree or pole. It was reported in 1 Kings 11:5 that Solomon worshipped Asherah after one of his foreign wives introduced her worship, and also Molek.

Ezekiel was swiftly shown the judgment of the Lord when He called for those who were appointed to execute judgment on the city. Six men appeared, each with a deadly weapon, and a man clothed in linen who had a writing kit at his side. This man was told to go throughout Jerusalem and put a mark on the foreheads of persons who grieved and lamented over all the detestable things that were done in it. (A man dressed in linen also appears several times in the books of Daniel and Revelation. A note after Revelation 19:8 states, *"Fine linen stands for the righteous acts of God's holy people."*) The other men were told to follow the man in linen and to slaughter everyone except those who had the mark, beginning in the sanctuary of the Temple. A distraught Ezekiel asked the Lord if He was going to destroy the entire remnant of Israel when He pours out His wrath on Jerusalem.

> He answered me, *"The sin of the people of Israel and Judah is exceedingly great; the land is full of bloodshed and the city is full of injustice. They say, 'The LORD has forsaken the land; the LORD does not see.' So I will not look on them with pity or spare them, but I will bring down on their own heads what they have done."*
>
> *Then the man in linen with the writing kit at his side brought back word, saying, "I have done as you commanded."*
> (Ezekiel 9:9-11)

After being told of the coming judgment, Ezekiel saw a throne of lapis lazuli above the vault that was over the heads of the cherubim, and the Lord said to the man in linen, *"Go in among the wheels beneath the cherubim. Fill your hands with burning coals from among the cherubim and scatter them over the city*" (Ezekiel 10:2). This act foretold the conflagration awaiting Jerusalem.

A cloud filled the temple that spread the radiance of the glory of the Lord. The cherubim rose upward as the glory of the Lord also rose and left the Temple to the east.[k] God had deserted Jerusalem and left it to its fate. He had not, however, deserted His people in exile. Ezekiel received from the Lord the following message of hope, the promise of the peoples' return to Israel and the receipt of an undivided heart and new spirit.

> *The word of the Lord came to me: "Son of man, the people of Jerusalem have said of your fellow exiles and all the other Israelites, 'They are far away from the Lord; this land was given to us as our possession.'*
>
> *"Therefore say: 'This is what the Sovereign Lord says: Although I sent them far away among the nations and scattered them among the countries, yet for a little while I have been a sanctuary for them in the countries where they have gone.'*
>
> *"Therefore say: 'This is what the Sovereign Lord says: I will gather you from the nations and bring you back from the countries where you have been scattered, and I will give you back the land of Israel again.*
>
> *"They will return to it and remove all its vile images and detestable idols. I will give them an undivided heart and put a*

---

[k] In traditional Christian angelology, there are many levels of angels, the highest being the seraphim and next the cherubim. The seraphim are mentioned only twice in the Hebrew Bible, both times involved in Isaiah's call narrative. They sang *"Holy, holy, holy is the Lord Almighty; the whole earth is full of his glory"* (Isaiah 6:3). The cherubim are mentioned about sixty times in the Hebrew Bible. Bahá'u'lláh described the cherubim when He wrote: *"By 'angels' is meant those who, reinforced by the power of the spirit, have consumed, with the fire of the love of God, all human traits and limitations, and have clothed themselves with the attributes of the most exalted Beings and of the Cherubim" The Kitáb-i-Íqán,* no. 86, 79.

new spirit in them; I will remove from them their heart of stone and give them a heart of flesh. Then they will follow my decrees and be careful to keep my laws. They will be my people, and I will be their God. But as for those whose hearts are devoted to their vile images and detestable idols, I will bring down on their own heads what they have done, declares the Sovereign Lord." (Ezekiel 11:14-21)

The vision lifted as Ezekiel turned to the exiles and told them everything that the Lord had shown him. The people generally disregarded the preexilic prophets because the foreseen fall of Jerusalem hadn't happened. However, Ezekiel knew that the time of prophetic fulfillment was almost upon them.

The word of the LORD came to me: "Son of man, the Israelites are saying, 'The vision he sees is for many years from now, and he prophesies about the distant future.'

"Therefore say to them, 'This is what the Sovereign LORD says: None of my words will be delayed any longer; whatever I say will be fulfilled, declares the Sovereign LORD.'" (Ezekiel 12:26-28)

The Lord told Ezekiel much more about the devastation to come, that the people would know that He was the Lord when the land became a desolate waste. But not quite yet.

"As for you, son of man, your people are talking together about you by the walls and at the doors of the houses, saying to each other, 'Come and hear the message that has come from the LORD.' My people come to you, as they usually do, and sit before you to hear your words, but they do not put them into practice. Their mouths speak of love, but their hearts are greedy for unjust gain. Indeed, to them you are nothing more than one who sings love songs with

a beautiful voice and plays an instrument well, for they hear your words but do not put them into practice.

"When all this comes true—and it surely will—then they will know that a prophet has been among them." (Ezekiel 33:30-33)

The news of Jerusalem's fall was received the next day! Then the people knew that a true prophet had been among them. Finally silenced were the false prophets who had claimed that Jerusalem would prevail, the House of David would endure, and the deportees would soon return to their homeland. Instead, the third wave of Israelites would soon embark upon the 700-mile trudge to Babylon.

Ezekiel received the news of Jerusalem's fall five years after his second vision of the glory of the Lord, in the seventh year of his exile. He described receipt of the news and the lifting of his muteness: *"In the twelfth year of our exile, in the tenth month on the fifth day, a man who had escaped from Jerusalem came to me and said, 'the city has fallen!' Now the evening before the man arrived, the hand of the LORD was on me, and he opened my mouth before the man came to me in the morning. So my mouth was opened and I was no longer silent"* (Ezekiel 33:21-22).

OUT OF THE NATIONS

The Exile was beginning and the nature of Ezekiel's ministry would change from harsh condemnation to reassurance that the Israelites would be restored. *"For I will take you out of the nations; I will gather you from all the countries and bring you back into your own land"* (Ezekiel 36:24).

Ezekiel's prophetic voice changed after his near-future prophecies were vindicated with the fall of Jerusalem and the Exile. There was an immediate change of tone as his verses started focusing on the far future. Previous to the fall of Jerusalem, he had condemned the people's idolatry. After the fall of Jerusalem, he was told to prophesy against the shepherds of Israel, meaning the religious leaders of Israel, not against the people. First, the shepherds were severely castigated.

The word of the Lord came to me: "This is what the Sovereign Lord says: Woe to you shepherds of Israel who only take care of yourselves! Should not shepherds take care of the flock? You eat the curds, clothe yourselves with the wool and slaughter the choice animals, but you do not take care of the flock. You have not strengthened the weak or healed the sick or bound up the injured. You have not brought back the strays or searched for the lost. You have ruled them harshly and brutally. So they were scattered because there was no shepherd, and when they were scattered, they became food for all the wild animals. My sheep wandered over all the mountains and on every high hill. They were scattered over the whole earth, and no one searched or looked for them." (Ezekiel 34:1-6)

The shepherds—those intransigent religious leaders—would be held accountable for the Lord's flock, which had been scattered. However, *"As a shepherd looks after his scattered flock when he is with them, so will I look after my sheep. I will rescue them from all the places where they were scattered on a day of clouds and darkness"* (Ezekiel 34:12, emphasis added). Jesus would later say that *"as lightning that comes from the east is visible even in the west, so will be the coming of the Son of Man,"* and in the distress of those days *"the sun will be darkened, and the moon will not give its light,"* and He would come *"on the clouds of heaven"* (Matthew 24:27, 29-30). A new shepherd, that is, a new Prophet of God, would come from the east.

Second, Ezekiel described how the sheep would be gathered from all countries and brought back to their own land.

"'For this is what the Sovereign Lord says: I myself will search for my sheep and look after them. As a shepherd looks after his scattered flock when he is with them, so will I look after my sheep. I will rescue them from all the places where they were scattered on a day of clouds and darkness. I will bring them out from the

nations and gather them from the countries, and I will bring
them into their own land. I will pasture them on the mountains
of Israel, in the ravines and in all the settlements in the land…
I will shepherd the flock with justice. (Ezekiel 34:11-13, 16,
emphasis added)

Ezekiel foresaw the spiritual governance of the flock. "*I will place over*
them **one shepherd**, *my servant David, and he will tend them; he will tend*
them and be their shepherd. I the LORD *will be their God,* **and my servant**
David will be prince among them. I the LORD **have spoken. I will make a**
covenant of peace with them…"(Ezekiel 34:23-25).

Jesus made no claim to be the *Prince of Peace*, saying instead, "*Do*
not suppose that I have come to bring peace to the earth. I did not come to
bring peace, but a sword" (Matthew 10:34). 'Abdu'l-Bahá referred to
Bahá'u'lláh as the Prince of Peace when He wrote:

The **Sun of Truth** *hath risen above the horizon of this world and*
cast down its bounty of guidance. Eternal grace is never inter-
rupted, and a fruit of that everlasting grace is universal peace.
Rest thou assured that in this era of the spirit, the Kingdom of
Peace will raise up its tabernacle on the summits of the world, and
the commandments of the **Prince of Peace** *will so dominate the*
arteries and nerves of every people as to draw into His sheltering
shade all the nations on earth. From springs of love and truth and
unity will the true Shepherd give His sheep to drink.[80]

A primary purpose of the Faith of Bahá'u'lláh is to bring universal
peace through the unity of humankind, a blessed level of consciousness
that will not tolerate war. "*It is not for him to pride himself who loveth his*
own country, but rather for him who loveth the whole world. The earth is
but one country, and mankind its citizens." [81] Bahá'u'lláh also put *justice*
foremost in His teachings when He wrote, "*The light of men is Justice.*
Quench it not with the contrary winds of oppression and tyranny. The purpose
of justice is the appearance of unity among men." [82]

There are also far-future prophecies embedded in Ezekiel's near-future ones. His oracle against Egypt is a case in point. It was issued about 571 BCE, fifteen years after his other oracles against countries surrounding Judah were issued during the siege of Jerusalem in 587. Its first three verses state:

> *The word of the LORD came again unto me, saying, Son of man, prophesy and say, Thus saith the Lord GOD; Howl ye,* **Woe worth the day!** *For the day is near, even the day of the LORD is near, a cloudy day; it shall be the time of the heathen.* (Ezekiel 30:1-3, KJV, emphasis added)

About twenty-five hundred years later, 'Abdu'l-Bahá gave a commentary on chapter 11 of the Revelation of John which mentions three woes and also the *woe* mentioned in the thirtieth chapter of Ezekiel as follows:

> *"The second woe is past; and, behold, the third woe cometh quickly."* [1] *The first woe was the advent of the Apostle of God, Muḥammad the son of 'Abdu'lláh, peace be upon Him. The second woe was that of the Báb, upon Him be glory and praise. The third woe is the great Day of the advent of the Lord of Hosts and the revelation of the promised Beauty. The explanation of this matter is provided in the* **thirtieth chapter of Ezekiel,** *where it is said: "The word of the Lord came again unto me, saying, Son of man, prophesy and say, Thus saith the Lord God; Howl ye,* **Woe worth the day!** *For the day is near, even the* **day of the Lord** *is near." It is therefore evident then that the day of woe is the day of the Lord; for in that day woe is upon the heedless, the sinners, and the ignorant. That is why it is said, "The second woe is past; and behold, the third one cometh quickly." This third woe is the day of the manifestation*

---

[1] Revelation 11:14, KJV

of Bahá'u'lláh, the Day of God, and it is near to the day of the appearance of the Báb.[83]

There are many prophesies in the Hebrew Bible about the restoration of the Jews to Israel. Ezekiel presents this theme again.

*"For I will take you out of the nations; I will gather you from all the countries and bring you back into your own land. I will sprinkle clean water on you, and you will be clean; I will cleanse you from all your impurities and from all your idols. **I will give you a new heart and put a new spirit in you;** I will remove from you your heart of stone and give you a heart of flesh. And I will put my Spirit in you and move you to follow my decrees and be careful to keep my laws. Then you will live in the land I gave your ancestors; you will be my people, and I will be your God."* (Ezekiel 36:24-28)

The inpouring into modern Israel would be accompanied by divine grace. God punishes, but God also extends grace. One of the mysteries of God is His ever-flowing grace, whether in this life or the life hereafter. A *new heart and spirit* suggest a new Revelation to come.

Ezekiel continued,

"'This is what the Sovereign Lord says: On the day I cleanse you from all your sins, I will resettle your towns, and the ruins will be rebuilt. The desolate land will be cultivated instead of lying desolate in the sight of all who pass through it. They will say, "This land that was laid waste has become like the garden of Eden; the cities that were lying in ruins, desolate and destroyed, are now fortified and inhabited." Then the nations around you that remain will know that I the Lord have rebuilt what was destroyed and have replanted what was desolate. I the Lord have spoken, and I will do it.'" (Ezekiel 36:33-36).

Under the poor governance of the Ottoman Empire, Palestine became desolate through overgrazing by goats and punitive tax measures that discouraged the development of agriculture and industry. The early Zionist emigrants drained the swamps, cultivated the land, and planted trees. The state of Israel has often been remarked upon for its verdant agricultural land and its vibrant business and technological sectors. Today flowering plants, bushes, and trees are planted everywhere, even on highway median strips.

THE VALLEY OF DRY BONES

Perhaps Ezekiel's best-known promise of restoration is his saga of the valley of dry bones, which is only fourteen verses long. In a vision, Ezekiel was set down in the middle of a valley that was full of human bones and was led back and forth among them. They were very dry, indicating that they were old. The Lord asked, *"Son of man, can these bones live?"* (Ezekiel 37:3) A perplexed Ezekiel responded that only He, the Sovereign Lord, knew. Next, Ezekiel was told to prophesy to the bones:

> *Then he said to me, "Prophesy to these bones and say to them, 'Dry bones, hear the word of the Lord! This is what the Sovereign Lord says to these bones: I will make breath enter you, and you will come to life. I will attach tendons to you and make flesh come upon you and cover you with skin; I will put breath in you, and you will come to life. Then you will know that I am the Lord.'"*
>
> *So I prophesied as I was commanded. And as I was prophesying, there was a noise, a rattling sound, and the bones came together, bone to bone. I looked, and tendons and flesh appeared on them and skin covered them, but there was no breath in them.*
> (Ezekiel 37:4-8)

Ezekiel was then told to prophesy to the breath, to breathe from the four winds, and to breathe it into the slain that they might live.

Therefore, he prophesied as commanded, and breath entered the bones until they came to life. They stood up on their feet like a vast army. The Lord explained to Ezekiel:

> *"Son of man, these bones are the people of Israel. They say, 'Our bones are dried up and our hope is gone; we are cut off.' Therefore prophesy and say to them: 'This is what the Sovereign Lord says: My people, I am going to open your graves and bring you up from them; I will bring you back to the land of Israel. Then you, my people, will know that I am the Lord, when I **open your graves** and bring you up from them. I will put my Spirit in you and you will live, and I will settle you in your own land. Then you will know that I the Lord have spoken, and I have done it, declares the Lord.'"* (Ezekiel 37:11-14, emphasis added)

The vision of the dry bones can first be seen as a straightforward prophecy of the return of the Jews from the diaspora to Israel starting in the nineteenth century. The dry bones can also be understood to mean progressive revelation from God because each new revelation builds on the verities of past ones and revitalizes the divine purpose of religion. The resurrection of the dry bones is an apt description of the renewal of religion that breathes new spiritual life when the previous religion has become like dry bones.

ONE NATION UNDER ONE KING

The Lord told Ezekiel to take a stick of wood and write on it, *"Belonging to Judah and the Israelites associated with him"* and on another stick of wood to write *"Belonging to Joseph (that is, to Ephraim) and all the Israelites associated with him"* (Ezekiel 37:16), then to join them together in one stick. Likewise, the Lord will take the Israelites out of the nations and will gather them back in their own land to be one nation. There would be one king and never again two nations or two kingdoms. *"They will be my people, and I will be their God"* (Ezekiel 37:23). And who will be the king? *"My servant David will be king over them, and they will all have one shepherd"* (Ezekiel 37:24). The people will live in their homeland forever, and

> *"**David** my servant will be their prince forever. I will make a covenant of peace with them; it will be an everlasting covenant. I will establish them and increase their numbers, and I will put my sanctuary among them forever. My dwelling place will be with them; I will be their God, and they will be my people. Then the nations will know that I the LORD make Israel holy, when my sanctuary is among them forever."* (Ezekiel 37:25-28, emphasis added)

Bahá'u'lláh shed mystical light on the mention of *David* above when He wrote, *"The Most Great Law is come, and the Ancient Beauty ruleth upon the throne of David. Thus hath My Pen spoken that which the histories of bygone ages have related."* [84] The Ancient Beauty is a title of Bahá'u'lláh, and the Most Great Law refers to His Dispensation.

Now we will move on to two particularly challenging prophecies of Ezekiel, the saga of Gog and Magog and the measuring of a new temple.

Chapter 6

EZEKIEL – GOG AND MAGOG

"The only true Explainer of the Book of God is the Holy Spirit, for no two minds are alike, no two can comprehend alike, no two can speak alike. That is to say, from the mere human standpoint of interpretation there could be neither truth nor agreement."

'Abdu'l-Bahá [85]

E zekiel's narrative of Gog in the land of Magog (chapters 38-39) is one of the most puzzling, concerning, and even frightening prophecies in the Hebrew Bible. Indeed, it's a labyrinth of fearsome themes and supernatural images. Ezekiel's Gog and Magog has engendered much commentary, not to mention ferocious argument, about a final, horrific war in the last days, or end times, of human history.

The saga of Gog and Magog seems to depict war waged on a restored Israel in the distant future from the time Ezekiel prophesied it. Let's approach the challenge presented by the wars of Gog in three sections: a summary of Ezekiel 38-39; various Christian approaches; and a perspective taken from both biblical and Bahá'í scriptures.

A SUMMARY OF EZEKIEL'S GOG AND MAGOG

Ezekiel was told by the Lord to set his face against Gog, the chief prince of the land of Magog, and to prophesy against him.

> *The word of the LORD came to me: "Son of man, set your face against Gog, of the land of Magog, **the chief prince** of Meshek and Tubal; prophesy against him and say: "This is what the Sovereign LORD says: I am against you, Gog, chief prince of Meshek and Tubal. **I will turn you around, put hooks in your jaws** and bring you out with your whole army—your horses, your horsemen fully armed, and a great horde with large and small shields, all of them brandishing their swords. Persia, Cush and Put will be with them, all with shields and helmets, also Gomer with all its troops, and Beth Togarmah from **the far north** with all its troops—**the many nations** with you.* (Ezekiel 38:1-6, emphasis added)

Gog was a title of *chief prince*, not an individual person. Gog in *the far north* would gather massive forces from Persia, Cush, Put, Gomer, and Beth Togarmah. Today, Persia is now called Iran; the areas of Cush and Put are now Ethiopia and Libya, respectively; Beth Togarmah seems to have been lands today known as central Turkey and Armenia; and Gomer seems to have been located in what is now northern Turkey and eastern Europe. Putting hooks or a bit in the jaw of an animal made it move in the direction the rider desired. The comments *I will turn you around* and *put hooks in jaws* suggests that Gog may be used by God to fulfill His purpose rather than Gog waging war of his own volition. *"In future years you [Gog] will invade a land that has recovered from war, whose people were gathered from many nations to the mountains of Israel, which had long been desolate"* (Ezekiel 38:8). The King James Version states, *"After many days thou shalt be visited: in the **latter years** thou shalt come into the land that is brought back from the sword, ..."* (Ezekiel 38:8, KJV, emphasis added).

Whoever Gog turned out to be, he would *"advance like a storm and be like a cloud covering the land"* (Ezekiel 38:9), *"will come from your place in **the far north*** (Ezekiel 38:15, emphasis added). It's hinted that this invasion will be by the will of God. *"You will advance against my people Israel like a cloud that covers the land. In days to come, Gog, I will bring you against my land, so that **the nations** may know me when I am proved holy through you before their eyes"* (Ezekiel 38:16, emphasis added). Gog and his horde will be driven by their evil scheme to invade a land of unwalled villages, a land of peaceful and unsuspecting people, to plunder and loot these people who had been gathered from among the nations.[m] Mention of *the many nations* hints of the global aspect of the mayhem of Gog and Magog.

The Lord told Ezekiel that Gog was the one of whom He had spoken in former days to His servants, the prophets of Israel. They had prophesied repeatedly that He would bring evil forces against His people. However, the attack from Gog on the land of Israel, even though by the will of God, will arouse His *hot anger.*

> *This is what will happen in that day: When Gog attacks the land of Israel, **my hot anger** will be aroused, declares the Sovereign Lord. In my zeal and fiery wrath I declare that at that time there shall be a great earthquake in the land of Israel. The fish in the sea, the birds in the sky, the beasts of the field, every creature that moves along the ground, and all the people on the face of the earth will tremble at my presence. The mountains*

---

[m] There is speculation that the plunder of Ezekiel 38:13 could refer to the massive reserve of natural gas off the coast of Haifa, Israel. As of this writing in 2023, this gas has enabled Israel to be energy self-sufficient and has the potential to help alleviate European dependency on Russian gas. The news service Al Jazeera reported on June 15, 2022, that the European Union, Israel, and Egypt had signed a tripartite gas deal with Israel in order to lessen reliance upon Russian gas. Israeli exports will be "significant," brought through a pipeline to an Egyptian terminal for liquefication and then transportation to Europe on tankers. https://www.aljazeera.com/news/2022/6/15/eu-signs-gas-deal-with-israel-egypt-in-bid-to-ditch-russia.

will be overturned, the cliffs will crumble and every wall will fall to the ground. I will summon a sword against Gog on all my mountains, declares the Sovereign Lord. Every man's sword will be against his brother. I will execute judgment on him with plague and bloodshed; I will pour down torrents of rain, hailstones and burning sulfur on him and on his troops and on the many nations with him. And so I will show my greatness and my holiness, and I will make myself known in the sight of many nations. Then they will know that I am the Lord. (Ezekiel 38:18-23, emphasis added)

The key word is *judgment,* judgment upon the *many nations* as well as on individuals.

The Lord tells Ezekiel to prophesy that He is against Gog and *"I will turn you around and drag you along. I will bring you from the far north and send you against the mountains of Israel"* Ezekiel 39:2). These forces will be defeated and the dead given as food to carrion birds and wild animals. Fire will be set upon Magog and those who live in supposed safety in the coastlands, and they will know that He is the Lord. *"I will make known my holy name among my people Israel. I will no longer let my holy name be profaned, and the nations will know that I the Lord am the Holy One in Israel. It is coming! It will surely take place, declares the Sovereign Lord. This is the day I have spoken of"* (Ezekiel 39:7-8).

Ezekiel was told that, after Israel's victory, for seven years the people will use the war weapons for fuel—shields, bows and arrows, clubs and spears. They will recover the loot from those who looted them, the plunder from those who plundered them. For seven months, the Israelis will search for bodies to bury. This will be followed by a more detailed seven-month search for bones to be buried. And so will the land be cleansed.

Gog and his soldiers will be buried in the valley called Hamon Gog (the hordes of Gog). *"On that day I will give Gog a burial place in Israel, in the valley of those who travel east of the Sea"* (Ezekiel 39:11). If *east of the sea* means the Dead Sea, the burials will be in a

Jordanian desert. After this total victory, the people are to assemble for a feast prepared for them by the Lord, a great sacrifice on the mountains of Israel.

To what purpose? *"I will display my glory among the nations, and all the nations will see the punishment I inflict and the hand I lay on them. From that day forward the people of Israel will know that I am the* LORD *their God"* (Ezekiel 39:21-22). The heathen are to know that the house of Israel went into exile because of their iniquity, uncleanliness, and trespasses. Therefore, God had hidden His face from them. *"Therefore this is what the Sovereign* LORD *says: I will now restore the fortunes of Jacob and will have compassion on all the people of Israel, and I will be zealous for my holy name"* (Ezekiel 39:25). The slavery of Joseph in Egypt eventually resulted in protection for his family that migrated to Egypt. Likewise, the people will dwell safely and unafraid in their land, gathered from out of their enemies' lands and their Lord sanctified in the sight of many nations.

The final two verses in Ezekiel 39 state: *"Then they will know that I am the* LORD *their God, for though I sent them into exile among the nations, I will gather them to their own land, not leaving any behind. I will no longer hide my face from them, for I will pour out my Spirit on the people of Israel, declares the Sovereign Lord"* (Ezekiel 39:28-29).

CHRISTIAN APPROACHES TO GOG AND MAGOG

Mainstream Protestant churches do not focus much, if at all, on the seemingly impenetrable prophecies from the books of Ezekiel, Daniel, and Revelation. Gog and Magog, in particular, are not dwelled upon.

The approach of the Catholic church is likewise circumspect. The Catholic writers Paul Thigpen and Marcus Grodi reflect this caution: "The Church teaches, of course, that the book of Revelation and the book of Daniel, with its similar imagery, belong among the Scriptures inspired by God. Nevertheless, much of what is contained in these books is exceedingly difficult to understand. The rule of interpreting a biblical text as far as possible in its 'plain sense' does not help much in many passages we find here. The 'plain sense' of a red dragon with seven heads and ten horns is just not very plain at all." [86]

Catholic doctrine recognizes a future great tribulation with the appearance of an antichrist and its deceptions, the Second Coming of Jesus that will be visible to all the world and His reign, the resurrection of the dead with the Last Judgment, and the overthrow of evil. However, Catholicism shies away from premillennialism,[n] the rapture,[o] speculative dates for any future event, and possible identities of Gog or an antichrist. Thigpen and Grodi wrote:

> Unlike the *Left Behind* and many other fundamentalist "prophecy scholars," the Catholic Magisterium[p] does not spend much time speculating about who will be the Antichrist or whether he is now living on earth. It does not try to match up the vivid scenarios in Revelation and Daniel with the evening news and the mutually contradictory, ever-changing predictions of politicians, scientists, and economists. It does not seek to provide a definitive explanation of the millennium, or "thousand years," referred to in Revelation.... After all, the plug-the-headline-into-the-Bible-verse game has always been a losing proposition.[87]

In contrast, the subject of Gog and Magog is of major concern for most evangelical and fundamentalist Protestant Christians, although not all of them dwell on this subject. For example, the Reverand Roger Barrier, who writes from a Southern Baptist perspective, issued a

---

[n] In Christian eschatology, premillennialism is the belief that Jesus will physically return to Earth before a thousand-year golden age of peace. This belief is based on a literal interpretation of Revelation 20:1-6.

[o] The rapture is the belief that believers in Christ will be suddenly taken from earth before the Great Tribulation and the millennium begin.

[p] The Magisterium refers collectively to those who exercise teaching authority, who are the pope and the bishops teaching in union with him.

caution similar to that of Thigpen and Grodi: "As we read about Gog and Magog in Ezekiel 38-39, we discover that understanding the biblical material is quite difficult." [88]

In evangelical thought, two wars are generally seen with Ezekiel 38-39:16 covering the first war as one regional event and Ezekiel 39:17-24 covering a second war that is global in scale. Gog is presented as a human being in the first war and is buried with his soldiers, but he is presented in the second as a superhuman being, or a human taken over by the antichrist, a great antagonist expected to fill the world with wickedness but to be conquered forever by Christ at His second coming. Gog's forces in the first war are primarily from atheistic and Islamic countries, but forces from all nations are involved in the second war and the battle of Armageddon in the Valley of Megiddo in Israel.

The land of Magog in the far north is generally believed to be Russia. Gog gathers his allies and invades modern Israel. The rapture will come just before the war of Gog and Magog starts. The rapture will be the carrying away of the church and of all persons who have died in Christ, as well as all who are alive and living in Christ. The biblical reference used for the rapture is from Paul in 1 Thessalonians 4:13-18:

> Brothers and sisters, we do not want you to be uninformed about those who sleep in death, so that you do not grieve like the rest of mankind, who have no hope. For we believe that Jesus died and rose again, and so we believe that God will bring with Jesus those who have fallen asleep in him. According to the Lord's word, we tell you that we who are still alive, who are left until the coming of the Lord, will certainly not precede those who have fallen asleep. For the Lord himself will come down from heaven, with a loud command, with the voice of the archangel and with the trumpet call of God, and the dead in Christ will rise first. After that, we who are still alive and are left will be caught up together with them in the clouds to meet the Lord in the air. And so we will be with the Lord forever. Therefore encourage one another with these words.

Then will come the *great tribulation* spoken of by Jesus. *"For then shall be great tribulation, such as was not since the beginning of the world to this time, no, nor ever shall be"* (Matthew 24:21, KVJ). The tribulation will affect the whole world and will last seven years, during which time God will pour out His wrath. There are differing views as to when during the tribulation the war of Gog will occur.

Gog and his allies will gather for the battle of Armageddon as noted in Revelation 16:16: *"Then they gathered the kings together to the place that in Hebrew is called Armageddon."* The mark of the beast will be the given to the antichrist's followers, and those who will not worship the beast will be killed (Revelation 13:15). The nations of the world will try to destroy Israel, but at that point Jesus returns and Satan is defeated. The description of the horrors of this war indicates a conflagration of bombs and rockets (*hailstones),* poison gas (*burning sulfur*), and massive destruction.

Jesus will then establish His kingdom on earth for a thousand years, the millennium, and judge the nations. The first resurrection was that of the righteous, both deceased and living, in the rapture before the tribulation began. The second resurrection will be that of the wicked from all ages which will take place after Satan is thrown into the lake of fire. The souls of the wicked will also be thrown into the lake of fire.

Ezekiel does not mention the antichrist, the rapture, the millennium, or Armageddon. Verses from several other books of the Bible are used to construct the evangelical approach to the latter days.

A BAHÁ'Í PERSPECTIVE

This section reflects my Bahá'í viewpoint on Gog and Magog and the latter days as I understand Ezekiel and the Bahá'í writings. My studies have shown that the Bible provides prophetic descriptions of three major Revelations brought since the time of Jesus—those of Muḥammad, the Báb, and Bahá'u'lláh.

The coming of a Prophet of God is called the Day of God, the Day of the Lord, and the Day of Judgment. St. John the Divine in the book of Revelation called this Day a *woe* because of the tests and upheavals that ensue with the coming of a Prophet of God. A new religion for the spiritual advancement of humanity is revolutionary and releases tremendous spiritual energy. Prolonged resistance to it can cause catastrophes. This is even more true today, the latter days, during the transition from the Adamic Cycle, also called the Prophetic Cycle, to the Bahá'í Cycle, also called the Cycle of Fulfillment.

The Adamic Cycle of six thousand years[89] lasted from the Prophets Adam through Muḥammad and ended in 1844. The Cycle of Fulfillment commenced in 1844 with the Báb, the forerunner of Bahá'u'lláh. This shift has brought major positive changes as well as unprecedented social disruption, travails, and chaos. The world we know is crumbling; we are experiencing the cataclysms caused by resistance to the divine forces of spiritual change. The upheavals caused by previous Days of God pale in comparison.

Armageddon is mentioned only once in the Bible: *"Then they gathered the kings together to the place that in Hebrew is called Armageddon"* (Revelation 16:16). The biblical scholar John Able wrote that Armageddon is not only a symbol of war *"but also as a Hebrew cover-name meaning a Mountain of Preaching (HAR-MAGIDON)."* [90] He explained that the Hebrew Bible mentions Megiddo ("Magido") as a valley just once, but mentions Megiddo as a capital of this valley many times. This city controlled the pass connecting the valley from the Sea of Galilee to the coast and many battles were fought there. Today, the city of Megiddo is an archaeological excavation site called Tel-Megiddo. Since the hill Megiddo is located on is only about 200 feet high, it is no mountain. "Instead, the Valley of Magido has only one real HAR that can be called a mountain. It stands in full view, dominating the valley, flanking it as its south-west escarpment. This mountain of **Mount Carmel is *Armageddon*.**" [91]

'Abdu'l-Bahá was recorded as saying the following in a talk in 1912:

We are on the eve of the battle of Armageddon, referred to in the 16th chapter of Revelation. The time is two years hence, when

*only a spark will set aflame the whole of Europe. The social unrest
in all countries, the growing religious skepticism antecedent to the
millennium are already here, will set aflame the whole of Europe
as is prophesied in the Book of Daniel and in the Book (Revelation) of John. By 1917 kingdoms will fall and cataclysms will
rock the earth.*[92]

The First World War broke out in 1914 and was the first global
conflict in human history. Towards the end of this war in late September 1918, the Battle of Megiddo was fought between the British and
Ottoman Turkish armies in northern Palestine in the Jezreel Valley,
which is also called the plain of Armageddon. This battle was the final
Allied offensive in Palestine, and the war officially ended six weeks later
with the Armistice of November 11. Rather than being the war to end
all wars, the First World War was soon followed by the Second World
War, then the Korean War, the Vietnam War, the Gulf War, the Iran-
Iraq War, the Russian war on Ukraine, the Hamas-Israel war, and many
other military conflagrations. Shoghi Effendi referred to the conclusion
of the First World War as "the first stage in a titanic convulsion long
predicted by Bahá'u'lláh." [93] The Battle of Armageddon has intensified
far beyond what was imaginable over one hundred years ago. Humanity
has been in the battle of Armageddon for a long time, and tribulation
has been continuously worsening.

Megiddo, that ancient town situated at the foot of the Carmel
Range overlooking the Jezreel Valley, is now a major tourist attraction.
Many tourists flock there to see where they believe the battle of Armageddon, *"the battle on the great day of God Almighty"* (Revelation 16:14),
will take place. However, as Able said, the biblical mention of Megiddo
is undoubtedly a reference to Mount Carmel. The *Mountain of Preaching* is an apt name for Mount Carmel, the place where Elijah issued his
challenge to the prophets of Baal and whose caves were inhabited by
Elijah and Elisha.

The presence of the administrative headquarters of the Bahá'í Faith
on Mount Carmel gives a new dimension to the battle of Armageddon.

This battle can be understood as being between the proverbial forces of light and darkness. The spiritual forces of a new revelation from God emanate around the world from the Bahá'í World Centre. This new light is countered by the forces of irreligion, immorality, worldly power, corruption, militarism, and unbridled materialism.

There are many parallels in Revelation with Ezekiel that give invaluable additional information and insight into these *last days* when God will bring *"new heavens and a new earth."* *"Then I saw 'a new heaven and a new earth' for the first heaven and the first earth had passed away. I saw the Holy City, the new Jerusalem, coming down out of heaven from God, prepared as a bride beautifully dressed for her husband"* (Revelation 21:1-2). Third Isaiah had said: *"See, I will create new heavens and a new earth. The former things will not be remembered, nor will they come to mind* (Isaiah 65:17). Unfortunately, it would take another book to present the parallels between the books of Isaiah, Ezekiel, and Revelation with the Bahá'í writings. Fortunately, four excellent books set forth the authors' understandings from a Bahá'í perspective—*Apocalypse Secrets: Bahá'í Interpretation of the Book of Revelation* by John Able, *Thy Kingdom Come: A Biblical Introduction to the Bahá'í Faith* by Thomas Tai-Seale, *The Apocalypse: An Exegesis* by Robert Riggs, and *The Logic of the Revelation of St. John* by Stephen Beebe.

The millennium is a major subject within the context of the latter days. 'Abdu'l-Bahá clarified the meaning of the thousand years, the millennium, which is mentioned six times in Revelation 20:1-8.[q] He was

---

[q] *"And I saw an angel coming down out of heaven, having the key to the Abyss and holding in his hand a great chain. He seized the dragon, that ancient serpent, who is the devil, or Satan, and bound him for a thousand years. He threw him into the Abyss, and locked and sealed it over him, to keep him from deceiving the nations anymore until the thousand years were ended. After that, he must be set free for a short time. I saw thrones on which were seated those who had been given authority to judge. And I saw the souls of those who had been beheaded because of their testimony about Jesus and because of the word of God. They had not worshiped the beast or its image and had not received its mark on their foreheads or their hands. They came to life and reigned with Christ a thousand years. (The rest of the dead did not come to life until the thousand years were ended.) This is the first resurrection. Blessed and holy are those who share in the first resurrection. The second*

responding to questions about when the millennium would come, and whether the questioner would live to see it, when He wrote:

> *Concerning the one thousand years as recorded in the Book: It signifieth the beginning of this Manifestation until the end of its predominance throughout the contingent world; because this Cause is great, its powers are growing and its signs are dazzling. It shall continue in elevation, exaltation, growth, promulgation and promotion until it shall reach the apex of its glory in one thousand years – as the Day of this Manifestation is one thousand years. Thou shalt see its conquering power, its manifest dominion, its eternal might and its everlasting glory.*[94]

Bahá'u'lláh stated in *The Kitáb-i-Aqdas* that *"Whosoever layeth claim to a Revelation direct from God, ere the expiration of a full thousand years, such a man is assuredly a lying imposter."* [95] Shoghi Effendi wrote of the Revelation of Bahá'u'lláh: "A Revelation hailed as the promise and crowning glory of past ages and centuries, as the consummation of the dispensations within the Adamic Cycle, inaugurating an era of at least a thousand years' duration, and a cycle destined to last no less than five thousand centuries, signalizing the end of the Prophetic Era and the beginning of the Era of Fulfillment." [96]

Now let's turn our attention to a few portions of the Olivet discourse, Matthew 24. This chapter is called the Olivet discourse because Jesus and His disciples were on the Mount of Olives. An excellent book for understanding this chapter from a Bahá'í perspective is *He Cometh with the Clouds* by Gary L. Matthews.[97] I'll focus on only a few verses.

---

death has no power over them, but they will be priests of God and of Christ and will reign with him for a thousand years. When the thousand years are over, Satan will be released from his prison and will go out to deceive the nations in the four corners of the earth—Gog and Magog—and to the four corners of the earth—Gog and Magog—and to gather them for battle. In number they are like the sand on the seashore" (Revelation 20:1-8).

Jesus gave a stunning description of our times, the transition from one major cycle to another, when He answered His disciples' questions about the end of the age in Matthew 24. Jesus warned of religious deception, wars and the rumors of wars, nations rising against nations, famines and earthquakes, persecution, false prophets, an increase of wickedness, and love grown cold.

The following verses deserve special attention. *"Nation will rise against nation, and kingdom against kingdom. There will be famines and earthquakes in various places. All these are the beginning of birth pains"* (Matthew: 24:7-8). *"And this gospel of the kingdom will be preached in the whole world as a testimony to all nations, and then the end will come"* (Matthew 24:14). The *nations* were cited repeatedly by Ezekiel and twice by Jesus. Nations are currently fighting nations, but the nations will also, eventually, be the foundation for global unity. Jesus then followed with, *"So when you see standing in the holy place 'the abomination that causes desolation,' spoken of through the prophet Daniel—let the reader understand—then let those who are in Judea flee to the mountains"* (Matthew 24:15-16). He did not mince words when He said, *"For then there will be great distress, unequaled from the beginning of the world until now—and never to be equaled again. If those days had not been cut short, no one would survive, but for the sake of the elect those days will be shortened"* (Matthew 24:21-22).

Jesus's disciples thought that He was talking about His own return. However, the Prophets of God are one in essential unity. Each Prophet is a return of the Christ spirit and in that sense a return of the previous Prophet, and each reinforces the spiritual verities taught by the former. Jesus was talking about the coming of Bahá'u'lláh who would arrive *"on the clouds of heaven, with power and great glory"* (Matthew 24:30). The *clouds* indicate the fog of confusion and the inability to see clearly. Bahá'u'lláh said of the day of His coming: *"Say! Tribulation is a horizon unto my Revelation. The day star of grace shineth above it, and sheddeth a light which neither the clouds of men's idle fancy nor the vain imaginations of the aggressor can obscure."* [98]

Jesus is quoted in the Gospel of Mark as saying, *"When you see 'the abomination that causes desolation' standing where it does not belong—let the reader understand—then let those who are in Judea flee to the mountains*" (Mark 13:14). (The *abomination that causes desolation* will be explained in Chapter 18.) To *flee to the mountains* is to seek the religious truth with institutions that will not crumble. When pillars of religion, government, and society fall after exposure of their corruption and worse, a distress *unequaled from the beginning of the world until now* is felt. Why haven't the benefits of science and social progress served us better? Because they haven't been accompanied by the spiritual verities of the ages and by the healing remedies of the Divine Physician, Bahá'u'lláh.

Jesus used the example of the days of Noah when people were going about their lives and ignoring Noah's warnings, until suddenly the flood came and took them away. Jesus warned: "*That is how it will be at the coming of the Son of Man. Two men will be in the field; one will be taken and the other left. Two women will be grinding with a hand mill; one will be taken and the other left*" (Matthew 24:39-41). This scenario describes how one person recognizes the new Day of God and serves it, and another person denies and resists it. One is taken into a new spiritual consciousness and the other is left behind in an outmoded consciousness that no longer assists his soul.

Ezekiel also balanced warnings with visions portraying new hope for humanity as we will explore in the next chapter.

Chapter 7

EZEKIEL – A NEW TEMPLE
FOR HUMANITY

---

*"We, verily, have ordained this Temple to be the source of
all existence in the new creation, that all may know of a certainty
My power to accomplish that which I have purposed through
My word 'Be', and it is!"*

Bahá'u'lláh [99]

Ezekiel had another seemingly enigmatic vision when he was shown
in detail a fully constructed, future temple in Jerusalem. Fortunately,
this vision is comparatively easy to explain and to be understood.

Ezekiel states that he received this vision in April 573 BCE. *"In
the twenty-fifth year of our exile, at the beginning of the year, on the
tenth of the month, in the fourteenth year after the fall of the city—on
that very day the hand of the LORD WAS ON ME AND HE TOOK ME THERE.
In visions of God he took me to the land of Israel and set me on a very high
mountain, on whose south side were some buildings that looked like a city"*
(Ezekiel 40:1-2).

Briefly summarized, Ezekiel was taken to a high mountain overlooking a city and saw a man whose appearance was like bronze. He was

equipped with a linen cord[r] and a measuring rod. Starting at the east gate of this visionary temple, the man of bronze measured its base, threshold, alcoves, walls, jambs, porticos, parapets, gates, courtyard, rooms, and other spaces. In mind-numbing detail throughout three chapters (Ezekiel 40-42), Ezekiel recounts following the man of bronze as he took these measurements and noted aspects of how the temple was built. The altar, furnishings, wall decorations, and carvings were also described in detail. The depiction of this temple is so exact that many drawings have been rendered of it.

THE GLORY OF THE LORD APPEARS IN THE TEMPLE

Just as it seems that there would be no end to the tedious measuring, a spectacular event occurred.

> *Then the man brought me to the gate facing east, and I saw the **glory of the God of Israel** coming from the **east**. His voice was like the roar of rushing waters, and the land was radiant with his glory. The vision I saw was like the vision I had seen when he came to destroy the city and like the visions I had seen by the Kebar River, and I fell facedown. The **glory of the LORD** entered the temple through the **gate facing east**. Then the Spirit lifted me up and brought me into the inner court, and the **glory of the LORD** filled the temple.*
>
> *While the man was standing beside me, I heard someone speaking to me from inside the temple. He said: "Son of man, this is **the place of my throne** and the place for the soles of my feet."*
> (Ezekiel 43:1-7, emphasis added)

---

[r] Linen was considered a pure fabric, and the Temple priests were clothed in linen. "He is to put on the sacred linen tunic, with linen undergarments next to his body; he is to tie the linen sash around him and put on the linen turban. These are sacred garments; so he must bathe himself with water before he puts them on" (Leviticus 16:4).

As the sun rises in the east and travels to the west, all the Manifestations of God have come from the *east* and their teachings have spread to the west. *"From the beginning of time until the present day,"* 'Abdu'l-Bahá affirmed, *"the light of Divine Revelation hath risen in the East and shed its radiance upon the West."* [100] Bahá'u'lláh, *the glory of God,* who was born in Persia, came from the *east* and was ultimately exiled to Akka. Bahá'u'lláh wrote about Akka as the *throne*:

> *Thereupon, a Voice was raised from the direction of Hijáz,* [s] *calling aloud and saying: "Great is thy blessedness, O Akká, in that God hath made thee the dayspring of His Most Sweet Voice, and the dawn of His most mighty signs. Happy art thou in that the* **Throne of Justice** *hath been established upon thee, and the Daystar of God's loving-kindness and bounty hath shone forth above thy horizon. Well is it with every fair-minded person that hath judged fairly Him Who is the Most Great Remembrance, and woe betide him that hath erred and doubted."* [101]

And,

> *Anas, son of Malík* [t] *may God be pleased with him—hath said: "The Apostle of God—may the blessings of God and His salutations be upon Him—hath said: 'By the shore of the sea is a city, suspended beneath* **the Throne,** *and named Akká. He that dwelleth therein, firm and expecting a reward from God—exalted be He—God will write down for him, until the Day of Resurrection, the recompense of such as have been patient, and have stood up, and knelt down, and prostrated themselves, before Him.'"* [102]

---

[s] The Hijáz is a region in the west of present-day Saudi Arabia best known for the holy cities of Mecca and Medina. As the site of Islam's most holy places, the Hijáz has significance in the Arab and Islamic historical and political landscape.

[t] Anas, son of Malik, was the longest-lived of the companions of Muḥammad. He was a prolific transmitter of hadiths, or traditions, about Muḥammad and His utterances that were not included in the Quran.

(See Appendix B for Shoghi Effendi's summary of various remarks about Akka from Sacred Scriptures.)

Returning to Ezekiel's vision of the new temple, he received instructions to describe the temple. *"Son of man, describe the temple to the people of Israel, that they may be ashamed of their sins. Let them consider its perfection, and if they are ashamed of all they have done, make known to them the design of the temple—its arrangement, its exits and entrances—its whole design and all its regulations and laws. Write these down before them so that they may be faithful to its design and follow all its regulations"* (Ezekiel 43:10-11).

The temple was not temporal. The biblical scholar Thomas Tai-Seale gave his understanding that symbolic interpretation is not only more likely than a literal one, but that

> the temple is a symbol for religion itself with its two components: the inner court, or spiritual reality of a religion, and the outer court, the form of religion. The measurement is done by the Prophet of God, who is the assayer of true religion. The reed is the symbol for the Prophet of God from Whom God's melody flows. The rod is the rod of His commandments. The prophecy is of a judgment. Those who are spiritually awake and live in the inner court of religion are counted by the assayer. Those who have only the form of religion—the part dominated by laws, customs, rites, and rituals—are not counted.[103]

'Abdu'l-Bahá commented on the symbolic interpretations of the outer and inner courts as follows:

> *The religion of God consists of two parts: One is the very foundation and belongs to the spiritual realm; that is, it pertains to spiritual virtues and divine qualities. This part suffers neither change nor alteration: It is the Holy of Holies, which constitutes the essence of the religion of Adam, Noah, Abraham, Moses, Christ, Muḥammad, the Báb, and Bahá'u'lláh, and which will endure*

throughout all the prophetic Dispensations. It will never be abrogated, for it consists in spiritual rather than material truth. It is faith, knowledge, certitude, justice, piety, high-mindedness, trustworthiness, love of God, and charity. It is mercy to the poor, assistance to the oppressed, generosity to the needy, and upliftment of the fallen. It is purity, detachment, humility, forbearance, patience, and constancy. These are divine qualities. These commandments will never be abrogated, but will remain in force and effect for all eternity. These human virtues are renewed in every Dispensation; for at the close of each Dispensation the spirit of the law of God, which consists in the human virtues, vanishes in substance and persists only in form.

The second part of the religion of God, which pertains to the material world and which concerns such things as fasting; prayer; worship; marriage; divorce; manumission; legal rulings; transactions; and penalties and punishments for murder, assault, theft, and injury, is changed and altered in every Dispensation and may be abrogated—for policies, transactions, punishments, and other laws are bound to change according to the exigencies of the time.[104]

Ezekiel saw water flowing from the south side as a trickle from under the threshold that continued to the north gate. There the man of bronze faced eastward and measured the flowing water first as ankle-deep, then waist-deep, and finally too deep to cross. Ezekiel was told that the water flowed toward the eastern region and entered the Dead Sea, an inland salt sea. A beautiful portrayal of the cleansing, healing power of the word of God follows.

Then he led me back to the bank of the river. When I arrived there, I saw a great number of trees on each side of the river. He said to me, "This water flows toward the eastern region and goes down into the Arabah, where it enters the Dead Sea. When it empties into the sea, the salty water there becomes fresh. Swarms of living creatures will live wherever the river

*flows. There will be large numbers of fish, because this water
flows there and makes the salt water fresh; so where the river
flows everything will live.... The fish will be of many kinds—
like the fish of the Mediterranean Sea. But the swamps and
marshes will not become fresh; they will be left for salt. Fruit
trees of all kinds will grow on both banks of the river. Their
leaves will not wither, nor will their fruit fail. Every month
they will bear fruit because the water from the sanctuary flows
to them. Their fruit will serve for food and their leaves for
healing.* (Ezekiel 47:6–12)

Waters freshened and waters left for salt are analogies for spiritual movement on one hand and spiritual stasis on the other. A flowing stream of water becomes purified as the flowing motion serves to decompose and dilute pollutants. Flowing water is the cleansing word of God. The various depths of the water suggest the levels of spiritual truths that are revealed through the progressive revelations of the Prophets of God. The refusal to accept a new revelation is stasis, the stillness of swamps and marshes that cannot be freshened when the word of God is rejected.

The biblical scholar John Able commented on the temple by first referring to the renowned Jewish scholar Louis Ginzburg, who recounted a tradition of Moses asking a mystical question of God:

"O Lord of the world! When will this Temple built here in heaven come down to earth below?" God replied: "I have made known the time of the event to no creature, either to the earlier ones or to the later, how then should I tell thee?" Moses said: "Give me a sign, so that out of the happenings in the world I may gather when that time will approach." God: I shall first scatter Israel as with a shovel over all the earth, so that they may be scattered among all nations in the four corners of the earth, and then shall I 'set My hand again the second time,' and gather them in that migrated with Jonah, the son of Amittai, to the land of Pathros, and those that dwell in the land of Shinar, Hamath, Elam, and the islands of the sea." [105]

Able then added his own analysis:

The visionary temple of heavenly New Jerusalem has been waiting for the people of Israel to return. Ever since 1844, this is what has been happening. The Temple of Bahá'u'lláh and his Bahá'í Faith has indeed *come down to earth below* and begun to build global divine civilization. Bahá'u'lláh has taken *the symbolic form of the human temple* and has been *calling from this manifest Temple,* as other messengers did before him. His *Tablet of the Temple* is written in graphic form of a pentacle that represents his human shape and addresses his own self as a *living Temple, from body part to body part,* stating:

> *Thus have we built the Temple with the hands of power and might.... Which is preferable, this, or a temple which is built of clay? Set your faces toward it.* [106]

The other striking parallel is that both Ezekiel and St. John the Divine saw the flow of water. *"Then the angel showed me* **the river of the water of life,** *as clear as crystal, flowing from the throne of God and of the Lamb down the middle of the great street of the city. On each side of the river stood the tree of life, bearing twelve crops of fruit, yielding its fruit every month. And the leaves of the tree are for the healing of the nations"* (Revelation 22:1-2, emphasis added). The *river of the water of life* would seem to indicate a new divine dispensation that would ultimately heal the strife between nations.

A NEW CITY

The measuring was not finished. There would be a new city in addition to the new temple. This new Jerusalem would have three gates on each of its four sides for a total of twelve gates. Each side would measure 4,500 cubits for a total circumference of 18,000. One approach to understanding these numbers is based on a general rule of numerology, which is to add numbers until a one-digit number results and to apply the symbolic meaning of the result. To work with the number 18,000, one would add one and eight and get nine. The number nine is symbolic of the Bahá'í Faith, whose symbol is a nine-pointed star. Shoghi Effendi wrote: "The number nine, which in itself is the number of perfection, is considered by the Bahá'ís as sacred, because it is symbolic of the perfection of the Bahá'í Revelation which constitutes the ninth in the line of existing religions, the latest and fullest Revelation which mankind has ever known." [107]

Over the course of religious history, Jerusalem would come to signify the new, or renewed, Word of God. The book of Revelation states: *"The one who is victorious I will make a pillar in the temple of my God. Never again will they leave it. I will write on them the name of my God and the name of the city of my God, the **new Jerusalem**, which is coming down out of heaven from my God; and I will also write on them my new name"* (Revelation 3:12, emphasis added).

Ezekiel's visionary temple was a sign of the Day of God, the Day of Bahá'u'lláh, when mankind would again come under the protection of God by recognizing and obeying His law. *"And the name of the city from that time on will be:* THE LORD IS THERE" (Ezekiel 48:35). There are many parallels between Ezekiel's description of Jerusalem and those given by St. John the Divine. Two of them are more than coincidental and of great interest.

*And he carried me away in the Spirit to a mountain great and high, and showed me the Holy City, Jerusalem, coming down out of heaven from God. It shone with **the glory of God**, and its brilliance was like that of a very precious jewel, like a jasper, clear as crystal.* (Revelation 21:10-11, emphasis added)

I did not see a temple in the city, because the Lord God Almighty and the Lamb are its temple. The city does not need the sun or the *moon to shine on it, for **the glory of God** gives it light, and the Lamb is its lamp. **The nations** will walk by its light, and the kings of the earth will bring their splendor into it. On no day will its gates ever be shut, for **there will be no night there**. The glory and honor of the nations will be brought into it.* (Revelation 21:22-26, emphasis added)

The *new Jerusalem* is the new dispensation brought by Bahá'u'lláh, *the glory of God.*

The Universal House of Justice elaborated on the meaning of *there will be no night there* as follows:

> The Bahá'í Dispensation is described in the words of its Founder as "a day that shall not be followed by night." Through His Covenant, Bahá'u'lláh has provided an unfailing source of divine guidance that will endure throughout the Dispensation. Authority to administer the affairs of the community and to ensure both the integrity of the Word of God and the promotion of the Faith's message is conferred upon the Administrative Order to which the Covenant has given birth.[108]

Another aspect of *there will be no night there* is that, for the first time in religious history, a line of divinely guided successors to Bahá'u'lláh was provided through 'Abdu'l-Bahá and then His Twin Successors, the Guardianship[u] and the Universal House of Justice.[v] This succession of

---

[u] Bahá'u'lláh had appointed 'Abdu'l-Bahá to succeed Him as head of the Faith. 'Abdu'l-Bahá, who died in 1921, appointed his grandson, Shoghi Effendi, as head of the Faith. Shoghi Effendi chose the most humble title he could think of, that of "Guardian of the Faith."

[v] When Shoghi Effendi died in 1957, he had not left a designated successor. Therefore, nine members of the Hands of the Cause of God (a title conferred upon 27 distinguished Bahá'ís by Shoghi Effendi), handled the affairs of the Faith. Six years later in 1963, the first Universal House of Justice, the global governing body of the Bahá'í Faith, was elected and has been continuously elected every five years since.

divine guidance has and will protect the Bahá'í Faith against the development of schisms, sects, and infighting over leadership. This protection of God will facilitate the major goal of the Bahá'í Faith—the unity of the nations.

Chapter 8

OBADIAH – DELIVERANCE ON MOUNT ZION

*Remember, L*ORD*, what the Edomites did on the day Jerusalem*
fell. "Tear it down," they cried, "tear it down to its foundations!"

Psalm 137:7

Obadiah was an exilic prophet, meaning that his mission occurred primarily during the time of the Exile, and he has the shortest book in the Hebrew Bible—one chapter with twenty-one verses. No biographical information or call narrative is given. Nevertheless, considering his fury with the Edomites' refusal to assist refugees fleeing Jerusalem, the most probable date for Obadiah is the early sixth century soon after the fall of Jerusalem in 586 BCE. An early sixth-century date for Obadiah is the favored position among scholars, which would have made him a contemporary of Jeremiah and Ezekiel. Perhaps he fled Judah ahead of the Babylonians, or maybe he went into the Exile with his countrymen. Writing from the Exile in Babylon would have given his work the best possibility for preservation and eventual inclusion in the canon of the Hebrew Bible.

There was a long, difficult history between the Israelites and the Edomites. Genesis tells how the twins Jacob and Esau, struggled with each other in the womb of their mother, Rebekah. When she asked the Lord why they fought, she was told that they were two nations of two different peoples, that one would be stronger than the other and that the elder would serve the younger. Upon adulthood, the wily Jacob cheated Esau out of his birthright, the blessing of their father Isaac that belonged to the eldest son (Genesis 25:19-27:45).

Esau settled in the hill country of Seir that stretched between the Dead Sea and the Gulf of Aqaba located south of the land of future Judah. In time, Esau came to be called the father of the Edomites. Centuries later, Moses's messengers asked the king of Edom for safe passage for Moses and His people through Edom on their trek to the Promised Land. *"But Edom answered: You may not pass through here; if you try, we will march out and attack you with the sword"* (Numbers 20:18). The Israelites replied that they would go along the main road on foot and would pay for water drunk by them and their livestock. *"Again they answered: You may not pass through"* (Numbers 20:20).

The land of Edom had a somewhat circular configuration that included a mountain range extending from the Dead Sea in the north to the Gulf of Aqaba on the Red Sea in the south. Its northern border was with Moab and the future Judah, and its eastern border was shared with the nomadic Nabateans. The western border was probably indeterminate in the Negev Desert. An international trade route, the King's Highway, ran from Luxor in Egypt to Sharm El Sheikh at the southern tip of the Sinai Peninsula and then to Petra and Damascus, from which trade routes extended east and west. Control of the section of the King's Highway that ran through Edom brought riches to the Edomites, who taxed every passing caravan. The wealthy Edomite city of Petra was carved out of a rock cliff and is today a major tourist attraction in southern Jordan.

The enmity between the Israelites and the Edomites continued for centuries. They battled each other frequently. Edom came under the control of Saul (1 Samuel 14:47), and David's forces supposedly killed all the fighting men in Edom (1 Kings 11:15-16). When the Hebrew kingdom split into two, the Edomites regained their strength and territory and conflicts between Judah and Edom were interspersed with periods of alliance against the Moabites and the Ammonites. The Edomites' harshest blow against the Israelites was their alliance with the Babylonians against Judah. The Edomites plundered areas of Judah, and they not only refused refuge to fleeing Judeans when Jerusalem fell but turned them over to the Babylonians.

Obadiah was undoubtedly already enraged about the perfidy of the Edomites before he received a message in a vision from the Lord that expressed His outrage. The Israelites and the Edomites were both descendants of Isaac and Rebekah, and the history of the Edomites as warring cousins would eventually set the stage for Obadiah's prophecies for today. The first 14 verses of Obadiah are set against this volatile background and join the tradition of past oracles that had been uttered against Edom.

ORACLES AGAINST EDOM

There was a long prophetic tradition of oracles expressing the wrath of God against wicked nations, and Edom was on many prophets' lists. Amos said, *"This is what the LORD says: 'For three sins of Edom, even for four, I will not relent. Because he pursued his brother with a sword and slaughtered the women of the land, because his anger raged continually and his fury flamed unchecked, I will send fire on Teman that will consume the fortresses of Bozrah"* [w] (Amos 1:11–12). The book of Isaiah devoted a chapter to God's vengeance on Edom which includes, *"God will stretch out over Edom the measuring line of chaos and the plumb line of desolation"* (Isaiah 34:11). Jeremiah wrote oracles against several nations, and the one against Edom included: *"Edom will become an object of horror; all who pass by will be appalled and will scoff because of all its wounds"* (Jeremiah

---

[w] Teman was a city in western Sinai believed to have been named after a grandson of Esau. Bozrah was the principal city of Edom and possibly its capital. It's located in modern-day Jordan.

49: 17). Ezekiel sternly condemned Edom and prophesied God's judgment against it. *"I will make you desolate forever; your towns will not be inhabited. Then you will know that I am the Lord"* (Ezekiel 35:9).

Obadiah continued in like vein and got right to the point. *"This is what the Sovereign* LORD *says about Edom—'Though you soar like the eagle and make your nest among the stars, from there I will bring you down,' declares the Lord"* (Obadiah 1:4). He speaks of thieves who take only what they want and grape pickers who leave few grapes. Obadiah warns how Edom will be deceived and overpowered by its friends. He continues:

> *"In that day," declares the* LORD,
> > *"will I not destroy the wise men of Edom,*
> > *those of understanding in the mountains of Esau?*
> *Your warriors, Teman, will be terrified,*
> > *and everyone in Esau's mountains*
> > *will be cut down in the slaughter.*
> *Because of the violence against your brother Jacob,*
> > *you will be covered with shame;*
> > *you will be destroyed forever."* (Obadiah 1:8-10)

The scene then shifts spectacularly to another time, to the day of the Lord when tyrannical nations like Edom will face divine judgment.

> *"The **day of the** LORD *is near for all nations.*
> *As you have done, it will be done to you;*
> > *your deeds will return upon your own head.*
>
> *Just as you drank on my holy hill,*
> > *so **all the nations** will drink continually;*
> *they will drink and drink*
> > *and be as if they had never been.*
> ***But on Mount Zion will be deliverance;***
> > *it will be holy,*
> > *and Jacob will possess his inheritance.*

Jacob will be a fire
and Joseph a flame;
Esau will be stubble,
and they will set him on fire and destroy him.
There will be no survivors from Esau."

The Lord has spoken. (Obadiah 1:15–18, emphasis added)

Obadiah proclaimed that the *day of the Lord* is near for *all the nations* and that *deliverance* would come from Mount Zion. Bahá'u'lláh wrote: *"The promises of God, as recorded in the holy Scriptures, have all been fulfilled. Out of Zion hath gone forth the Law of God, and Jerusalem, and the hills and land thereof, are filled with the glory of His Revelation. Happy is the man that pondereth in his heart that which hath been revealed in the Books of God, the Help in Peril, the Self-Subsisting.*[109]

The book of Obadiah ends by stating: *"Deliverers will go up on Mount Zion to govern the mountains of Esau. And the kingdom will be the Lord's"* (Obadiah 1:21).

THE END OF EDOM

The Edomite nation came to an end with poetic justice. It did not prosper under Babylonian rule. Soon after the days of Obadiah, the Edomites were displaced from portions of their land by the Nabateans from the east, who took over Petra and Bozrah. The Edomites moved into the western Sinai where they became known as the Idumeans, and they also were pushed north into Judah just fifteen miles south of Hebron. Then in the second century, John Hyrcanus, a prince of the Hasmonean family who ruled the Jewish Maccabean nation,[x] solved the problem of the

---

[x] The Maccabees were the leaders of a Jewish rebel army in Judea that gained autonomy from the Greeks in 164 BCE and lost it one hundred years later in 63. John Hyrcanus reigned from 134 to 104.

polytheistic, quarreling Edomites for once and for all. After taking their major cities, he forced their conversion to Judaism!

Unfortunately, the Edomite line of Jews produced Herod I, who ruled Judah under the Roman Empire. He is remembered for his colossal building projects that included an expansion of the Second Temple and the Temple mount. Herod is also remembered for his tyranny and cruelty, his murder of family members, and his alleged attempt to kill the infant Jesus (Matthew 2:1–18). Herod died a slow, excruciatingly painful death from kidney failure and a medical condition that appeared to have been Fournier's disease.[y]

---

[y] Findings presented at the Clinical Pathological Conference in January 2002 suggest that Herod succumbed to a combination of chronic kidney disease and an unusual genital infection called Fournier's gangrene.

Chapter 9

SECOND ISAIAH –
COMFORT YE, COMFORT YE
MY PEOPLE

"I am the One Whom the tongue of Isaiah hath extolled,
the One with Whose name both the Torah and the Evangel
were adorned."

Bahá'u'lláh[110]

Biblical scholars mostly agree that book of Isaiah contains distinct works of at least three men from three separate periods. Isaiah himself could only have authored Chapters 1 to 39, called First Isaiah, Proto-Isaiah, and the historical Isaiah. Chapters 40 to 55, called Second Isaiah and Deutero-Isaiah, were written by a person living in Babylonia during late exilic times. Chapters 56 to 66, called Third Isaiah and Trito-Isaiah, were written by an individual living in postexilic Jerusalem. The identities of Second and Third Isaiah are not known.

The message of Second Isaiah is in essential harmony with that of First Isaiah. No biographical data has been discovered for the prophet of Second Isaiah, but biblical scholars generally agree that he lived during the Exile, probably in Babylon. The middle section of the book of Isaiah, chapters 40 through 55 that are called Second Isaiah, may have been a collective effort, although I will refer to Second Isaiah in the singular. His message proclaims in soaring language the tremendous scale of God's power in creation and human history.

Steeped in the tradition of First Isaiah, Second Isaiah reflected much of his predecessor's theological beliefs. Yet Second Isaiah was separated in time, distance, and circumstances from First Isaiah, and he developed his own approach for the challenges of his time. The Exile had begun by the time of Second Isaiah, and this made paramount the reassurance of the comfort and mercy of God. The redemptive message was that God would bring deliverance and salvation to His people. Not only would the Hebrews of the Exile be restored to Jerusalem, but clear signals were given about future Prophets of God, including Jesus, the Báb, and Bahá'u'lláh.

The beauty and scope of Second Isaiah are staggering. This prophet painted a portrait of the condition and future of his people with a sweeping brush of compassion, certitude, and optimism. Punishment had been meted out, the sentence was being served, and never again would God so chastise His people like that.

> *"To me this is like the days of Noah,*
>   *when I swore that the waters of Noah*
>   *would never again cover the earth.*
> *So now I have sworn not to be angry with you,*
>   *never to rebuke you again.*
> *Though the mountains be shaken*
>   *and the hills be removed,*
> *yet my unfailing love for you will not be shaken*
>   *nor my covenant of peace be removed,"*
>   *says the* LORD, *who has compassion on you.* (Isaiah 54:9–10)

COMFORT YE, COMFORT YE MY PEOPLE

Second Isaiah reveals much of his message in the first five verses, his poignantly soothing and reassuring words of comfort. Are there more evocative words of comfort than the following?

> *Comfort ye, comfort ye my people, saith your God. Speak ye comfortably to Jerusalem, and cry unto her, that her warfare is accomplished, that her iniquity is pardoned: for she hath received of the* LORD's *hand double for all her sins.*
>
> *The voice of him that* **crieth in the wilderness, Prepare ye the way of the** LORD, *make straight in the desert a highway for our God. Every valley shall be exalted, and* **every mountain and hill shall be made low:** *and* **the crooked shall be made straight,** *and the rough places plain: And the* **glory of the** LORD *shall be revealed, and* **all flesh shall see it together:** *for the* **mouth of the** LORD *hath spoken it.* (Isaiah 40:1-5, KJV, emphasis added)

The debt for past iniquity has been paid double. Foresight is given of John the Baptist as the voice that *crieth in the wilderness*, the voice that prepared the way for the Lord Jesus. The *way of the* LORD would mean Jesus, who would bring a new covenant with God. All four of the Gospels refer to Isaiah 40:3, one of them as follows:

> *In those days John the Baptist came, preaching in the wilderness of Judea and saying, "Repent, for the kingdom of heaven has come near." This is he who was spoken of through the prophet Isaiah:*
>
> > *"A voice of one calling in the wilderness,*
> > *'Prepare the way for the Lord, make straight paths for him.'"* [z]
> > (Matthew 3:1-3)

---

[z] Isaiah 40:3

John the Baptist preached repentance because the kingdom of heaven was at hand and baptized those who repented. Priests and Levites were sent to ask him who he was, to ask if he was Elijah. John denied being the Elijah. Then who was he? *"John replied in the words of Isaiah the prophet, 'I am the voice of one calling in the wilderness. Make straight the way for the LORD'"* (John 1:23).

Every mountain was to be made low. 'Abdu'l-Bahá explained the significance of mountains when He wrote: *"The mountains are men of high renown, whose famous names sink into insignificance, when the dawn of the Manifestation fills the world with light. The pomp of Annas and Caiaphas is outshone by the simple glory of the Christ. The earthquake is the wave of spiritual life, that moves through all living things and makes creation quiver."* [111]

One of the awesome aspects of Second Isaiah is that he apparently foretold both the coming of Jesus and Bahá'u'lláh in verses 40:1-5. The *glory of the LORD* is Bahá'u'lláh, Whose words have been translated into hundreds of languages and disseminated around the world. Because of the internet and other marvels of the communications revolution, *all flesh shall see it together.*

Symbolically, a new Covenant exalts the valleys and lowers the hills and mountains, the terrain of men's outmoded beliefs and the religious authorities who ill serve their people. A new Covenant makes *the crooked straight*, the *crooked* being idolatries, superstitions, and outmoded laws, and the *straight* a new dispensation from God with spiritual teachings and laws for that day.

The prophet continued, *"A voice says, 'Cry out.' And I said, 'What shall I cry?'"* (Isaiah 40:6) That all people are like grass was the answer, unfaithful like withering grass and falling flowers, but the word of God would endure forever.

O Zion, that bringest good tidings, get thee up into the high mountain; O Jerusalem, that bringest good tidings, lift up thy voice with strength; lift it up, be not afraid; say unto the cities of Judah, Behold your God!

> *Behold, the* LORD *God will come with strong hand, and his arm shall rule for him: behold, his reward is with him, and his work before him.* (Isaiah 40.9-10, KJV)

Bahá'u'lláh commented on these verses. Note His use of Zion and Jerusalem as symbology.

> *O Shaykh! Peruse that which Isaiah hath spoken in His Book. He saith: "Get thee up into the high mountain, O Zion, that bringest good tidings; lift up Thy Voice with strength, O Jerusalem, that bringest good tidings. Lift it up, be not afraid; say unto the cities of Judah: 'Behold your God! Behold the Lord God will come with strong hand, and His arm shall rule for Him.'" This Day all the signs have appeared. A Great City hath descended from heaven, and Zion trembleth and exulteth with joy at the Revelation of God, for it hath heard the Voice of God on every side. This Day Jerusalem hath attained unto a new Evangel, for in the stead of the sycamore standeth the cedar. Jerusalem is the place of pilgrimage for all the peoples of the world, and hath been named the Holy City. Together with Zion and Palestine, they are all included within these regions. Wherefore, hath it been said: "Blessed is the man that hath migrated to Akká."* [112]

The people had been forgiven and their future awaited. But had they learned their lessons about monolatrous idolatry after their defeat by the Babylonians? The Lord asked some ultimate questions, thus presenting a challenge to absolute honesty and humbleness:

> *"To whom will you compare me?*
>   *Or who is my equal?" says the Holy One.*
> *Lift up your eyes and look to the heavens:*
>   *Who created all these?*
> *He who brings out the starry host one by one*
>   *and calls forth each of them by name.*

Because of his great power and mighty strength,
not one of them is missing." (Isaiah 40:25-26)

The Israelites in the Exile were confronted with a new array of deities. Isaiah saw firsthand the temptations of Babylonian idolatry as the Hebrews built their new lives in the Exile. Isaiah countered with rebukes reminiscent of those given by the preexilic prophets.

"This is what the LORD says—
Israel's King and Redeemer, the LORD Almighty:
I am the first and I am the last;
apart from me there is no God.
Who then is like me? Let him proclaim it.
Let him declare and lay out before me
what has happened since I established my ancient people,
and what is yet to come—
yes, let them foretell what will come.
Do not tremble, do not be afraid.
Did I not proclaim this and foretell it long ago?"
(Isaiah 44:6-8)

Isaiah added ridicule to his arsenal.

Bel *bows down,* **Nebo** *stoops low; their idols are borne by beasts of burden. The images that are carried about are burdensome, a burden for the weary. They stoop and bow down together; unable to rescue the burden, they themselves go off into captivity.* (Isaiah 46:1-2)

Bel was a name for Marduk, the preeminent god of Babylon, and *Nebo* was a high-ranking god. They are portrayed as burdens to the beasts who haul their wooden images, and they are shown as inanimate objects unable to deliver the Babylonians from defeat at the hands of the Persians.

The people are commanded not to complain, not to think that their actions are hidden from the Lord, and not to believe that their cause is disregarded by the Lord. Something momentous would happen. Wonders were in store.

CYRUS II AND THE PROMISE OF RETURN

First Isaiah foresaw the Assyrians as God's tool for the punishment of the northern kingdom. Jeremiah and Ezekiel identified the Babylonians as God's instrument of chastisement of the southern kingdom. Now came a change in fortune for the Jews. Second Isaiah announced that the Persian king Cyrus II (c. 559–530 BCE), also known as Cyrus the Great, would be God's instrument to end the Exile by conquering the Babylonians. *"I have stirred up one from the north, and he comes—one from the rising sun who calls on my name. He treads on rulers as if they were mortar, as if he were a potter treading the clay"* (Isaiah 41:25). The armies of Cyrus came from the north of Babylon, from the far northwest of Persia.

Redemption was coming. At least five times Second Isaiah acknowledged Cyrus as God's tool for the restoration of Israel. Joyful verses flow as though redemption had already arrived. *"Sing for joy, you heavens, for the LORD has done this; shout aloud, you earth beneath. Burst into song, you mountains, you forests and all your trees, for the LORD has redeemed Jacob, he displays his glory in Israel"* (Isaiah 44:23).

The joyful verses continue with the affirmations that the Lord is the maker of all things who stretches out the heavens and spreads out the earth by Himself, who foils the signs of false prophets, who turns the learning of the wise into nonsense, and who fulfills the predictions of His messengers, the Prophets of God, who says that Jerusalem and the towns of Judah shall be rebuilt. He says of Cyrus: *"He is my shepherd and will accomplish all that I please; he will say of Jerusalem, 'Let it be rebuilt,' and of the temple, 'Let its foundations be laid'"* (Isaiah 44:28).

Second Isaiah wrote that the Lord spoke of Cyrus as His *anointed*, which was the only time in the Hebrew Bible that a non-Hebrew was so honored. *"This is what the* LORD *says to his **anointed**, to Cyrus, whose right hand I take hold of to subdue nations before him.... I summon you by name and bestow on you a title of honor, though you do not acknowledge me"* (Isaiah 45:1, 4, emphasis added). Cyrus was the only non-Hebrew person in the Hebrew Bible who was anointed.

The Babylonian empire had been in the throes of theological strife because its king Nabonidus (c. 556–539) had elevated the moon-god Sin to supreme god of the empire, thereby displacing the god Marduk. The disaffected priests of Marduk believed that their god had recognized Cyrus as righteous and had ordered him to move against Babylon so that he could be reinstated at the top of the deific hierarchy. Cyrus marched through the Babylonian empire with little opposition. Perhaps it was the priests of Marduk who opened the gates of Babylon to the Persian army that took the city without a battle in 539. Cyrus was hailed as champion by both the priests of Marduk and the Hebrews, although he worshipped neither Marduk nor the Lord. He was a devout Zoroastrian.

Hope and expectancy abounded within the Jewish community that their fortunes would improve under Persian rule. Could the return to Judah really be possible as Second Isaiah had foreseen? Could the anger of God truly have been abated?

The memories of the siege of Jerusalem had been handed down to the second and third generations in the Exile. These recollections, like those of the Holocaust twenty-six hundred years later, chilled the collective Jewish soul. The book of Lamentations tells of besieged Jerusalem with starving infants and children, the nobility sitting on ash heaps and embracing dung heaps, corpses in the streets, and cannibalism. How does one have hope when faith in God has been dashed by His apparent absence in the hour of extreme peril?

Or had He been absent? Second Isaiah nurtured the small wellspring of hope rising in the exilic community by telling the people repeatedly not to fear, not to be afraid, and not to be dismayed. *"Do not fear, for I have redeemed you; I have summoned you by name; you are mine"* (Isaiah 43:1). And the promise was made:

This is what the LORD says—
your Redeemer, the Holy One of Israel:
"For your sake I will send to Babylon
and bring down as fugitives all the Babylonians,
in the ships in which they took pride.
I am the LORD, YOUR HOLY ONE,
Israel's Creator, your King." (Isaiah 43:14)

Most of the educated Hebrews of Judah, such as the scholars, scribes, and priests who were the guardians of Hebrew worship, traditions, and scripture, had been sent to Babylon. Therefore, they must be returned to Judah so that succeeding portions of the divine plan could unfold. The Restoration was imperative. This was made clear in no uncertain terms.

Some of the exiled Judahites had adopted Mesopotamian polytheism and found it expedient to exchange the Canaanite gods for Babylonian ones. Assimilated into the local culture, they were not motivated to partake of the Restoration. The Exile had served as a filter for Hebrew identity and faithfulness to the Covenant of Moses, although the struggle for such would continue in Jerusalem and Judah.

SOMETHING NEW

The earlier prophets had striven to renew and strengthen spiritual obedience to the Mosaic Dispensation while sometimes time-shifting into future dispensations. Second Isaiah strongly reiterated faith in the one God, but he focused comparatively little on renewing past religious revelation and more on anticipating what was to come—with expectancy and excitement.

Do you not know?
Have you not heard?
Has it not been told you from the beginning?
Have you not understood since the earth was founded?

He sits enthroned above the circle of the earth,
*   and its people are like grasshoppers.*
He stretches out the heavens like a canopy,
*   and spreads them out like a tent to live in.*
He brings princes to naught
*   and reduces the rulers of this world to nothing.*
(Isaiah 40:21-23)

Even youths grow tired and weary,
*   and young men stumble and fall;*
but those who hope in the L*ORD*
*   will renew their strength.*
They will soar on wings like eagles;
*   they will run and not grow weary,*
*   they will walk and not be faint.* (Isaiah 40:30-31)

Past trials were not to be dwelt upon because the new was coming:

"Forget the former things;
*   do not dwell on the past.*
See, I am doing a new thing!
*   Now it springs up; do you not perceive it?*
I am making a way in the wilderness
*   and streams in the wasteland."* (Isaiah 43:18-19)

The Lord is the all-knowing from the beginning; His purpose is a force that none can stand against.

I make known the end from the beginning,
**   from ancient times, what is still to come.**
I say, 'My purpose will stand,
*   and I will do all that I please.'*
From the east I summon a **bird of prey;**
*   from a far-off land, a man to fulfill my purpose.*

What I have said, that I will bring about;
what I have planned, that I will do.
(Isaiah 46:10-11, emphasis added)

The divine time of God is not our concept of time that is circumscribed by yesterday, today, and tomorrow, and by clocks and calendars. Divine knowledge since creation was declared in these words: *"I make known the end from the beginning, from ancient times, what is still to come."* The summoned *bird of prey* turned out to be the Persian King Cyrus, who was destined to fulfill God's plan that the Jews return from Babylon to Jerusalem.

THE SERVANT SONGS

And where would we look for what is still to come? Good possibilities are found in the four segments of Second Isaiah that are known as the servant songs wherein the prophet wove a mosaic of insights into what and who was to come. The sets of verses generally identified with the servant include Isaiah 42:1-4, 49:1-6, 50:4-11, and 52:13-15 to 53:12. These four sets of verses dispersed throughout Second Isaiah hold keys to the *"new things, of hidden things unknown to you"* (Isaiah 48:6).

Little in the Hebrew Bible has been pondered and debated as much as the identification of the servant, sometimes called the suffering servant, and interpretation of the servant songs. Traditional Christian theology recognizes the servant passages as references to Jesus and His suffering and crucifixion as ordained by God. There are many theological approaches to the servant songs, and various Bahá'í writers have added their insights. Perhaps more than one Prophet from more than one religion is described in the servant songs.

The first servant song (Isaiah 42:1–4) is only four verses in length. The servant is introduced as the one on whom God will put His Spirit and who will bring justice to the nations.

"Here is my servant, whom I uphold,
  my chosen one in whom I delight;
I will put my Spirit on him,
  and he will bring justice to the nations.
He will not shout or cry out,
  or raise his voice in the streets.
A bruised reed he will not break,
  and a smoldering wick he will not snuff out.
In faithfulness he will bring forth justice;
  he will not falter or be discouraged
till he establishes justice on earth.
  In his teaching the islands will put their hope." (Isaiah 42:1-4)

These verses are mentioned in the Gospel of Matthew in connection with one of Jesus's earlier incidents of healing and teaching that aroused the enmity of the Pharisees. Jesus had gone into a synagogue on the Sabbath and encountered a man with a shriveled hand. The Pharisees asked Jesus if it was lawful to heal on the Sabbath. Jesus answered by asking if the owner of a sheep fell into a pit on the Sabbath, would he not pull it out. *"How much more valuable is a person than a sheep! Therefore it is lawful to do good on the Sabbath"* (Matthew 12:12). He then restored the man's shriveled hand to the soundness of the other. Knowing that the Pharisees were plotting how to kill Him, Jesus quietly left, followed by a large crowd. He healed those who were ill and warned them not to tell others about Him.

This was to fulfill what was spoken through the prophet Isaiah:

"Here is my servant whom I have chosen,
  the one I love, in whom I delight;
I will put my Spirit on him,
  and he will proclaim justice to the nations.

He will not quarrel or cry out;
no one will hear his voice in the streets.
A bruised reed he will not break,
and a smoldering wick he will not snuff out,
till he has brought justice through to victory.
In his name the nations will put their hope." aa
(Matthew 12:17-21)

Approaches to understanding may need to be multi-layered. Consider the verses that immediately follow this first servant song.

"I, the LORD, have called you in righteousness;
I will take hold of your hand.
I will keep you and will make you
to be a covenant for the people
and a light for the Gentiles
to open eyes that are blind,
to free captives from prison
and to release from the dungeon those who sit in darkness.

"I am the LORD; that is my name!
I will not yield my glory to another
or my praise to idols.
See, the former things have taken place,
and new things I declare;
before they spring into being
I announce them to you." (Isaiah 42:6-9)

In 1902, an address written by the preeminent Bahá'í scholar of the late nineteenth and early twentieth centuries, Mírzá Abu'l-Faḍl, was read at a celebration of 'Abdu'l-Bahá held in Washington, D.C. Mírzá

aa Isaiah 42:1-4

Abu'l-Faḍl remarked at length on many verses from the book of Isaiah and in particular on the above verses as follows:

> Consider how, in the first few verses of the 42nd chapter of Isaiah, it is clearly shown that in the last day, God, the Exalted, shall elect the Bearer of the Banner of His servitude, confer upon Him the Holy Spirit of His Divinity, unfurl the standard of the Supreme Covenant and Testament in His Name, and shall protect Him, with His Strong Hand, from the deceit of the violators and the devices of the people of rancor; that Servant of the Lord shall become a Banner for the people's salvation and a Light for hearts and souls; shall restore the blind and deliver the captives; direct those who sit in darkness unto light; place all the creatures under the standard of universal peace, security and absolute emancipation, and make the tongues of all the east and west fluent in new hymns and wonderful glorifications! [113]

'Abdu'l-Bahá had been born 'Abbás, but He took the name Servant of Bahá. This was the only title He ever permitted Himself. According to Mírzá Abu'l-Faḍl, the "Bearer of the Banner of His servitude" was 'Abdu'l-Bahá.

The second servant song has six verses (Isaiah 49:1-6). The pronoun "I" indicates that the servant himself is speaking. Let's consider it in two parts.

> *Listen to me, you islands;*
>   *hear this, you distant nations:*
> *Before I was born the LORD called me;*
>   *from my mother's womb he has spoken my name.*
> *He made my mouth like a **sharpened sword**,*
>   *in the shadow of his hand he hid me;*
> *he made me into **a polished arrow***
>   *and concealed me in his **quiver**.*
> (Isaiah 49:1-2, emphasis added)

The tongues of the Prophets of God are like sharpened swords that cut through traditional, outmoded beliefs and customs of their times. A *polished arrow* could mean the communication of a Prophet of God Whose teachings strike into the hearts of men. A *quiver* would hold the many such arrows launched, or it could be an analogy for the progression of each *arrow* being a Day of the Lord when it is nocked in the bow and sent forth by the divine archer.

Second Isaiah continued:

> *And now the* Lord *says—*
>   *he who formed me in the womb to be his servant*
> *to bring Jacob back to him*
>   *and gather Israel to himself,*
> *for I am honored in the eyes of the* Lord
>   *and my God has been my strength—*
> *he says:*
>
> *"It is too small a thing for you to be my servant*
>   *to restore the tribes of Jacob*
>   *and bring back those of Israel I have kept.*
> *I will also make you* **a light for the Gentiles**,
>   *that my salvation may reach to the ends of the earth."*
> (Isaiah 49:5-6, emphasis added)

Jesus became a *light for the Gentiles* as early Christianity spread throughout the Middle East and eventually throughout the world. Paul and other early Christians had first preached primarily to the Jews, but they were generally not as receptive to this new message as many gentiles were.

As we move along, let's keep in mind that the *new things I declare* were announced in the plural.

The third Servant song also has six verses (Isaiah 50:4-9). The words are confident and suggest the inner voice of Jesus as He as ponders His mission.

The Sovereign LORD *has given me a well-instructed tongue,*
   to know the word that sustains the weary.
He wakens me morning by morning,
   wakens my ear to listen like one being instructed.
The Sovereign LORD *has opened my ears;*
   I have not been rebellious,
   I have not turned away.
I offered my back to those who beat me,
   my cheeks to those who pulled out my beard;
I did not hide my face
   from mocking and spitting.
Because the Sovereign LORD *helps me,*
   I will not be disgraced.
Therefore have I set my face like flint,
   and I know I will not be put to shame.
He who vindicates me is near.
   Who then will bring charges against me?
   Let us face each other!
Who is my accuser?
   Let him confront me!
It is the Sovereign LORD *who helps me.*
   Who will condemn me?
They will all wear out like a garment;
   the moths will eat them up. (Isaiah 50:4-9)

The tribulations of Jesus, especially the physical punishment He suffered before and during the crucifixion, fit the travails of the suffering servant. When the Sanhedrin brought him to Pilate and Pilate asked Him if He was king of the Jews, Jesus's response was not as passive as it might seem. *"You have said so"* (Matthew 26:64, Mark 15:2). For He had not only turned the question back on Pilate but followed it with a declaration of His identity: *"But I say to all of you: From now on you will see the Son of Man sitting at the right hand of the Mighty One and coming on the clouds of heaven"* (Matthew 26:64).

The afore-mentioned verse seems not only to refer to Jesus, but also to someone to come. In His response to Pilate, Jesus appeared to be quoting Daniel 7:13. *"In my vision at night I looked, and there before me was one like a son of man, coming with the clouds of heaven. He approached the Ancient of Days and was led into his presence."* The seventh chapter of Daniel, which is fully discussed in Chapter 17 of this volume, is devoted to Daniel's prophecy known as "a time, times, and half a time." This prophecy points to the year 1844.

The fourth servant song of 15 verses (Isaiah 52:13-15 to 53:1-12) is seen by the renowned Polish-American rabbi Abraham J. Heschel[ab] as presenting the Jewish perspective that the servant was not an individual but was the Nation of Israel that had received double for all her sins. Heschel wrote, "Israel's suffering is not a penalty, but a privilege, a sacrifice; its endurance is a ritual, its meaning is to be disclosed to all men in the hour of Israel's redemption. Deliverance, redemption, is what the Lord has in store for Israel, and through Israel for all men. Her suffering and agony are the birth pangs of salvation which, the prophet proclaims, is about to unfold." [114]

Perhaps these verses about the fourth servant suggest Jesus, the Báb, and Bahá'u'lláh in various places. Let's reflect on these verses a few at a time.

See, my servant will act wisely;
*   he will be raised and lifted up and highly exalted.*
Just as there were many who were appalled at him—
*   his appearance was so **disfigured** beyond that of any human being*
*   and his form **marred** beyond human likeness—*
so he will sprinkle many nations,
*   and kings will shut their mouths because of him.*

[ab] Rabbi Heschel (1907–1972) was a Jewish theologian and philosopher who presented the prophetic and mystical aspects of Judaism in a unified philosophy of religion based on ancient and medieval Jewish tradition. He attempted to renew traditional Jewish piety for modern times.

For what they were not told, they will see,
   and what they have not heard, they will understand.
(Isaiah 52:13-15, emphasis added)

The *disfigured* appearance and *marred* body describe the results of the Báb's execution by a volley of 750 bullets although, miraculously, His face was spared. "At this volley the bullets produced such an effect that the breasts [of the Báb and Anís] were riddled, and their limbs were completely dissected, except their faces, which were but little marred." [115]

Bahá'u'lláh's body was twice marred for life. The first was caused by bearing the Qará-Guhar and Salásil chains, which weighed about a hundred pounds, which He bore on His shoulders while imprisoned in the Síyáh-Chál. These chains cruelly cut into His shoulders, leaving scars and indentations there for the rest of His life. The second episode occurred during Bahá'u'lláh's banishment to Adrianople. His half-brother Mírzá Yaḥyá, who was jealous of the respect that Bahá'u'lláh received, poisoned him. Bahá'u'lláh was severely ill,[ac] and an aftermath of this poisoning was a tremor in his hand that showed in His handwriting for the rest of His life.[116]

The fourth servant song continued as follows:

He was despised and rejected by mankind,
   a man of suffering, and familiar with pain.
Like one from whom people hide their faces

[ac] "So grave was His condition that a foreign doctor, named Shishman, was called in to attend Him. The doctor was so appalled by His livid hue that he deemed His case hopeless, and, after having fallen at His feet, retired from His presence without prescribing a remedy. A few days later that doctor fell ill and died. Prior to his death Bahá'u'lláh had intimated that doctor Shishman had sacrificed his life for Him. To Mírzá Áqá Ján, sent by Bahá'u'lláh to visit him, the doctor had stated that God had answered his prayers, and that after his death a certain Dr Chupan, whom he knew to be reliable, should, whenever necessary, be called in his stead."

he was despised, and we held him in low esteem.
Surely he took up our pain
    and bore our suffering,
yet we considered him punished by God,
    stricken by him, and afflicted.
*But he was **pierced** for our transgressions,*
    he was crushed for our iniquities;
the punishment that brought us peace was on him,
    and by his wounds we are healed.
*We all, like **sheep**, have gone astray,*
    each of us has turned to our own way;
and the LORD has laid on him
    the iniquity of us all. (Isaiah 53:3–6, emphasis added)

Throngs of the common people were attracted to Jesus, but He was despised by the ecclesiastics who felt threatened by Him. Judging from the accounts in the Gospels, only a few disciples and followers stayed with Him at the end. That Jesus took up our pain and bore our suffering, took on *the iniquity of us all,* is a foremost Christian belief. Jesus was *pierced* by the spear of the centurion. Jesus often used *sheep* as a metaphor for people in need of spiritual nurturance. *"Feed my sheep"* (John 21:17).

The fourth song continues:

He was oppressed and afflicted,
    yet he did not open his mouth;
he was led like a lamb to the slaughter,
    and as a sheep before its shearers is silent,
    so he did not open his mouth.
By oppression and judgment he was taken away.
    Yet who of his generation protested?
For he was cut off from the land of the living;
    for the transgression of my people he was punished.
(Isaiah 53:7–8)

The King James version of the Bible records Isaiah 53:8 as: *"He was taken from prison and from judgment: and who shall declare his generation? for he was cut off out of the land of the living: for the transgression of my people was he stricken."*

Jesus was never imprisoned. He was taken from the Garden of Gethsemane to Pontius Pilate, then to punishment at the hands of soldiers, and then to His crucifixion. However, the Báb was taken from prison in 1848 to face questioning from the crown prince of Persia and Islamic clerics.[117]

The fourth song continues:

> *He was assigned **a grave with the wicked,***
> *and with the rich in his death,*
> *though he had done no violence,*
> *nor was any deceit in his mouth.*
> *Yet it was the LORD's will to crush him and cause him to suffer,*
> *and though the LORD makes his life an offering for sin,*
> *he will see his offspring and prolong his days,*
> *and **the will of the LORD will prosper in his hand.***
> (Isaiah 53:9-10, emphasis added)

The body of the Báb was thrown by the soldiers into the city moat with the bodies of executed criminals, *a grave with the wicked,* and was surreptitiously retrieved by a few followers on the third day.[118]

Bahá'u'lláh wrote a tablet called "The Book of the Covenant" in which He appointed his oldest son, 'Abdu'l-Bahá, Center of the Covenant after His passing. 'Abdu'l-Bahá was also designated by Bahá'u'lláh the sole interpreter of His writings. Despite the exiles of Bahá'u'lláh and 'Abdu'l-Bahá, and the intense persecutions of Bahá'ís, it has become apparent that *the will of the LORD will prosper in his hand.*

A PARALLEL TO PSALM 45

Psalm 45 offered a prophetic look at both Bahá'u'lláh and His wife, Ásíyíh Khánum.[119] Second Isaiah also wrote about Ásíyíh Khánum, who had only nine years of a normal married, family life. Then the Bábí movement started sweeping across the land and the persecutions and exiles began. Her faith in God and her husband's Cause was absolute as she shared the trials and tragedies of His exile for the rest of her life. Second Isaiah's first three verses about her state:

> *"Sing, barren woman,*
> *you who never bore a child;*
> *burst into song, shout for joy,*
> *you who were never in labor;*
> *because more are the children of the desolate woman*
> *than of her who has a husband,"*
> *says the LORD.*
> *"Enlarge the place of your tent,*
> *stretch your tent curtains wide,*
> *do not hold back;*
> *lengthen your cords,*
> *strengthen your stakes.*
> *For you will spread out to the right and to the left;*
> *your descendants will dispossess nations*
> *and settle in their desolate cities.* (Isaiah 54:1-3)

Second Isaiah assured her that *"your Maker is your husband—the LORD Almighty is his name—the Holy One of Israel is your Redeemer; he is called the God of all the earth."* (Isaiah 54:5). And the Lord's kindness would never desert her.

> *For the mountains shall depart, and the hills be removed;*
> *but my kindness shall not depart from thee, neither shall the*

covenant of my peace be removed, saith the LORD *that hath mercy on thee.*

O thou afflicted, tossed with tempest, and not comforted, behold, I will lay thy stones with fair colours, and lay thy foundations with sapphires.

And I will make thy windows of agates, and thy gates of carbuncles, and all thy borders of pleasant stones.

And all thy children shall be taught of the LORD; *and great shall be the peace of thy children.*

In righteousness shalt thou be established: thou shalt be far from oppression; for thou shalt not fear: and from terror; for it shall not come near thee. (Isaiah 54:10-14)

The last verse of this chapter 54 assures Ásíyíh <u>Kh</u>ánum: *"No weapon that is formed against thee shall prosper; and every tongue that shall rise against thee in judgment thou shalt condemn. This is the heritage of the servants of the* LORD, *and their righteousness is of me, saith the* LORD*"* (Isaiah 54:17).

'Abdu'l-Bahá wrote unequivocally that this chapter is about His mother, Ásíyíh <u>Kh</u>ánum:

As to thy question concerning the 54th chapter of Isaiah: This chapter refers to the Exalted Leaf, the mother of 'Abdu'l-Bahá. As a proof to this it is said: "For more are the children of the desolate, than the children of the married wife." Reflect upon this statement and then upon the following: "And thy seed shall inherit the Gentiles and make the desolate cities to be inhabited." And truly the humiliation and reproach which she suffered in the path of God is a fact which no one can refute. For the calamities and afflictions mentioned in the whole chapter are such afflictions which she suffered in the path of God, all of which she endured with patience and thanked God therefor and praised Him, because He had enabled her to endure afflictions for the sake of Bahá. During all this time, the men and women (nakazeen) persecuted her in an incomparable manner, while she was patient, God-fearing, calm, humble and contented through the favor of her Lord and by the bounty of her Creator.[120]

Major accounts are given of Ásíyíh <u>Kh</u>ánum, the wife of Bahá'u'lláh, twice in the Hebrew Bible—Psalm 45[ad] and Isaiah 54:1-17.

I cannot resist leaving Second Isaiah without noting that it was he who wrote, *"There is no peace,"* says the *LORD, "for the wicked"* (Isaiah 48:22).

[ad] *The Coming of the Glory, Vol. I,* Chapter 12, 152-156.

Chapter 10

THE RESTORATION

"*I am Cyrus, king of the universe, the great king,*
the powerful king...
I collected together all of their people and returned them
to their settlements, ...
I returned them unharmed to their cells, in the sanctuaries
that make them happy."

Cyrus II [ae]

Let's take time out from the Hebrew prophets to look at the Restoration, the return from Exile to Jerusalem, which was a major event in Hebrew history. The events of the Restoration in the second half of the fifth century BCE are recorded in the books of Ezra and Nehemiah, which are the final chapters of the historical narrative of the Hebrew

---

[ae] The Cyrus Cylinder was found in 1879 in Babylon and is one of the foremost discoveries from the ancient Middle East. It is a clay cylinder that gives a Persian account of the conquest of Babylon by Cyrus II in 539 BCE, the repatriation of displaced people, and the restoration of temples throughout Mesopotamia and other areas previously occupied by the Babylonians. Cyrus refers to the dilapidated condition of many of the shrines of the foreign gods and cited this as one reason for returning these gods' peoples to their homelands. https://www.britishmuseum.org/research/collection_online/collection_object_details.aspx.

Bible. Unfortunately, there is no other biblical record of the return from the Exile. Ezra and Nehemiah had strong points of view that may not have reflected the actual situation.

The exiled Hebrews had not gone in chains to slavery but had been deported to settle not only in Babylon but also in areas of the Babylonian empire that needed development. While exile was bitter, the conditions back home in war-ravaged Judah were far worse. Mary Joan Winn Leith, an archaeologist who specializes in the Persian period, noted that demographic studies based on excavated and surveyed sites of that period indicate that the population of rural Judah fell from 32,250 in the late preexilic years to about 10,800 for the next couple of hundred years, and the population of Jerusalem fell to a "miniscule 475 to 500" during this time.[121] In chapters 39 and 52 of the book of Jeremiah, the prophet described the siege and fall of Jerusalem to the forces of Nebuchadnezzar and the division of the people for exile. Nebuzaradan, the commander of the guard, sent some of the poorest people into the exile along with those who had remained in the city, the rest of the craftsmen, and people who had deserted to the king of Babylon. However, *Nebuzaradan left behind in the land of Judah some of the poor people, who owned nothing; and at that time he gave them vineyards and fields* (Jeremiah 39:10). The land was not as empty as Ezra and Nehemiah would imply.

The rural poor and farmers who remained in Judah received a fresh start through land redistribution carried out by the Babylonian authorities after the wealthy landowners were deported. Much land went fallow, though, because of the lack of manpower to farm it, and vineyard terraces crumbled for lack of maintenance. The economy sank into depression and goods and services were no longer available as before. Levels of literacy fell because most of the literate upper classes had been deported.

The exiled Judeans lived together in their own communities and had a measure of self-governance that enabled them to retain their Hebrew identity, genealogical records, religious traditions, and history. The lives of these educated and formerly wealthy priests, nobles, skilled artisans, and professional people were far easier than those of their countrymen in Judah. Despite the relative comfort of their new lives, though, they wanted to go home.

Jeremiah had written to the Judean exiles after the 597 deportation and urged them to settle down and invest themselves in their new lives.[122] The same advice would have applied to the exiles of 586. Those individuals who took Jeremiah's advice prospered economically and socially. Some of them succeeded too well and lost their identity as they assimilated into Babylonian culture and adopted the worship of local gods. The Canaanite idols, the child sacrifices to Moloch, and the offerings to Asherah, the queen of heaven, may have been left behind, but the pantheon of Babylonian deities must have been tempting. There had only been one temple in the whole of Judah, but Babylon and other cities and towns each had numerous temples that were dedicated to Babylonian deities. Many Hebrews who had been caught up in monolatry turned to Mesopotamian gods and assimilated into Mesopotamian culture.

For other exiles, though, the Exile was a period spent in reflection and contrition. There's a consensus among biblical historians that scholars and scribes finalized the Torah and other books of the Hebrew Bible during the Exile. Without temple rituals, the scriptures became a treasured resource that assumed major importance and gave even more impetus to literacy. The result was the rise of synagogues where the Torah was taught and became the focal point of worship. The observance of the Sabbath took on more significance as deeper meanings of Mosaic law were understood.

In the Middle East, the gods were inextricably connected with particular cities and the people in them. It had been no different for the Hebrews, whose religious identity had formerly been tied to their homeland and the temple. The Exile brought realization that the God of Abraham and Moses was ubiquitous, that He accompanied His people wherever they went. The one God was not confined by geography. The faithful remnant underwent a purification of belief and worship to the extent that neither Zerubbabel, a leader of the first return to Jerusalem, nor Ezra, a descendant of the last high priest of the Jerusalem temple who led another group of returnees, nor Nehemiah, a reformer and governor of Judah who wrote memoirs about the return to Jerusalem, mentioned idolatry as a problem. However, the prophet of Third Isaiah (see Chapter 14) condemned idolatry in the same tones as a preexilic prophet, which indicates that the records and memoirs of Ezra and Nehemiah did not tell the whole story.

THE DECREE OF CYRUS IN 539 BCE

Cyrus the Great consolidated his power over all the areas of the former Babylonian empire and created the largest empire that the Middle East had yet known, stretching two thousand miles from the Mediterranean Sea to Pakistan. He conquered the Babylonians in 539 and within a year he issued the Edict of Restoration that released ethnic exiled groups to return to their ancestral homes. Although this decree did not mention the Hebrews by name, they were included. For them, this decree inaugurated the period of the Second Temple. History remembers Cyrus as a thoughtful ruler, pragmatic and progressive by the standards of his day. He recognized that deported populations would flourish best in their own homeland and thus be more productive for the empire. The book of Ezra starts as follows:

> *In the first year of Cyrus king of Persia, in order to fulfill the word of the LORD spoken by Jeremiah, the LORD moved the heart of Cyrus king of Persia to make a proclamation throughout his realm and also to put it in writing:*
>
> *"This is what Cyrus king of Persia says:*
>
>> *"'The LORD, the God of heaven, has given me all the kingdoms of the earth and he has appointed me to build a temple for him at Jerusalem in Judah. Any of his people among you may go up to Jerusalem in Judah and build the temple of the LORD, the God of Israel, the God who is in Jerusalem, and may their God*

be with them. And in any locality where survivors may now be living, the people are to provide them with silver and gold, with goods and livestock, and with freewill offerings for the temple of God in Jerusalem.'" (Ezra 1:1-4)

According to the book of Ezra, Zerubbabel and Joshua led the first group of returnees, and Ezra left for Jerusalem perhaps a couple of decades afterward. Cyrus not only encouraged the rebuilding of the temple but he reportedly returned the numerous gold and silver articles that Nebuchadnezzar had pillaged from the temple decades previously. Cyrus also directed that those Hebrews who were not returning were to contribute financially to the effort.

A MIXED HOMECOMING

The return to Jerusalem was not a mass exodus because the majority of the Hebrews chose not to return within a period of one hundred years after the edict. They had been born in Babylonia, had reasonably secure and prosperous lives there, and did not want to face the hardships of the four-month journey and then the tasks of rebuilding not only their lives but a ruined city.

Who did return? Foremost would have been the priestly class that wanted to resume their duties in a restored temple. Close on their heels would have been the Hebrews who had undergone a religious revival and believed it was their duty to God and the Covenant to return to Jerusalem. Then there would have been the usual pioneers—younger sons who could not inherit land, merchants, speculators, and adventurers.

Under the leadership of Zerubbabel, who was born in Babylon and may have been a grandson of King Jehoiachin, and Joshua, noted to be a high priest, the first group of Jews left Babylon in the mid-530s BCE. They arrived in a land that was a pale shadow of its former self. The biblical scholar Israel Finkelstein estimated the entire population of Judah, including Jerusalem, to be 12,000 during the early Persian period in Judah. This would have been an approximate decline of two-thirds of the estimated population before the Babylonian conquest.[123] Finkelstein also estimated Jerusalem's population to have fallen to about a few hundred people.[124]

Zerubbabel laid the foundation for the second temple fourteen months after arrival. However, the celebration of the laying of the foundation seems to have been bittersweet. Most of the people shouted for joy, *"But many of the older priests and Levites and family heads, who remembered the former temple, wept aloud when they saw the foundation of this temple being laid, while many others shouted for joy"* (Ezra 3:12). The second temple would be much smaller than the Temple of Solomon. The reality was that the Temple of Solomon would not be replicated.

The returnees to their ancestral land also met a certain level of resistance from those individuals who had remained. Times had changed and the land had been redistributed by the Babylonian administrators. Families who had worked those lands for two or three generations would not have willingly relinquished them. In addition, Persian administrators who succeeded the Babylonian ones would not have tolerated social or agricultural upheavals. Ezra's book is silent about this aspect of the return and other problems that it must have caused for the people who had remained either on the land or in Jerusalem. Trouble ensued. Some of the returnees had arrived with a superior attitude and rejected offers of help.

When the enemies of Judah and Benjamin heard that the exiles were building a temple for the Lord, *the God of Israe, they came to Zerubbabel and to the heads of the families and said, "Let us help you build because, like you, we seek your God and have been sacrificing to him since the time of Esarhaddon king of Assyria, who brought us here."*

"But Zerubbabel, Joshua and the rest of the heads of the families of Israel answered, 'You have no part with us in building a temple to our God. We alone will build it for the Lord, the God of Israel, as King Cyrus, the king of Persia, commanded us'" (Ezra 4:1-3).

The self-defined religiously reformed and purified remnant lost an opportunity to ease the integrative process and improve relations with the Samaritans, who had been slowly converting to Judaism since their forced resettlement on the land by the Assyrians. The repercussions of this rejection were seen in Jesus's day when the Samaritans were considered a lower-class people, set apart and to be avoided.

A deep division developed between the returnees and the people who had remained in Judah. The community of returnees gained a disproportionate amount of power in Jerusalem but probably not in the countryside. The newly arrived priesthood assumed religious power, and religious issues were of no concern to the Persian administrators as long as the temple taxes were paid and there was no sedition. Some of the returnees also assumed leadership positions in the Persian administration, such as Zerubbabel being appointed governor of the subprovince of Yehud (Judah).

Not surprisingly, when the Samaritans and other local people were not accepted into the new Jewish community and welcomed to the effort to rebuild the temple, they became enemies who caused many problems. *"Then the peoples around them set out to discourage the people of Judah and make them afraid to go on building. They bribed officials to work against them and frustrate their plans during the entire reign of Cyrus king of Persia and down to the reign of Darius king of Persia"* (Ezra 4:4-5). Opposition to the rebuilding of the temple caused seventeen years of delays.

THREE MORE DECREES

It would take three more decrees from two other Persian kings (Darius I, who reigned 522-486 BCE, and Artaxerxes I, who reigned 465–424) before the rebuilding of the temple, the city, and the city walls could all be completed. The route of these three decrees was complicated. First, Tattenai, the Persian governor of Trans-Euphrates, the land west of the Euphrates River that reached to Syria and Yehud, questioned the temple-building activity and sent a request to Darius I, known as Darius the Great, to verify the decree of Cyrus II. The scroll with the decree

Cyrus II had issued was found that gave his authorization for the temple to be rebuilt.

> *King Darius then issued an order, and they searched in the archives stored in the treasury at Babylon. A scroll was found in the citadel of Ecbatana in the province of Media, and this was written on it:*
>
> *Memorandum:*
>
> *In the first year of King Cyrus, the king issued a decree concerning the temple of God in Jerusalem: Let the temple be rebuilt as a place to present sacrifices, and let its foundations be laid.* (Ezra 6:1-3)

This decree was issued about 518 and was essentially a renewal of Cyrus's permission to rebuild the temple. It also stipulated the return of the gold and silver taken from the temple by Nebuchadnezzar. Tattenai and his officials were ordered to stay away from the temple building and not interfere, and they were also to pay the expenses from the royal treasury from the revenues of Trans-Euphrates so that the construction work would not falter. Then came the final touch. Darius decreed that if anyone defied this edict, a beam was to be pulled from his house and he was to be impaled on it. *"May God, who has caused his Name to dwell there, overthrow any king or people who lifts a hand to change this decree or to destroy this temple in Jerusalem. I Darius have decreed it. Let it be carried out with diligence"* (Ezra 6:12).

Work had ceased on the temple in the face of local opposition and attention turned to the rebuilding of homes, farms, and businesses. However, the prophets Haggai and Zechariah, who lived in Jerusalem, took the people sternly to task and motivated them to finish the job. *"So the elders of the Jews continued to build and prosper under the preaching of Haggai the prophet and Zechariah, a descendent of Iddo. They finished building the temple according to the command of the God of Israel and the decrees of Cyrus, Darius and Artaxerxes, king of Persia. The temple was completed on the third day of the month Adar, in the sixth year of the reign of King Darius"* (Ezra 6:14-15). The temple was completed in 516/515, which may have fulfilled Jeremiah's prophecy in his letter to the exiles living in Babylon: *"This is what the Lord says: 'When seventy years are completed for Babylon, I will come to you and fulfill my good promise to bring you back to this place'"* (Jeremiah 29:10). There were 70 years from the destruction of Solomon's Temple in 586 to the year 516.

Opposition continued, though. There was strong resistance to the rebuilding of Jerusalem and its walls, which had been started in the early fifth century after the temple was completed. Reports were sent by opponents to Artaxerxes I in 465, the first year of his reign. These opponents labeled Jerusalem that *"rebellious and wicked city"* which, when rebuilt, would no longer pay taxes, tribute, or duty, *"and eventually the royal revenues will suffer"* (Ezra 4:12-13). Citing that they were loyally under obligation to the palace, they wrote they did not want to see the king dishonored and urged that the archival records citing Jerusalem as a seditious city be reviewed.

Artaxerxes responded to this letter with an order that the reconstruction work be stopped and the city not rebuilt until he himself ordered it. However, this order of 465/464 is not considered to be the third decree of Artaxerxes.

The third decree was issued by Artaxerxes in 457 when he had changed his mind and authorized the rebuilding of Jerusalem. He encouraged Ezra, a priest and scribe living in Babylon, to lead a group of returnees to Jerusalem. Ezra was a *"teacher well versed in the Law of Moses, which the LORD, the God of Israel, had given. The king had granted him everything he asked, for the hand of the Lord his God was on him"* (Ezra 7:6).

Ezra arrived in Jerusalem in the fifth month of the seventh year of Artaxerxes's reign, which put his arrival in the year 457. Ezra had been sent by Artaxerxes to inquire about Judah and Jerusalem regarding the law of the Israelite God and to evaluate the religious understanding of His people. He was given silver and gold by the king and was authorized to also take any gold and silver offered by the province of Babylon and the freewill offerings of the Jews and the priests. In addition, all the treasurers of Trans-Euphrates were to provide with diligence whatever Ezra asked for the journey. This decree also provided for the restoration of local government on a scale not mentioned in any other decrees. Ezra was approved to appoint magistrates and judges to administer justice to all the people of Trans-Euphrates, that is, to those who knew Mosaic law, and to teach those who were not educated in it. The letter ended with a dire warning: *"Whoever does not obey the law of your God and the law of the king must surely be punished by death, banishment, confiscation of property, or imprisonment"* (Ezra 7:26). Ezra became a moving force behind the rebuilding of Jerusalem and its governmental institutions.

The fourth decree is considered to be the one given to Nehemiah, a cupbearer to Artaxerxes. In the twentieth year of Artaxerxes's reign, about 445, Nehemiah was profoundly distressed by news that the returnees were in great trouble and disgrace because the walls of Jerusalem were still in ruins. Artaxerxes inquired of his sadness and asked Nehemiah what he wanted. He asked to be sent to Jerusalem to rebuild its walls. The book of Nehemiah recounts how he was sent to Jerusalem with a safe-conduct pass and letters authorizing the purchase of timber for the walls and his residence. Nehemiah arrived in Jerusalem in 445 to rebuild the walls and an imperial fortress called the citadel of the temple. He successfully directed the rebuilding of Jerusalem's walls in the face of opposition that had still persisted, but no more decrees were needed. Nehemiah also served as governor of Judah for twelve years.

SOCIAL PROBLEMS

Ezra was forced to deal with the situation of intermarriage with the neighboring people, a practice that had never ceased although marrying Canaanite and other non-Hebrew women had long been forbidden since the days of Moses. It's written that Ezra tore his clothes and prostrated himself before the Temple, praying:

"I am too ashamed and disgraced, my God, to lift up my face to you, because our sins are higher than our heads and our guilt has

reached to the heavens. From the days of our ancestors until now,
our guilt has been great. Because of our sins, we and our kings and
our priests have been subjected to the sword and captivity, to pil-
lage and humiliation at the hand of foreign kings, as it is today."
(Ezra 9:6-7)

The prayer continued at length and the people gathered about him confessed their sins. It's stated that Ezra issued a proclamation throughout the land for all the exiles to assemble in Jerusalem within three days or forfeit their property and be expelled from the assembly of the exiles. The men arrived and Ezra addressed them. They had been unfaithful to the Lord by marrying foreign women and now they must separate themselves from them. The guilty were to appear before the elders and judges of each town.

The book of Nehemiah records disturbing religious and social problems. Farmers were mortgaging their fields, vineyards, and homes to purchase grain during famine. Other field laborers were borrowing money to pay taxes on the fields and vineyards that belonged to others, and inability to repay these debts resulted in their children being subjected to slavery. Debt slavery had reared its ugly head again with Jews enslaving Jews. Nehemiah confronted the slaveholders:

"When I heard their outcry and these charges, I was very angry. So
I called together a large meeting to deal with them and said: 'As far
as possible, we have bought back our fellow Jews who were sold to
the Gentiles. Now you are selling your own people, only for them to
be sold back to us!' They kept quiet, because they could find nothing
to say." (Nehemiah 5:7-8)

Nehemiah demanded that interest on loans be ceased and the fields, vineyards, olive groves, and houses be returned to the indebted, as well as all past interest charged them. The owners agreed to do so, and Nehemiah summoned the priests, nobles, and officials to take an oath to that effect.

Ezra had been tasked to teach the law. Nehemiah tried to used his power and influence to see that the laws of Moses were kept, especially those of the Sabbath, whose observance had greatly declined. Success in promoting adherence to Mosaic law, though, entailed a separation between those who obeyed and those who did not.

The Restoration, as momentous an event that it was, unfortunately exacerbated social inequality and a multitude of other problems in Judah where the community of returned exiles was frequently at odds with the indigenous population that had remained in Judah. The immigrants from Babylon were comparatively wealthy and they maintained their status as social and economic elites. Leith described the extent of the returnees' wealth in the Restoration.

> A class-based breakdown of the population and the distribution of wealth illuminates both the social tensions and the inner-temple struggles to which the biblical record alludes. The majority of the population consisted primarily of peasants and artisans, along with petty criminals and underemployed itinerant workers who lived off their wits or off charity. Ethnographers and historians suggest that the governing class— particularly the priestly families in postexilic Judah—averaged about 1 percent of the population but controlled as much as quarter of the national income. Together, the ruler (the Persians) and the governing class (primarily the Zadokite priestly families)[af] in general could have received not less than half the national income.[125]

Two populations had emerged—an inner core of upper-class returnees who claimed religious purity, and the remaining outer core of people whom the upper class considered unworthy. The Israelite struggle to monotheism had been largely achieved, at least among the returnees. Now the struggle was perceived as one for purity, or righteousness. The

---

[af] The Zakodite priests were Levites.

disproportionate power of the priesthood would, in time, contribute to the rise of sectarianism in Judaism. By the time of Jesus there were the Sadducees, the Pharisees, the Essenes, and other sects. There would also be the development of religious zealotry as a defense against Greek and Roman influences.

The legacies of Ezra and Nehemiah were religious reform. They attempted to make the laws of religion the laws of society. Genealogical records were used to determine who was a "true Israelite" rather than a professed believer. Membership in the resulting inner core would require a certain withdrawal from society and a growing dependence on strict interpretation of Mosaic laws that would deaden the spirit of the Mosaic Dispensation, which Jesus often condemned.

OTHER CONSIDERATIONS

The basic problem with the historicity of the Restoration as recorded in the books of Ezra and Nehemiah is that apparently neither Ezra nor Nehemiah wrote these two books, which for several hundred years were actually one book called Ezra-Nehemiah before they were split. Most biblical scholars agree that the books of Chronicles I and II, Ezra, and Nehemiah were written by an anonymous person (or group) who was appropriately named the Chronicler. It's likely that the Chronicler had access to the memoirs and writings of Ezra and Nehemiah, two leaders who would have wanted their legacies to be remembered.

There's the adage among historians that whoever wins the battle gets to tell his version of it. Much research has been pursued by biblical scholars and archaeologists on the Persian period in Judah and papers subsequently written about it. They seem to raise more questions than they answer. For example, Finkelstein wrote unequivocally, "To sum up this issue, there is no archaeological evidence for the city wall of Nehemiah." [126] He further wrote:

> The Persian-period finds in Jerusalem and the search for Nehemiah's wall are additional cases in which archaeologists

have given up archaeology in favor of an uncritical reading of the biblical text. The dearth of archaeological finds and the lack of extra-biblical texts on Persian-period Yehud open the way to circular reasoning in reconstructing the history of this period. The finds indicate that in the Persian and Early Hellenistic periods Jerusalem was a small unfortified village that stretched over an area of c. 20 dunams, with a population of a few hundred people—that is, not much more than 100 adult men. This population—and the depleted population of the Jerusalem countryside in particular and the entire territory of Yehud in general—could not have supported a major reconstruction effort of the ruined Iron II fortifications of the city. In addition, there is no archaeological evidence whatsoever for any reconstruction or renovation of fortifications in the Persian period. On a broader issue, the archaeological evidence from Jerusalem casts severe doubt on the notion that much of the biblical material was composed in the Persian and Early Hellenistic periods.[127]

Perhaps the experience of the Restoration was an idealized memory by the time it was committed to writing.

Chapter 11

HAGGAI – BUILD THAT TEMPLE

*"Gone are the vigorous denunciations of the earlier prophets;
gone are their idyllic hopes. Still, one must remember
that Haggai spoke to a disheartened people who scarcely
needed another word of woe. Haggai's very concrete messages
at least gave the people something to hang on to
as they sought desperately to reestablish themselves
in the land of their fathers."*

Jay C. Williams[128]

One sign of the winding down of the classical prophets in postexilic Judah is the brevity of their books compared with those of their predecessors. The Exile and the Restoration brought religious renewal to a certain extent, yet the frosts of the fall and winter of the Mosaic Dispensation would increase their grip as evidenced by reliance on the letter of the law rather than its spirit.

The returnees had been in Judah less than two decades when the prophet Haggai made himself known in the second year of the reign of King Darius I of Persia, 520 BCE. *"In the second year of King Darius, on the first day of the sixth month, the word of the LORD came through the prophet Haggai to Zerubbabel"* (Haggai 1:1). Most conveniently for biblical scholars, Haggai continued to state exactly, to the day, when he received the word of the Lord. His book is the second shortest of the prophetic volumes with just two chapters. No biographical data is given for Haggai beyond his designation as *"the prophet Haggai"* and *"the Lord's messenger"* (Haggai 1:1, 13). Haggai's ministry lasted a brief four months but it was charged with three weighty points of focus—a firm directive to complete the Second Temple, the building of the spiritual temple, and a new Revelation of God to come.

Haggai lived contemporaneously with the prophet Zechariah in Jerusalem, and Zechariah reinforced Haggai's appeals to finish rebuilding the temple. The four months of Haggai's ministry started with his exhortations to finish the construction. After all, permission and funds had been received from Darius the Great, who had confirmed the decree of Cyrus the Great that the temple be rebuilt. Haggai received a message from the Lord for Zerubbabel, the governor of Judah, and Joshua, the high priest, as follows:

> *This is what the LORD Almighty says: "These people say, 'The time has not yet come to rebuild the LORD's house.'"*
>
> *Then the word of the LORD came through the prophet Haggai: "Is it a time for you yourselves to be living in your paneled houses, while this house remains a ruin?"* (Haggai 1:2-4)

Haggai then reviewed how the returnees had not prospered in any area since their attention had turned from completing the temple to restoring their homes, farms, and businesses. They had planted much but harvested little, had eaten but never enough, had drunk but never a sufficient amount, had clothed themselves but were never warm, and had lost their wages to holes in their purses. Why had prosperity eluded them?

> *This is what the Lord Almighty says: "Give careful thought to your ways. Go up into the mountains and bring down timber*

and build my house, so that I may take pleasure in it and be hon-
ored," says the Lord. You expected much, but see, it turned out to
be little. What you brought home, I blew away. Why?" declares
the LORD Almighty.

"Because of my house, which remains a ruin, while each of
you is busy with your own house. Therefore, because of you the
heavens have withheld their dew and the earth its crops. I called
for a drought on the fields and the mountains, on the grain, the
new wine, the olive oil and everything else the ground produces,
on people and livestock, and on all the labor of your hands."
(Haggai 1: 7-11)

Thus the Lord stirred the spirit of Zerubbabel, Joshua, and the
people. The work began twenty-three days later on the twenty-fourth
day of the sixth month of the second year of Darius's reign and was
completed four years later. The Second Temple would be vitally important to the development of later Judaism. The works of the prophets
were venerated, along with other Hebrew literature, during the Second
Temple period.

Haggai's verses may have been more than a straightforward order
to finish constructing the temple. Hushidar Motlagh saw another layer
of interpretation and commented on Haggai 1:2-10 as follows: "The
prophecy indicates that we have built our own house for a long time,
that we have depended on human institutions for many centuries with
little benefits; it is time now to build the divine Institution and depend
on God's House of Justice." [129] Motlagh also wrote that the Lord's
house "symbolizes God's plan for humankind. Every Messenger and
Redeemer has offered to build that house—one of justice and order—on
our planet, but people have refused to accept it." [130]

YOU CAN'T GO HOME AGAIN

Just a few weeks after work had resumed on the Second Temple, on
the twenty-first day of the seventh month, Haggai again heard the

word of the Lord. He was told to speak to Zerubbabel, Joshua, and the people and ask: *"Who of you is left who saw this house in its former glory? How does it look to you now? Does it not seem to you like nothing?"* (Haggai 2:3) Haggai was warning that "you can't go home again." [131] When one tries to return to a place from the past, it won't be the same as it had been. Time inexorably moves forward. The Plan of God inexorably moves forward. The purpose of the Restoration was not to recreate Jerusalem and the temple as they had been in the past but to prepare for the future.

Haggai counseled the people to be strong and to continue the work because, *"This is what I covenanted with you when you came out of Egypt. And my Spirit remains among you. Do not fear"* (Haggai 2:5). Comparisons were not to be made between Solomon's Temple and the Second Temple because there was a deeper, symbolic meaning into which Haggai plunged.

> *"This is what the LORD Almighty says: 'In a little while I will once more shake the heavens and the earth, the sea and the dry land. I will **shake all nations**, and what is **desired by all nations** will come, and I will fill this house with glory,' says the LORD Almighty. 'The **silver** is mine and the **gold** is mine,' declares the LORD Almighty. 'The **glory of this present house will be greater than the glory of the former house,**' says the LORD Almighty. 'And in this place I will grant peace,' declares the LORD Almighty."*
> (Haggai 2:6-9, KJV, emphasis added)

The advent of Bahá'u'lláh would help these verses to be better understood. His Dispensation is now shaking the nations and our social order in accordance with His words: *"By My Self! The day is approaching when We will have rolled up the world and all that is therein, and spread out a new order in its stead. He, verily, is powerful over all things."* [132] Bahá'u'lláh thus warned, *"The world's equilibrium hath been upset through the vibrating influence of this most great, this new World Order. Mankind's ordered life hath been revolutionized through the agency of this unique, this wondrous System—the like of which mortal eyes have never witnessed.*" [133] The shaking of *all nations* indicates the universality of the upheaval.

The *desired by all nations* might refer to one of the titles of Bahá'u'lláh as stated by Shoghi Effendi: "He was formally designated Bahá'u'lláh, an appellation specifically recorded in the Persian Bayán, signifying at once the glory, the light and the splendor of God, and was styled the 'Lord of Lords,' the 'Desire of the Nations, …'" [ag,134] If this is accurate, the reference to *glory* would refer to Bahá'u'lláh.

Bahá'u'lláh considered *gold and silver* not only worthless but a distraction, even a danger to the people. *"Know ye of a certainty that all the treasures of the earth, all the gold, the silver, and the rare and precious gems they contain, are, in the sight of God, of His chosen ones and His loved ones, as worthless as a handful of clay."* [135]

Haggai may have been foreseeing the Dispensation of Bahá'u'lláh when he alluded to the greatness of *the glory of this future house* would be greater than that of the previous house. In addition, *peace* would be a major goal of the Bahá'í Faith. The book containing transcriptions of 140 of 'Abdu'l-Bahá's talks given in the United States in 1912 is titled *The Promulgation of Universal Peace.*

'Abdu'l-Bahá commented on *gold* with reference to Bahá'u'lláh, although He was not referring to Haggai's statement when He explained that Moses used a rod of the plant, Muḥammad used a rod of iron, and Bahá'u'lláh used a rod of gold:

[ag] The complete quotation reads: "He was formally designated Bahá'u'lláh, an appellation specifically recorded in the Persian Bayán, signifying at once the glory, the light and the splendor of God, and was styled the "Lord of Lords," the "Most Great Name," the "Ancient Beauty," the "Pen of the Most High," the "Hidden Name," the "Preserved Treasure," "He Whom God will make manifest," the "Most Great Light," the "All-Highest Horizon," the "Most Great Ocean," the "Supreme Heaven," the "Pre-Existent Root," the "Self-Subsistent," the "Day-Star of the Universe," the "Great Announcement," the "Speaker on Sinai," the "Sifter of Men," the "Wronged One of the World," the "Desire of the Nations," the "Lord of the Covenant," the "Tree beyond which there is no passing."

In brief, it is said that: "And he that talked with me had a golden rod to measure the city and the gates thereof and the walls thereof." The purport is this, that certain souls guided (people) with a rod of the plant, that is, a reed wherewith he shepherded the sheep, like unto the rod of Moses; other trained (the people) with a rod of iron and drove them, as in the time of Mohammed (The scepter of Mohammed was the sword). In this Greatest Day the rod of the plant and the rod of iron are changed into a rod which is of pure gold and is from the endless treasuries of the Kingdom of God.[136]

The divine goal of the Restoration seems not to have been a significantly renewed Judaism within its previous mold. The cycles within a dispensation of God, or religion, do not allow for religious revival to the extent of permanently reversing the slide into fall and winter. Following the symbolic cycle of the seasons, the summer of the Mosaic Dispensation was probably during the days of the united kingdom, and the division of the kingdom, followed by the conquests of the Assyrians and the Babylonians, was fertile ground for the spiritual fall and winter that followed.

THE SIGNET RING

The final message of Haggai had a touch of apocalyptic thought in that it foresaw the defeat of many monarchs, the shattering of the power of kingdoms, and civil war among the fighters. This would be followed by the restoration of the Davidic kingdom.

The word of the Lord came to Haggai a second time on the twenty-fourth day of the month: "Tell Zerubbabel governor of Judah that I am going to shake the heavens and the earth. I will overturn royal thrones and shatter the power of the foreign kingdoms. I will overthrow chariots and their drivers; horses and their riders will fall, each by the sword of his brother.

"On that day,' declares the LORD Almighty, 'I will take you,
my servant Zerubbabel, son of Shealtiel,' declares the LORD, 'and I
will make you like my signet ring, for I have chosen you,' declares
the LORD Almighty." (Haggai 2:20-23)

Signet rings were worn by kings and other persons of authority as identity when used to seal documents. There had long been hope that the Davidic kingdom would be reinstated. However, even though Zerubbabel was an heir to the Davidic kingdom as a grandson of Jehoiachin, he was also the Persian-appointed governor of Judah and had undoubtedly been selected because of his demonstrated loyalty to the Persian empire. Any movement on Zerubbabel's part to claim the throne would have cost him his life and brought Persian troops back in force. So why were false hopes supposedly raised by allusions to a situation that would never be?

The Bahá'í scholar William Sears pursued the mystery of Zerubbabel and discovered that, "The word Zerubbabel, according to the Oxford University Press red-letter edition of the King James version of the Bible, means 'Begotten in Babylon'. Other references say it means 'Scattered in Babylon'. [Alexander] Cruden, in his *Unabridged Concordance*, declares it to mean 'Banished in Babylon' or 'Stranger in Babylon' ('Born' in other editions)." [137] Bahá'u'lláh was banished to Baghdad, sixty miles north of the ancient ruins of Babylon. He was a stranger in Baghdad, and He was begotten in that city because Baghdad is where He declared His identity in 1863 CE as the Promised One foretold by the Báb. Within days, He left on the next leg of His exile to Constantinople, and four months later to Adrianople, which 'Abdu'l-Bahá called "this most remote place of banishment." [138] Bahá'u'lláh, His family, and followers were scattered in Babylon, in Constantinople, in Adrianople, and then in Akka, Palestine. The Davidic monarchy would not be reestablished on earth because it had played its role. However, it appears that Bahá'u'lláh had a mystical relationship with the Davidic monarchy.

From His imprisonment in Akka, Bahá'u'lláh wrote an epistle addressed to the clergy and people of various faiths that announced His rule on the throne of David.

> *The Most Great Law is come, and the **Ancient Beauty** ruleth upon **the throne of David**. Thus hath My Pen spoken that which the histories of bygone ages have related. At this time, however, David crieth aloud and saith: 'O my loving Lord! Do Thou number me with such as have stood steadfast in Thy Cause, O Thou through Whom the faces have been illumined, and the footsteps have slipped!'* [139]

The *Ancient Beauty* is one of the names of Bahá'u'lláh, and the *throne of David* was another clarifier of the identity of Bahá'u'lláh.[140]

Now we turn to Haggai's compatriot, the prophet Zechariah, who provided several dimensions of insight into the temple of God. He also had apocalyptic visions reminiscent of Ezekiel's.

Chapter 12

ZECHARIAH –
LET YOUR HANDS BE STRONG

*"All down the ages the prophets of God have been sent into the
world to serve the cause of truth—Moses brought the law of
truth, and all the prophets of Israel after him sought to spread it."*

'Abdu'l-Bahá[141]

Regarding the book of Zechariah, it seems that it encompassed the
ministries of three separate prophets who are called First, Second,
and Third Zechariah, respectively. The ministry of the prophet First
Zechariah (called Zechariah in this chapter) also started in the second
year of the reign of Darius, 520 BCE, just two months after Haggai
delivered his first known oracle. As with Haggai, some exact dates are
given such as, *"In the eighth month of the second year of Darius, the word
of the LORD came to the prophet Zechariah son of Berekiah, the son of Iddo"*
(Zechariah 1:1). His last recorded date was the fourth year and the
fourth day of the ninth month of Darius's reign, *"In the fourth year of
King Darius, the word of the LORD came to Zechariah on the fourth day of the
ninth month, the month of Kislev"* (Zechariah 7:1). This means that Zechariah's ministry lasted a little over two years. There is consensus among

biblical scholars that the book of Zechariah is actually two books—First Zechariah (chapters 1-8) that was written by the prophet of Darius's reign, and Second and Third Zechariah (chapters 9-14) that was composed much later by two or more unknown writers.

Zechariah's first message from the Lord reminded the people of their sinful past and the price that ignoring the preexilic prophets had cost them. The Lord admonished the people not to be like their ancestors who had disregarded the prophets but to turn from their *evil ways* and *evil practices*.

> *"The LORD was very angry with your ancestors. Therefore tell the people: This is what the LORD Almighty says: 'Return to me,' declares the LORD Almighty, 'and I will return to you,' says the LORD Almighty. Do not be like your ancestors, to whom the earlier prophets proclaimed: This is what the LORD Almighty says: 'Turn from your **evil ways** and your **evil practices**.' But they would not listen or pay attention to me, declares the LORD. Where are your ancestors now? And the prophets, do they live forever? But did not my words and my decrees, which I commanded my servants the prophets, overtake your ancestors?"*
> (Zechariah 1:2-6, emphasis added)

The emphasis on right behavior and turning to the Lord would continue but no longer coupled with threats of catastrophe for noncompliance. A certain gentleness was combined with remembrance of days past. The succession of the Hebrew prophets would not end for about another century. The warnings of the Lord's coming punishment had run their course with the conquests by the Assyrians and the Babylonians, and the ensuing Exile, left little room for argument. But much was still left to be imparted to His people. Zechariah received apocalyptic visions with strange imagery and seemingly unfathomable meanings reminiscent of Ezekiel, Daniel, and Haggai. Three months after Zechariah started his mission, he received eight visions during the course of one night, the twenty-fourth day of the eleventh month in the second year of Darius. They are told in six chapters (Zechariah 1:7-6:15). We shall examine four of these visions.

COMFORT ZION AND CHOOSE JERUSALEM

Zechariah saw many horses colored red, brown, and white. A man standing among the myrtle trees explained, *"They are the ones the LORD has sent to go throughout the earth"* (Zechariah 1:10). The horses reported to an angel standing among the myrtle trees that they had gone throughout the earth and found the whole world at rest and in peace. The angel thus implored the Lord, *"LORD Almighty, how long will you withhold mercy from Jerusalem and from the towns of Judah, which you have been angry with these seventy years?' So the LORD spoke kind and comforting words to the angel who talked with me"* (Zechariah 1:12-13). The angel spoke for the Lord:

> *"Therefore this is what the LORD says: 'I will return to Jerusalem with mercy, and there my house will be rebuilt. And the measuring line will be stretched out over Jerusalem,' declares the LORD Almighty.*
>
> *"Proclaim further: This is what the LORD Almighty says: 'My towns will again overflow with prosperity, and the LORD will again comfort Zion and choose Jerusalem.'"* (Zechariah 1:16-17, emphasis added)

As discussed previously, *Jerusalem* can mean a new religion. We will soon see how the *measuring line* will turn out to be an evaluation of this new religion.

Zechariah often received the word of the Lord through an angel. The Judeo-Christian concept of angels is a spiritual hierarchy of beings, a special creation that is intermediate between God and humans and dwells in the heavens. Traditionally angels are believed to have no capacity to defy God but only to obey Him. 'Abdu'l-Bahá gave another understanding of angels, a twofold interpretation, as follows:

> *The meaning of 'angels' is the **confirmations of God and His celestial powers.** Likewise angels are **blessed beings** who have severed all ties with this nether world, have been released from the chains of self and the desires of the flesh, and anchored their hearts to the heavenly realms of the Lord. These are of the Kingdom, heavenly; these are of God, spiritual; these are revelers of God's abounding grace; these are dawning-points of His spiritual bestowals.*[142]

Most of the *confirmations of God and His celestial powers,* that is, angels, are mostly not noticed by us in our material lives of attachment to this world even though these confirmations have graced our lives. The second definition of angels, the *blessed beings* of detachment and severance, offers every human being the achievable goal of becoming an angel. It appears that angels are humans who have accomplished severance from self as described by 'Abdu'l-Bahá, and anchored their hearts to the realms of God.

A MEASURING LINE FOR JERUSALEM

Zechariah saw a man with a *measuring line* who was determining the dimensions of Jerusalem. The angel who was speaking with Zechariah was leaving when another angel came to the first one and exclaimed:

> *"Run, tell that young man, Jerusalem will be a city without walls because of the great number of people and animals in it. And I myself will be a **wall of fire** around it,' declares the LORD, 'and I will be its glory within.'*
>
> *"Come! Come! Flee from the land of the north," declares the LORD, "for I have scattered you to the four winds of heaven," declares the LORD.*

*Come, **Zion!** Escape, you who live in Daughter Babylon! For this is what the LORD Almighty says: "After the Glorious One has sent me against the nations that have plundered you—for whoever touches you touches the apple of his eye—I will surely raise my hand against them so that their slaves will plunder them. Then you will know that the LORD Almighty has sent me.*

*"**Shout and be glad,** Daughter Zion. For I am coming, and I will live among you," declares the LORD. "**Many nations** will be joined with the LORD in that day and will become my people. I will live among you and you will know that the LORD Almighty has sent me to you. The LORD will inherit Judah as his portion in the holy land and will again choose Jerusalem. Be still before the LORD, all mankind, because he has roused himself from his holy dwelling."* (Zechariah 2:4-13, emphasis added)

The symbols jump from the page. Fire is an agent of both purification and destruction. The use of the *fire* here could be a reference to the Holy Spirit, which appeared to all the Manifestations of God in different forms—the Sacred Fire (Zoroaster), the Burning Bush (Moses), the Dove (Jesus), the angel Gabriel (Muḥammad), and the Maiden (Bahá'u'lláh). Consider the beauty of Bahá'u'lláh's musing on the fire of the Holy Spirit:

*I know not, O my God, what the **Fire** is which Thou didst kindle in Thy land. Earth can never cloud its splendor, nor water quench its flame. All the peoples of the world are powerless to resist its force. Great is the blessedness of him that hath drawn nigh unto it, and heard its roaring.*[143]

We have previously seen how *Jerusalem* is often used as a symbol for the renewed word of God that is delivered in each dispensation. Bahá'u'lláh wrote:

The time foreordained unto the peoples and kindreds of the earth is now come. The promises of God, as recorded in the holy Scriptures, have all been fulfilled. **Out of Zion hath gone forth the Law of God,** *and Jerusalem, and the hills and land thereof, are filled with the glory of His Revelation. Happy is the man that pondereth in his heart that which hath been revealed in the Books of God, the Help in Peril, the Self-Subsisting.*[144]

When Bahá'u'lláh wrote *Out of Zion hath gone forth the Law of God,* I think that He was referring to His Revelation, whose covenant would be fulfilled by the establishment of the Universal House of Justice whose Seat is located on Mount Carmel. His Most Holy Book, the *Kitáb-i-Aqdas,* the Book of Laws, would be published by the Universal House of Justice. Jerusalem would come to signify the new, or renewed, Word of God.

'Abdu'l-Bahá confirmed that verses 2:10-13 (starting with *Shout and be glad)* refer to the time of Bahá'u'lláh. *"As to the questions thou hast asked: Concerning…Zechariah, chapter 2, verses 10, 11, 12 and 13, and in St. Luke, chapter 21, verses 20 to the end, these refer to the century of the Blessed Beauty.*[145] The verses of Luke 21:20-38 are parallel in many ways with those of Matthew 24.

SEVEN CHANNELS, SEVEN LAMPS, AND TWO OLIVE TREES

The angel showed Zechariah another scene and asked him what he saw.

*I answered, "I see a solid **gold lampstand** with a bowl at the top and **seven lamps** on it, with **seven channels** to the lamps. Also there are **two olive trees** by it, one on the right of the bowl and the other on its left." (Zechariah 4:2-3, emphasis added)*

The *seven lamps* could represent the Prophets of the seven major religions of the Adamic Cycle who were symbolically fed through *seven channels* from the *gold lampstand.* If so, these seven lamps would be the seven major faiths that have survived—Hinduism, Sabeanism, Buddhism, Judaism, Zoroastrianism, Christianity, and Islam[146]—that were nurtured from the same lampstand, or divine source. The angel continued:

> *"This is the word of the* LORD *to* **Zerubbabel:** *'Not by might nor by power, but by my Spirit,' says the* LORD *Almighty.*
>
> *"What are you,* **mighty mountain?** *Before Zerubbabel you will become level ground. Then he will bring out the* **capstone** *to shouts of 'God bless it! God bless it!'"*
>
> *Then the word of the* LORD *came to me: "The hands of* **Zerubbabel** *have laid the foundation of this temple; his hands will also complete it. Then you will know that the* LORD *Almighty has sent me to you.*
>
> *"Who dares despise the day of small things, since* **the seven eyes** *of the* LORD *that range throughout the earth will rejoice when they see the chosen* **capstone** *in the hand of Zerubbabel?"*
>
> *Then I asked the angel, "What are these* **two olive trees** *on the right and the left of the lampstand?"*
>
> *Again I asked him, "What are these two olive branches beside the two gold pipes that pour out golden oil?"*
>
> *He replied, "Do you not know what these are?"*
>
> *"No, my lord," I said.*
>
> *So he said, "These are the two who are anointed to serve the* LORD *of all the earth."* (Zechariah 4:6-14, emphasis added)

In the previous chapter, we reviewed William Sears's reasons for determining that Haggai was speaking of Bahá'u'lláh when he spoke of

Zerubbabel. If Sears was correct, his reasoning could apply to Zechariah also using Zerubbabel's name.

Society's institutions and religions are often symbolized as mountains, and the old world order, the global state of affairs in our time, could be likened to the *mighty mountain* of perceived, but false, power. They will be flattened as repeatedly warned in the Bahá'í Scriptures. A *capstone* is completion, the apex of a structure, and the Bahá'í Revelation is the apex of God's Revelations that closed the Adamic Cycle and opened the Cycle of Fulfillment. The *seven eyes,* the seven extant religions, will rejoice at the capstone, the religion of Bahá'u'lláh.

'Abdu'l-Bahá explained that *two olive trees* were Muḥammad and His nephew 'Alí, who would be the guiding lights for Islam during its dispensation of 1,260 years. Although 'Abdu'l-Bahá was referring to Revelation 11:4 in the following explanation, His comments also explain Zechariah's references to the *two olive trees.*

> *"And I will give power unto my two witnesses, and they shall prophesy a thousand two hundred and three-score days...."* [ah] *By these two witnesses are intended Muhammad the Messenger of God and 'Alí the son of Abú Ṭálib. A "witness" means one by whose affirmation matters are ascertained. The commandments of these* **two witnesses** *were to be followed for* **1,260 days,** *each day corresponding to a year. Now, Muḥammad was the root and 'Alí the branch, like Moses and Joshua....*
>
> *"These are* **the two olive trees, and the two candlesticks** *standing before the God of the earth."* [ai] *These two Souls have been likened to olive trees, since all the lamps of that time were lit at night with olive oil. In other words, these are two Souls from whom the oil of divine wisdom—which is the cause of the illumination of the world—will appear, and through whom the*

[ah] Revelation 11:3, KJV
[ai] Revelation 11:4, KJV

lights of God will shine bright and resplendent. Thus have they also been likened to candlesticks. The candlestick is the locus of the light and the place from whence it emanates. In the same way, the light of guidance would shine resplendent from these luminous Countenances.[147]

Chapter 18 of this volume clarifies Daniel's prophecy concerning the 42 months/years, *the 1,260 days*, which would culminate in the year 1844 CE.

THE TEMPLE OF THE LORD

The word of the Lord came to Zechariah and he was told to take silver and gold from three exiles who had arrived from Babylon (Heldai, Tobijah, and Jedaiah) and to make a crown to be set upon the head of the high priest, Joshua.

And speak unto him [Joshua], *saying, Thus speaketh the* LORD *of hosts, saying, Behold the man whose name is* **The Branch**; *and he shall grow up out of his place, he shall build* **the temple of the** LORD: *Even he shall build the temple of the* LORD; *and he shall bear the glory, and shall sit and rule upon his throne; and he shall be a priest upon his throne: and the counsel of peace shall be between them both. And they that are far off shall come and build in the temple of the* LORD, *and ye shall know that the* LORD *of hosts hath sent me unto you. And this shall come to pass, if ye will diligently obey the voice of the* LORD *your God.* (Zechariah 6:12-13, 15, KVJ, emphasis added).

The Branch is Bahá'u'lláh according to Isaiah 11:1, *"A shoot will come up from the stump of Jesse; from his roots a Branch will bear fruit the rod out of stem of Jesse,"* and the many verses that follow. 'Abdu'l-Bahá gave a full explanation of Isaiah 11:1-12 that is discussed at length in Volume II.[148]

In incomparably beautiful prose, Bahá'u'lláh also elaborated upon the temple of His Revelation as the reflection of God.

> *Say: Naught is seen in My temple but the Temple of God, and in My beauty but His Beauty, and in My being but His Being, and in My self but His Self, and in My movement but His Movement, and in My acquiescence but His Acquiescence, and in My pen but His Pen, the Mighty, the All-Praised. There hath not been in My soul but the Truth, and in Myself naught could be seen but God.*[149]

The *haykal*, which means temple, is also referred to as the temple of man. Bahá'u'lláh had one of His most important tablets, the "Súriy-i-Haykal" (Surih of the Temple), together with His tablets addressed to Pope Pius IX, Napoleon III, Czar Alexander II, Queen Victoria, and Násiri'd-Dín Sháh, copied in the form of a pentacle symbolizing the temple of man. The introduction to *The Summons of the Lord of Hosts* states:

> It was this composite work which, shortly after its completion, Bahá'u'lláh instructed be written in the form of a pentacle, symbolizing the human temple. To it He added, as a conclusion, what Shoghi Effendi has described as "words which reveal the importance He attached to those Messages, and indicate their direct association with the prophecy of the Old Testament":
>
> > Thus have We built the Temple with the hands of power and might, could ye but know it. **This is the Temple promised unto you in the Book.** Draw ye nigh unto it. This is that which profiteth you, could ye but comprehend it. Be fair, O peoples of the earth! Which is preferable, this, or a temple which is built of clay? Set your faces towards it. Thus have ye been commanded by God, the Help in Peril, the Self-Subsisting.[150]

Since Bahá'u'lláh had immediately before referred to the Old Testament, I think we can assume that *the Book* refers to that Scripture. In addition, the esteemed scholar Adib Taherzadeh, after noting the above-mentioned five tablets copied as a pentacle, wrote: "Associating this with the prophecy of Zechariah in the Old Testament, Bahá'u'lláh concludes the *Súriy-i-Haykal* with these words:

> *Thus have We built the temple with the hands of power and might, could ye but know it. This is the Temple promised unto you in **the Book**. Draw ye nigh unto it. This is that which profiteth you, could ye but comprehend it. Be fair, O peoples of the earth! Which is preferable, this, or a temple which is built of clay? Set your faces towards it. Thus have ye been commanded by God, the Help in Peril, the Self-Subsisting.*[151]

VERSES FOR THE AGES

Zechariah wrote beautiful, inspirational verses that have reverberated throughout the centuries and whose symbology can now be better understood. For example,

> *This is what the* LORD *says: "I will return to Zion and dwell in Jerusalem. Then Jerusalem will be called the Faithful City, and the mountain of the* LORD *Almighty will be called the Holy Mountain."* (Zechariah 8:3)

This short ministry of Zechariah was momentous. It was followed by the prophets of Second and Third Zechariah, who added their own counsels and visions of the future.

Chapter 13

SECOND AND THIRD ZECHARIAH – FLICKERS OF THE FUTURE

*"When God sent forth His Prophet Muḥammad, on that day
the termination of the prophetic cycle was foreordained in the
knowledge of God. Yea, that promise hath indeed come true and
the decree of God hath been accomplished as He hath ordained.
Assuredly we are today living in the Days of God."*

The Báb[152]

Biblical scholars generally refer to chapters 9 to 11 as Second Zechariah, or Deutero-Zechariah, and chapters 12 to 14 as Third Zechariah, or Trito-Zechariah. Each has its own introduction setting it apart from previous chapters and themes. Second and Third Zechariah are usually dated to the fifth and fourth centuries BCE, respectively. Some biblical scholars suggest that chapters 9 to 14 were written by disciples of First Zechariah.

Second Zechariah appears to make use of the books of Isaiah, Jeremiah, and Ezekiel, and the themes from First Zechariah. The prophets of Second and Third Zechariah and other postexilic prophets conducted their missions against a background of stress with theocratic authorities who saw their work as threatening to the traditional priesthood. The archaeologist and biblical historian Mary Joan Winn Leith described the situation as follows:

> The postexilic age did have charismatic prophets, but their activities and works were often suppressed in theocratic circles as the work of renegades. Moreover, postexilic authors writing in both the theocratic and charismatic vein pseudonymously clothed themselves in the garb of eminent classical forebears, giving a new text validity by embedding it in the words of a venerated ancient prophet.... Such protests came from a group or groups who rejected Zadokite priestly claims and proposed an alternative religious program in which direct vindication from God of an aggrieved party was an essential element.[153]

This tension helps to explain why the prophets of Second and Third Zechariah, Second and Third Isaiah, and probably others were not identified by name but whose writings were attached to those prophets with whom they had affinity. Leith also points out that this postexilic prophetic movement expanded preexilic prophecy from a Hebrew mindset, that considered the Lord to be theirs alone, to a more universal deity. Even though various scenes were set in biblical Judah, God was expanded from being an actor in Hebrew history to being an actor on a global level. Traditionally a Middle Eastern deity belonged only to people settled in a particular city or region, but the God of the Hebrews went with His people into the Exile. From there, He would be seen as extending His power, law, and authority throughout the world. Leith wrote that the postexilic prophets were visionaries who

> saw punishment and redemption in terms of otherworldly categories, which ultimately became central in fully formed

apocalyptic thought. The timescale for God's judgment begins to expand, as does the sphere of divine judgment, which now includes all the nations, a more universalist view of God's interest.... Some expect God to personally intervene in history (Zech. 14); dreams and visions abound, often populated by angelic interpreters, a form of assistance that earlier prophets seldom required.[154]

The priests and the faithful who returned to Jerusalem to rebuild the temple set up what they believed to be a truer form of Jewish worship than what had survived in Judah after the conquest. The returnees denied other versions of Judaism as practiced by those who were left behind. This set the stage for theological schisms on one hand and a rigid form of Judaism on the other.

Biblical scholars do not agree as to when the additions to the book of Zechariah were written, but they do generally agree that they are among the most difficult of the prophetic works to understand. The biblical scholar Rex Mason expressed his frustration:

So much is obscure in these chapters that interpretation of them can only be tentative. The view that they came from a sharply eschatological party that found itself increasingly at odds with the priesthood and the Temple, and so looked for a more and more radical intervention of God, would account for much that is here. If that were so, it would mean that some of the factors that later gave rise to the Qumran community were already being felt by those from whom chaps. 9-14 came, perhaps in the third century BCE.[155]

Despite the difficulties with probing into the essence of these additions, there are stretches of lucidity that offer moments of identity with previous prophets and new insights into future times. The spirit and power of the Mosaic Dispensation was waning. Parallel to that reality, prophetic emphasis on returning to Mosaic law waned. There was a change of emphasis on apocalyptic visions of a far future and God's continuing hand in human history.

A PROGRESSION IN PROPHECY

Second Zechariah does not mention the temple or any of the subjects of his predecessor's visions. He made no references to Persian monarchs or ethical teachings. His focus was on a divine cleansing of humanity for the future with a universal emphasis.

Like Amos, Jeremiah, and Ezekiel, Second Zechariah started with dire prophetic oracles against several entities such as Tyre, Sidon, Ashkelon, Gaza, and other places. He ends this series of diatribes with a momentous promise: *"But I will encamp at my temple to guard it against marauding forces. Never again will an oppressor overrun my people, for now I am keeping watch"* (Zechariah 9:8). Then comes a flicker of the future, a possible reference to Jesus hailed as a king when He rode into Jerusalem on a donkey, although His kingdom was not of this world.

> *Rejoice greatly, Daughter Zion!*
>   *Shout, Daughter Jerusalem!*
> *See, your king comes to you,*
>   *righteous and victorious,*
> *lowly and riding on a **donkey**,*
>   *on a colt, the foal of a donkey.* (Zechariah 9:9)

The Gospel of John referred to this verse as follows:

> *The next day the great crowd that had come for the festival heard that Jesus was on his way to Jerusalem. They took palm branches and went out to meet him, shouting,*
>
> > *"Hosanna!"*
> > *"Blessed is he who comes in the name of the Lord!"*
> > *"Blessed is the king of Israel!"*

Jesus found a young donkey and sat on it, as it is written:

> *"Do not be afraid, Daughter Zion;*
> *see, your king is coming,*
> *seated on a donkey's colt."* aj

At first his disciples did not understand all this. Only after Jesus was glorified did they realize that these things had been written about him and that these things had been done to him. (John 12:12-16)

Shortly before His last visit to Jerusalem, Jesus had prepared His disciples for His passing. He made the intriguing promise: *"I have much more to say to you, more than you can now bear. But when he, the Spirit of truth, comes, he will guide you into all the truth. He will not speak on his own; he will speak only what he hears, and he will tell you what is yet to come"* (John 16:12-13). After speaking of the days to come, Jesus summarized: *"I have told you these things, so that in me you may have peace. In this world you will have trouble. But take heart! I have overcome the world"* (John 16:33).

There is a tradition, or hadith, in Islam that Sádiq, a son of Muḥammad, said: *"Knowledge is twenty and seven letters. All that the Prophets have revealed are two letters thereof. No man thus far hath known more than these two letters. But when the Qá'im shall arise, He will cause the remaining twenty and five letters to be made manifest."* 156

Bahá'u'lláh quoted this hadith and then wrote His own thoughts: *"Consider; He hath declared Knowledge to consist of twenty and seven letters, and regarded all the Prophets, from Adam even unto the 'Seal,' as Expounders of only two letters thereof and of having been sent down with these two letters. He also saith that the Qá'im will reveal all the remaining twenty and five letters. Behold from this utterance how great and lofty is His station! His rank excelleth all of the Prophets, and His*

---

aj Zechariah 9:9 NIV

Revelation transcendeth the comprehension and understanding of all their chosen ones." [157]

Jesus blessed the peacemakers when He said, *"Blessed are the peacemakers, for they will be called children of God"* (Matthew 5:9); however, world peace was not part of His dispensation. As discussed previously, the core of Jesus's ministry was the life everlasting and the individual's relationship with God. The kingdom of which Jesus often spoke was not of this world. Second Zechariah suggests a progression from Jesus to Bahá'u'lláh when the next verse foretells universal peace.

> *He will proclaim peace to the nations.*
> *His rule will extend from **sea to sea***
> *and from **the River** to the ends of the earth.*
> *As for you, because of the blood of my covenant with you,*
> *I will free your prisoners from **the waterless pit.***
> (Zechariah 9:10)

World unity and peace would be a primary focus of Bahá'u'lláh's Revelation, and He brought the "manual" to achieve global harmony— His Writings and the Administrative Order (see Appendix C).

Second Zechariah's phrase from *sea to sea* is reminiscent of Micah 7:12, *"In that day people will come to you from Assyria and the cities of Egypt, even from Egypt to the Euphrates and from sea to sea and from mountain to mountain."* The *River* could be the Euphrates, along whose bank Bahá'u'lláh spent ten years while imprisoned in Baghdad and from which His Faith started its spread throughout the world. The *waterless pit* could be the Siyah-Chal, a drained underground cistern in Tehran where Bahá'u'lláh was imprisoned for four months with several of His followers in 1853.

SHEEP AND SHEPHERDS

Another prophecy laments spiritual corruption of the priesthood, who were the religious shepherds responsible for the spiritual welfare of the people. Second Zechariah was told by God to stand in His place shepherding the flock to experience what He had been experiencing.

> *This is what the LORD my God says: "Shepherd the flock marked for slaughter. Their buyers slaughter them and go unpunished. Those who sell them say, 'Praise the LORD, I am rich!' Their own shepherds do not spare them. For I will no longer have pity on the people of the land," declares the LORD. "I will give everyone into the hands of their neighbors and their king. They will devastate the land, and I will not rescue anyone from their hands."* (Zechariah 11:4-6)

The sheep, a symbol for the people, had been marked for slaughter, slavery, or victimization of other crimes that enriched the shepherds. Three evil shepherds were defeated by the Lord using two staffs called Favor and Union. But was the flock grateful? No! *"The flock detested me, and I grew weary of them and said, I will not be your shepherd. Let the dying die, and the perishing perish. Let those who are left eat one another's flesh"* (Zechariah 11:8-8).

The Covenant of Moses had been grievously broken in innumerable ways over the centuries and would not be fully restored in the hearts of the people. Therefore, mention was made to the coming of the bearer of the next divine Covenant. This anecdote alluded to the first recorded violation of the Christian Covenant, which was the betrayal of Jesus by Judas Iscariot.

> *Then I took my staff called Favor[ak] and broke it, revoking the covenant I had made with all the nations. It was revoked on that day, and so the oppressed of the flock who were watching me knew it was the word of the LORD.*
>
> *I told them, "If you think it best, give me my pay; but if not, keep it." So they paid me* **thirty pieces of silver.**

[ak] In the KJV, the staff is called Beauty.

And the L<small>ORD</small> *said to me, "Throw it to the **potter**"—the hand-some price at which they valued me! So I took the thirty pieces of silver and threw them to the potter at the house of the* L<small>ORD</small>.

Then I broke my second staff called Union, breaking the family bond between Judah and Israel. (Zechariah 11:10-14, emphasis added)

The Mosaic Covenant would be replaced with another. Allusion to this replacement, to the coming of Jesus, is made by the mention of *thirty pieces of silver*. A remorseful Judas had tried to return the thirty pieces of silver he had been paid to betray Jesus, but it was blood money and the chief priests used it to purchase a *potter's field* for burial of foreigners (Matthew 26:15, 27:3-7).

The last words of Second Zechariah were:

"Woe to the worthless shepherd,
who deserts the flock!
May the sword strike his arm and his right eye!
May his arm be completely withered,
his right eye totally blinded!" (Zechariah 11:17)

Over two thousand years later Bahá'u'lláh would write: *"From two ranks amongst men power hath been seized: kings and ecclesiastics."* [158]

ASPECTS OF THE MARTYRDOM OF JESUS

Third Zechariah touched upon aspects of Jesus's martyrdom.

"And I will pour out on the house of David and the inhabitants of Jerusalem a spirit of grace and supplication. They will look on me, the one they have pierced, and they will mourn for him as one mourns for an only child, and grieve bitterly for him as one grieves for a firstborn son." (Zechariah 12:10)

Jesus was a descendant of the house of David. In time, grievous mourning for Him will be offset by the realization of the inner meaning of the *fountain* of Jesus's message. In addition, an amazing statement is made that the era of the Hebrew prophets would close with the Dispensation of Jesus.

> *"On that day a **fountain** will be opened to the house of David and the inhabitants of Jerusalem, to cleanse them from sin and impurity.*
>
> *"On that day, I will banish the names of the idols from the land, and they will be remembered no more," declares the* LORD *Almighty. "I will remove both the prophets and the spirit of impurity from the land. And if anyone still prophesies, their father and mother, to whom they were born, will say to them, 'You must die, because you have told lies in the Lord's name.' Then their own parents will stab the one who prophesies.*
>
> *"On that day every prophet will be ashamed of their prophetic vision. They will not put on a prophet's garment of hair in order to deceive. Each will say, 'I am not a prophet. I am a farmer; the land has been my livelihood since my youth.'"* (Zechariah 13:1-5, emphasis added)

The Gospel of Matthew records that after Jesus breathed His last, the temple curtain was rent from top to bottom (Matthew 27:51). Symbolically, this meant that the Covenant of Moses had been replaced by the Covenant of Jesus. Since the Hebrew prophets belonged to the Mosaic Dispensation, Third Zechariah saw that their days would be completed. The Jewish perspective is that Third Zechariah and Malachi were the last of the Hebrew prophets. The Christian perspective is that John the Baptist was the last prophet before the arrival of Jesus. *"The Law and the Prophets were proclaimed until John. Since that time, the good news of the kingdom of God is being preached, and everyone is forcing their way into it"* (Luke 16:16).

A DAY OF THE LORD IS COMING

Third Zechariah made several references to the day of the Lord including, *"A day of the LORD is coming, Jerusalem, when your possessions will be plundered and divided up within your very walls"* (Zechariah 14:1). Apocalyptic images followed of destruction of the city with half the people sent into exile. There will be fighting among the nations, and the Lord's feet will stand on the Mount of Olives as it splits in two from east to west, forming a great valley. People would flee they as fled the earthquake in the days of King Uzziah. But resolution to mankind's perpetual wars and religious conflicts would come.

> *... Then the LORD my God will come, and all the holy ones with him.*
>
> *On that day there will be neither sunlight nor cold, frosty darkness. It will be a unique day—a day known only to the LORD—with no distinction between day and night. When evening comes, there will be light.*
>
> *On that day living water will flow out from Jerusalem, half of it east to the Dead Sea and half of it west to the Mediterranean Sea, in summer and in winter.*
>
> *The LORD will be king over the whole earth. On that day there will be one LORD, and his name the only name.* (Zechariah 14:5-9, emphasis added)

Water is a universal symbol for spiritual cleansing, the word of God, and the Holy Spirit. Jeremiah related living water to the divine word when he relayed the voice of God as saying: *"My people have committed two sins: They have forsaken me, the spring of living water, and have dug their own cisterns, broken cisterns that cannot hold water"* (Jeremiah 2:13). The Apostle John wrote of the living water as the Holy Spirit:

On the last and greatest day of the festival, Jesus stood and said in a loud voice, "Let anyone who is thirsty come to me and drink. Whoever believes in me, as Scripture has said, rivers of **living water** *will flow from within them." By this he meant the Spirit, whom those who believed in him were later to receive. Up to that time the Spirit had not been given, since Jesus had not yet been glorified.* (John 7:37-39, emphasis added)

Jerusalem, as a symbol for a new religion, could refer to both Christianity and the Bahá'í Faith in their respective times. Both spread to *the east of the Dead Sea* and west to *the Mediterranean Sea.* Then we come to the *king, one Lord,* and the *one name.* One of the titles of Bahá'u'lláh is King of Kings.[159] Bahá'u'lláh wrote: *"Ye are but vassals, O kings of the earth! He Who is the King of Kings hath appeared, arrayed in His most wondrous glory, and is summoning you unto Himself, the Help in Peril, the Self-Subsisting."* [160]

Bahá'u'lláh sometimes referred to Himself as the **Lord of Lords**. One example was when He wrote to Pope Pius IX: *"O Pope! Rend the veils asunder. He Who is the* **Lord of Lords** *is come overshadowed with clouds, and the decree hath been fulfilled by God, the Almighty, the Unrestrained."* [161]

The *only name* is a vital clue to a possible meaning. The name of Bahá'u'lláh is spelled and pronounced the same everywhere in the world. Variants of the name Moses include Moishe (Yiddish), Moshe (Hebrew), Moussa and Mustafa (Arabic), and Musa (Turkish and Persian). Differences in the name Jesus include Yeshua (Hebrew), Isa (Arabic), Jésus (French), Jesús (Spanish), Gesù (Italian), Isus (Ukrainian), and Jesu (Yoruba). But the name Bahá'u'lláh is the same throughout the world, which is most fitting for the Prophet whose mission was to prepare humankind for the oneness of God, the oneness of the Prophets of God, and the oneness of the human race. In addition, seventy percent of the world's population uses Roman script, which does not vary the spelling of Bahá'u'lláh.

Chapter 14

THIRD ISAIAH – THE DAY THAT SHALL NOT BE FOLLOWED BY NIGHT

"Arise, shine, for your light has come,
and the glory of the LORD rises upon you."

Isaiah 60:1

Chapters 56 through 66 of the book of Isaiah were written by one or more anonymous prophets after the return from the Exile, perhaps during the time frame of 520 to 500 BCE. The date could have been later when temple worship had become routine and the Second Temple was not regarded with the reverence it must have enjoyed in its early years. According to Third Isaiah, the Restoration had not resulted in a Jewish population united in monotheism.

Haggai and First Zechariah did not mention idols or idolatry, which might infer that they were no longer an issue. However, Third Isaiah sounds preexilic in his condemnation of idolatrous worship in his time. According to him, even child sacrifice was still being practiced. Was this the case only among the Judeans who had stayed in the rural areas?

Had Jerusalemites who had stayed backslid without the guidance of the priests? Had some of the second- and third-generation descendants of the returnees relapsed? The prophet doesn't answer these questions but we can feel the singe of his red-hot anger.

> *You burn with lust among the oaks*
> *and under every spreading tree;*
> *you sacrifice your children in the ravines*
> *and under the overhanging crags.*
> *The idols among the smooth stones of the ravines are your portion;*
> *indeed, they are your lot.*
> *Yes, to them you have poured out drink offerings*
> *and offered grain offerings.*
> *In view of all this, should I relent?* (Isaiah 57:5-6)

Perhaps the religious reforms of Ezra and Nehemiah had not been as successful as their books suggest. The struggle against idolatry would continue when the Greeks conquered the Holy Land in the fourth century and brought their gods with them, and when the Romans conquered the Greeks and brought their gods. Would this struggle ever end? Yes, eventually.

As did all the prophets, Third Isaiah spoke strongly for justice. *"This is what the LORD says: 'Maintain justice and do what is right, for my salvation is close at hand and my righteousness will soon be revealed'"* (Isaiah 56:1). He scorched the perpetrators of injustice with his words from the Lord: *"No one calls for justice; no one pleads a case with integrity. They rely on empty arguments, they utter lies; they conceive trouble and give birth to evil"* (Isaiah 59:4), and *"So justice is far from us, and righteousness does not reach us. We look for light, but all is darkness; for brightness, but we walk in deep shadows"* (Isaiah 59:9).

Third Isaiah excoriated the Jews for seeking recognition from the Lord for fasting, but exploiting their workers during fasts and quarreling and fighting during fasts. How could they behave this way and yet expect their voices to be heard on high? *"Is not this the kind of fasting I have chosen: to loose the chains of injustice and untie the cords of the yoke, to set the oppressed free and break every yoke?"* (Isaiah 58:6)

True to prophetic mode, Third Isaiah used the circumstances and imagery of his time, but common threads run through them that apply to our times.

THE LIGHT AND THE GLORY

Third Isaiah said that again the Lord looked and saw that there was no justice, that there was no one intervening for justice. Therefore, *"He put on righteousness as his breastplate, and the helmet of salvation on his head; he put on the garments of vengeance and wrapped himself in zeal as in a cloak"* (Isaiah 59:17). He would repay according to what had been done. The time would come when God's Messenger would not only be recognized but the word of God brought through Him would be obeyed.

> *From the west, people will fear the name of the LORD,*
> *and from **the rising of the sun**, they will revere his glory.*
> *For he will come like a pent-up flood*
> *that the breath of the LORD drives along.*
> *"The Redeemer will come to Zion,*
> *to those in Jacob who repent of their sins," declares the LORD.*
>
> *"As for me, this is my covenant with them," says the Lord. "My Spirit, who is on you, will not depart from you, and my words that I have put in your mouth will always be on your lips, on the lips of your children and on the lips of their descendants—from this time on and forever," says the Lord.* (Isaiah 59:19-21, emphasis added)

The *rising of the sun* from the east has long been used as a symbol of the coming of a new Revelation from God, which has always risen in the East and spread to the West. For example, Nabil-i-Azám, the incomparable historian of early Bahá'í history, called the early followers of the Báb the dawn-breakers. Shoghi Effendi wrote: "When Bahá'u'lláh arrived at

'Akká, through the power of God He was able to hoist His banner. His light at first had been a star; now it became a mighty sun, and the illumination of His Cause expanded from the East to the West." [162]

The verses of Third Isaiah soar with promises of the coming of the light and glory of the Lord. For example,

> "Arise, shine, for your **light** has come,
>   and **the glory of the** LORD rises upon you.
> See, **darkness** covers the earth
>   and thick darkness is over the peoples,
> but the LORD rises upon you
>   and his glory appears over you.
> Nations will come to your light,
>   and kings to the brightness of your dawn.
>
> Your sun will never set again,
>   and your moon will wane no more;
> the LORD will be your everlasting light,
>   and your days of sorrow will end. (Isaiah 60:1-3)

In context with *the glory of the Lord*, the *light* means that of the new dispensation to come and the *darkness* is rejection of its spiritual light. This denial permeates our twenty-first century that is ridden with war, disease, poverty, ignorance, pollution, political corruption, and the profit motive run amuck. Society is breaking down as the forces of irreligion, greed, and power compete for souls. Bahá'u'lláh described these conditions from the vantage point of the nineteenth century: *"The signs of impending convulsions and chaos can now be discerned, inasmuch as the prevailing order appeareth to be lamentably defective."* [al,163] In

---

al The complete quotation is, "The winds of despair are, alas, blowing from every direction, and the strife that divideth and afflicteth the human race is daily increasing. The signs of impending convulsions and chaos can now be discerned, inasmuch as the prevailing order appeareth to be lamentably defective. I beseech God, exalted be His glory, that He may

time, however, perpetual peace will be embraced by the governments of the world.

> *I will make peace your governor*
> *and well-being your ruler.*
> *No longer will violence be heard in your land,*
> *nor ruin or destruction within your borders,*
> *but you will call your walls Salvation*
> *and your gates Praise.* (Isaiah 60:17-18)

Third Isaiah gave an interesting discourse on the sun and moon and how in this dispensation their light will not dim.

> *The sun will no more be your light by day,*
> *nor will the brightness of the moon shine on you,*
> *for the LORD will be your everlasting light,*
> *and your God will be your glory.*
> *Your sun will never set again,*
> *and your moon will wane no more;*
> *the LORD will be your everlasting light,*
> *and your days of sorrow will end.*
>
> *Then all your people will be righteous*
> *and they will possess the land forever.*
> *They are the shoot I have planted,*
> *the work of my hands,*
> *for the display of my splendor.*
> *The least of you will become a thousand,*
> *the smallest a mighty nation.*
> *I am the Lord;*
> *in its time I will do this swiftly."* (Isaiah 60:19-22)

---

graciously awaken the peoples of the earth, may grant that the end of their conduct may be profitable unto them, and aid them to accomplish that which beseemeth their station."

The Lord will be our everlasting spiritual light, and the sun of religion will not set in the Bahá'í dispensation. Consider that Bahá'u'lláh wrote when speaking of this Day of God, *"For the Day of God is none other but His own Self, Who hath appeared with the power of truth. This is the Day that shall not be followed by night, nor shall it be bounded by any praise, would that ye might understand!"* [164]

Shoghi Effendi gave a poignant example of recognition of the Day not being followed by the night of disunity and dissension. He wrote in *God Passes By*, his incomparable history of the first one hundred years of the Bahá'í Faith, as follows:

> The immediate effect of the ascension of Bahá'u'lláh had been, as already observed, to spread grief and bewilderment among his followers and companions, and to inspire its vigilant and redoubtable adversaries with fresh hope and renewed determination.
>
> Yet, as the appointed Center of Bahá'u'lláh's Covenant and the authorized Interpreter of His teaching had Himself later explained, the dissolution of the tabernacle wherein the soul of the Manifestation of God had chosen temporarily to abide signalized its release from the restrictions which an earthly life had, of necessity, imposed upon it. Its influence no longer circumscribed by any physical limitations, its radiance no longer beclouded by its human temple, that soul could henceforth energize the whole world to a degree unapproached at any stage in the course of its existence on this planet. [165]

Shoghi Effendi further explained that Bahá'u'lláh's mission had been carried out fully in every respect, and, "Above all the Covenant that was to perpetuate the influence of that Faith, insure its integrity, safeguard it from schism, and stimulate its world-wide expansion, had been fixed on an inviolable basis." [166] The morning after Bahá'u'lláh's ascension, 'Abdu'l-Bahá wrote a stirring message of faith.

The stirring proclamation 'Abdu'l-Bahá had penned, addressed to the rank and file of the followers of His Father, on the morrow of His ascension, as well as the prophecies He Himself had uttered in His Tablets, breathed a resolve and a confidence which the fruits garnered and the triumphs achieved in the course of a thirty-year ministry have abundantly justified.

The cloud of despondency that had momentarily settled on the disconsolate lovers of the Cause of Bahá'u'lláh was lifted. The continuity of that unerring guidance vouchsafed to it since its birth was now assured. The significance of the solemn affirmation that this is "the Day which shall not be followed by night" was now clearly apprehended. An orphan community had recognized in 'Abdu'l-Bahá, in its hour of desperate need, its Solace, its Guide, its Mainstay and Champion.[167]

The sun that will not set and the moon that will not wane mentioned by Third Isaiah undoubtedly has many meanings. Its foremost could be the Covenant of Bahá'u'lláh that provided for the stewardship of 'Abdu'l-Bahá and Shoghi Effendi, and then for the election of the Universal House of Justice.[168]

THE ACCEPTABLE YEAR OF THE LORD

Third Isaiah seems to have accurately foretold the coming of Jesus when he said:

The Spirit of the LORD GOD is upon me; because the LORD hath anointed me to preach good tidings unto the meek; he hath sent me to bind up the brokenhearted, to proclaim liberty to the captives, and the opening of the prison to them that are bound;

*To proclaim the **acceptable year of the LORD**, and the day of vengeance of our God; to comfort all that mourn;*

To appoint unto them that mourn in Zion, to give unto them beauty for ashes, the oil of joy for mourning, the garment of praise for the spirit of heaviness; that they might be called trees of righteousness, the planting of the LORD, that he might be glorified. (Isaiah 61:1-3, KVJ, emphasis added)

The *acceptable year of the LORD* can be seen as the day of the Lord when a new dispensation is given. Centuries later, Jesus attended synagogue in Nazareth on the Sabbath. He stood up to read and the scroll of Isaiah was given to Him.

*And there was delivered unto him the book of the prophet Esaias. And when he had opened the book, he found the place where it was written, "The Spirit of the Lord is upon me, because he hath anointed me to preach the gospel to the poor; he hath sent me to heal the brokenhearted, to preach deliverance to the captives, and recovering of sight to the blind, to set at liberty them that are bruised, to preach the **acceptable year of the LORD.**"*

And he closed the book, and he gave it again to the minister, and sat down. And the eyes of all them that were in the synagogue were fastened on him.

And he began to say unto them, "This day is this scripture fulfilled in your ears." (Luke 4:17-21, KJV, emphasis added)

A NEW NAME

Third Isaiah wrote that the Prophet of God for our day would be called by *a new name that the mouth of the LORD shall name.*

For Zion's sake will I not hold my peace, and for Jerusalem's sake I will not rest, until the righteousness thereof go forth as brightness, and the salvation thereof as a lamp that burneth.

*And the Gentiles shall see thy righteousness, and all kings thy glory: and thou shalt be called by **a new name, which the mouth of the LORD shall name**.* (Isaiah 62:1-2, KJV, emphasis added)

Third Isaiah also conveyed an explicit promise of *new heavens and a new earth*:

"See, I will create
*   **new heavens and a new earth.***
The former things will not be remembered,
*   nor will they come to mind."* (Isaiah 65:17)

Bahá'u'lláh explained the meaning of heaven when He wrote. *"By 'heaven' is meant the heaven of divine Revelation, which is elevated with every Manifestation, and rent asunder with every subsequent one."*[169] And He referred to a new earth when He wrote, *"In like manner, endeavour to comprehend the meaning of the 'changing of the earth.' Know thou, that upon whatever hearts the bountiful showers of mercy, raining from the 'heaven' of divine Revelation, have fallen, the earth of those hearts hath verily been changed into the earth of divine knowledge and wisdom."*[170]

The book of Revelation gives additional clues about the new heaven and new earth. *"Then I saw "a new heaven and a new earth," for the first heaven and the first earth had passed away, and there was no longer any sea. I saw the Holy City, the new Jerusalem, coming down out of heaven from God, prepared as a bride beautifully dressed for her husband"* (Revelation 21:1-2).

'Abdu'l-Bahá commented at length on the new heaven and new earth as mentioned by St. John the Divine.

Consider how unmistakably "the first heaven" and "the first earth" refer to the outward aspects of the former religion. For it is said that "the first heaven and earth were passed away; and there was no more sea". That is, the earth is the arena of the last judgement, and in this arena there will be no more sea, meaning that the law and teachings of God will have spread throughout the earth, all mankind will have embraced His Cause, and the earth will have been entirely peopled by the faithful. Thus there will be no more sea, for man dwells upon solid land and not in the sea—that is, in that Dispensation the sphere of influence of that religion will encompass every land that man has trodden, and it will be established upon solid ground whereon the feet do not falter.

Likewise, the religion of God is described as the Holy City or the New Jerusalem. Clearly, the New Jerusalem which descends from heaven is not a city of stone and lime, of brick and mortar, but is rather the religion of God which descends from heaven and is described as new. For it is obvious that the Jerusalem which is built of stone and mortar does not descend from heaven and is not renewed, but that what is renewed is the religion of God.[171]

After announcement of the creation of new heavens and a new earth, Third Isaiah continued:

"See, I will create
new heavens and a new earth.
The former things will not be remembered,
nor will they come to mind.
But be glad and rejoice forever
in what I will create,
for I will create Jerusalem to be a delight
and its people a joy.
I will rejoice over Jerusalem
and take delight in my people;
the sound of weeping and of crying
will be heard in it no more." (Isaiah 65:17-19)

The people will flourish in prosperity. Conditions of social justice and peace are described. The thoughts of First Isaiah about peace are echoed by Third Isaiah with the wolf and lamb feeding together, and the lion eating straw with the ox. *"They will neither harm nor destroy on all my holy mountain, says the LORD"* (Isaiah 65:25). The final words of Third Isaiah are:

> *"As the new heavens and the new earth that I make will endure before me," declares the LORD, "so will your name and descendants endure. From one New Moon to another and from one Sabbath to another, all mankind will come and bow down before me," says the LORD. "And they will go out and look on the dead bodies of those who rebelled against me; the worms that eat them will not die, the fire that burns them will not be quenched and they will be loathsome to all mankind."* (Isaiah 66:22-24)

To reduce any prophetic work from the Hebrew Bible, especially the book of Isaiah, to a few subjects with relevant verses, is woefully inadequate. The collective Isaiah spoke on many levels and alluded to many realities at various points in time.

Chapter 15

JOEL – BLOW THE TRUMPET

"O Haydar-'Alí! I swear by the righteousness of God! The Blast hath been blown on the Trumpet of the Bayán as decreed by the Lord, the Merciful, ... This is the Day in which the earth shineth with the effulgent light of thy Lord."

Bahá'u'lláh[172]

Little is known about the man named Joel who was called to be a prophet. His book starts with *"The word of the LORD that came to Joel son of Pethuel"* (Joel 1:1) but gives no further hint of his identity. Joel was obviously a learned man; his writings brim over with arresting imagery and demonstrate familiarity with the prophetic heritage that preceded his mission. Speculation for the time of Joel has ranged from the ninth through the fifth centuries BCE. Biblical commentators who advocate for an earlier time claim that Amos, Micah, and Isaiah called upon Joel's words, not vice versa. For example, both Isaiah and Micah wrote, *"They will beat their swords into plowshares and their spears into pruning hooks"* (Isaiah 2:4, Micah 4:3). Joel reversed the meaning in his metaphorical use of an army to portray spiritual forces when he wrote, *"Beat your plowshares into swords and your pruning hooks into spears. Let the weakling say, 'I am strong!' Come quickly, all you nations from every side, and assemble there"* (Joel 3:10-11).

Scholars who argue for the fourth century rely upon Joel's oracle against the nations that mentions the Greeks: *"You sold the people of Judah and Jerusalem to the Greeks, that you might send them far from their home-land"* (Joel 3:6). However, the Greeks did not conquer Palestine until about 332, which is a bit late for the line of Hebrew prophets to have continued. Joel does, however, refer obliquely to temple worship, which suggests the Second Temple period. This author opts for a postexilic date during the Persian occupation because Joel did not mention any of the issues crucial to preexilic prophets, primarily the sins of the people and looming defeat from the Assyrians or the Babylonians. Joel was totally focused on a very far future.

The book of Joel is short with only three chapters, which conforms to a noticeable trend to briefer ministries and shorter works as the age of the classical prophets ebbed. However, all three chapters focus on the day of the Lord, which is not only mentioned five times but each time is the central point of the discourse. The day of the Lord is Joel's only message. The sins of Israel, the Exile, and the Restoration were not relevant to his mission. He showed no interest in a revitalization of the Mosaic Dispensation, renewed adherence to Mosaic law, or purification of temple worship.

The book of Joel starts by describing in vivid, intense language an overwhelming invasion of locusts. Plagues of locusts had long been a biblical theme because they were a devastating threat. Locust swarms could block the sun and strip the land of crops, foliage, and pasture grass. Famine would ensue. Biblical locusts were often used as symbolic har-bingers of disaster because they were an indomitable force that could not be fought. Joel uses this metaphor when addressing the elders of the land about the blight of a catastrophic plague.

> *What the locust swarm has left*
> *the great locusts have eaten;*
> *what the great locusts have left*

the young locusts have eaten;
  what the young locusts have left
    other locusts have eaten. (Joel 1:4)

Locusts are an apt symbol for the darkening of a religion during its winter and for stripping society of its spiritual life and connection with God. The people are like drunks and must be awoken because a nation with a mighty army has invaded the land with the teeth of a lion and the fangs of a lioness.

It has laid waste my vines
  and ruined my fig trees.
It has stripped off their bark
  and thrown it away,
    leaving their branches white. (Joel 1:7)

The fields are barren, the grain destroyed, the vines shriveled up, and the fig trees withered. The people's joy has withered away but they do not awaken.

Grief and despair will not solve the problem; the situation calls for repentance with the donning of sackcloth, and recognition that the spiritual situation must be addressed because the *day of the* LORD is near.

Declare a holy fast;
  call a sacred assembly.
Summon the elders
  and all who live in the land
to the house of the LORD *your God,*
  and cry out to the LORD.

Alas for that day!
  For the day of the LORD ***is near;***
    it will come like destruction from the Almighty.
(Joel 1:14-15, emphasis added)

Joel has described the extreme straits of society with symbols of famine, storehouses in ruin, and suffering livestock, and he has implored the elders to lead the people in turning to God. *"To you, LORD, I call, for fire has devoured the pastures in the wilderness and flames have burned up all the trees of the field. Even the wild animals pant for you; the streams of water have dried up and fire has devoured the pastures in the wilderness* (Joel 1:19-20). And again Joel sounds his warning that the *day of the Lord* is coming.

> *Blow **the trumpet** in Zion;*
> *sound the alarm on my holy hill.*
>
> *Let all who live in the land tremble,*
> *for the **day of the LORD** is coming.*
> *It is close at hand—*
> *a day of darkness and gloom,*
> *a day of clouds and blackness.*
> (Joel 2:1-2, emphasis added)

This is the trumpet mentioned by Jesus. When Jesus's disciples asked Him about the signs of His coming and the end of the age. He warned of false prophets, wars and rumors wars, famines, and earthquakes, all of which would be the beginning of birth pains. He spoke of the abomination that causes desolation mentioned by Daniel (see Chapter 18). And He warned of flights that could mean mass migrations and great distress unequalled from the beginning of the world and never to be equaled again. Then Jesus listed the symbolic signs of His coming.

> *"Immediately after the distress of those days*
>
> *""The sun will be darkened,*
> *and the moon will not give its light;*
> *the stars will fall from the sky,*
> *and the heavenly bodies will be shaken."'* [am]

[am] Isaiah 13:10, 34:4

"Then will appear the sign of the Son of Man in heaven. And then all the peoples of the earth will mourn when they see the Son of Man coming on the clouds of heaven, with power and great glory.[an] *And he will send his angels with a loud **trumpet call**, and they will gather his elect from the four winds, from one end of the heavens to the other.* (Matthew 24:29-31, emphasis added)

Joel describes a mighty army coming as never before seen in ancient times, nor ever to be seen in ages to come. This army appears like horses as they gallop like cavalry, making noises like chariots as they leap over mountaintops. They are a mighty army that charges like warriors and scales walls like soldiers, never swerving from their course. Nations are in anguish as the invasion plunges through defenses and climbs into houses, entering like thieves through the windows.

> *Before them the earth shakes,*
> *the heavens tremble,*
> *the **sun and moon are darkened**,*
> *and the stars no longer shine.*
> *The Lord thunders*
> *at the head of his army;*
> *his forces are beyond number,*
> *and mighty is the army that obeys his command.*
> ***The day of the Lord is great;***
> ***it is dreadful.***
> ***Who can endure it?*** (Joel 2:10-11, emphasis added)

The onslaught is not to be defeated. The light of the previous dispensation has been lost. Religious leaders have little to offer as dark forces take over society. Zephaniah had pronounced the *day of the Lord* in stark

---

[an] Daniel 7:13-14

terms similar to Joel's, in an apocalyptic context of breathtakingly stark imagery (Zephaniah 1:14-18).[173]

Bahá'u'lláh commented on Joel 2:11 in His tablet *Epistle to the Son of the Wolf.* This Tablet was written to a Persian whose father had given the orders for the execution of two esteemed Bahá'ís in 1879. Bahá'u'lláh mostly spoke beyond this son and addressed all humanity as follows:

> *Joel saith: "For the Day of the Lord is great and very terrible; and who can abide it?" Firstly, in the sublime utterance set forth in the Gospel He saith that none is aware of the time of the Revelation, that none knoweth it except God, the All-Knowing, Who is cognizant of all. Secondly, He setteth forth the greatness of the Revelation. Likewise, in the Qur'án He saith: "Of what ask they of one another? Of the Great Announcement." This is the Announcement, the greatness of which hath been mentioned in most of the Books of old and of more recent times. This is the Announcement that hath caused the limbs of mankind to quake, except such as God, the Protector, the Helper, the Succorer, hath willed to exempt. Men have indeed with their own eyes witnessed how all men and all things have been thrown into confusion and been sore perplexed, save those whom God hath chosen to exempt.*[174]

Bahá'u'lláh also gave several meanings for the sun, the moon, and the stars as follows:

> *The term "suns" hath many a time been applied in the writings of the "immaculate Souls" unto the Prophets of God, those luminous Emblems of Detachment. ...[T]he terms "sun," "moon," and "stars" primarily signify the Prophets of God, the saints, and their companions, those Luminaries, the light of Whose knowledge hath shed illumination upon the worlds of the visible and the invisible.*
>
> *In another sense, by these terms is intended the divines of the former Dispensation, who live in the days of the subsequent*

Revelations, and who hold the reins of religion in their grasp. If these divines be illumined by the light of the latter Revelation, they will be acceptable unto God, and will shine with a light everlasting. Otherwise, they will be declared as darkened, even though to outward seeming they be leaders of men, inasmuch as belief and unbelief, guidance and error, felicity and misery, light and darkness, are all dependent upon the sanction of Him Who is the Daystar of Truth.[175]

"In another sense, by the terms 'sun', 'moon', and 'stars' are meant such laws and teachings as have been established and proclaimed in every Dispensation such as the laws of prayer and fasting." [176]

The trumpet blast is the symbol used by Jesus (above) and Muḥammad for the call of the Manifestation which is heard in both heaven and earth. Bahá'u'lláh commented on the trumpet as mentioned in the Quranic verse 50:20: *"And there was a blast on the trumpet—lo! it is the threatened Day! And every soul is summoned to a reckoning—with him an impeller and a witness."* Bahá'u'lláh wrote: *"Nay, by 'trumpet' is meant the trumpet-call of Muḥammad's Revelation, which was sounded in the heart of the universe, and by 'resurrection' is meant His own rise to proclaim the Cause of God."* [177]

Joel's scenes of destruction represent the social and religious collapse caused by resistance to spiritual forces brought by a Manifestation of God. Joel next gives an interlude of comforting words about the future.

"And afterward,
   I will pour out my Spirit on all people.
Your sons and daughters will prophesy,
   your old men will dream dreams,
   your young men will see visions.
Even on my servants, both men and women,
   I will pour out my Spirit in those days." (Joel 2:28-29)

Then Joel returned to the familiar metaphorical references of the sun turned to darkness and the moon to blood previous to the coming of the day of the Lord.

The sun will be turned to darkness
    and the moon to blood
    before the coming of the great and dreadful day of the LORD.
And everyone who calls
    on the name of the LORD *will be saved;*
for on Mount Zion and in Jerusalem
    there will be deliverance, as the LORD *has said,*
    even among the survivors whom the LORD *calls.* (Joel 2:31-32)

This apocalyptic saga has contributed to a certain literal belief about an end of days that culminates in a final judgment, or trial.

"In those days and at that time,
    when I restore the fortunes of Judah and Jerusalem,
*I will gather **all nations***
    *and bring them down to the **Valley of Jehoshaphat.***
*There I will put them **on trial***
    for what they did to my inheritance, my people Israel,
because they scattered my people among the nations
    and divided up my land." (Joel 3:1-2, emphasis added)

The name Jehoshaphat means "God shall judge," and the Valley of Jehoshaphat, located outside Jerusalem, has long been regarded as the place of judging of the nations (Joel 3:2, 12). It is also referred to as the "valley of decision" (Joel 3:14). The Valley of Jehoshaphat is now known at the Kidron Valley. Joel stated that *all nations* will be put *on trial* in the *Valley of Jehoshaphat*. Swing the sickle because the harvest is ripe, Joel said, before shifting the scene to another pronouncement of the *day of the Lord* when the Valley of Jehoshaphat is called the *valley of decision.*

"Multitudes, multitudes
   *in the **valley of decision!***
*For the **day of the** LORD is near*
   in the valley of decision."
The sun and moon will be darkened,
   and the stars no longer shine.
The LORD *will roar from Zion*
   and thunder from Jerusalem;
   the earth and the heavens will tremble.
But the LORD *will be a refuge for his people,*
   a stronghold for the people of Israel.
(Joel 3:14-16, emphasis added)

The prophet Amos, one of the first of the canonical prophets, wrote: *"The* LORD *roars from Zion and thunders from Jerusalem; the pastures of the shepherds dry up, and the top of Carmel withers* (Amos 1:2). Bahá'u'lláh wrote as follows:

> *Amos saith: "The Lord will roar from Zion, and utter His Voice from Jerusalem; and the habitations of the shepherds shall mourn, and the top of Carmel shall wither." Carmel, in the Book of God, hath been designated as the Hill of God, and His Vineyard. It is here that, by the grace of the Lord of Revelation, the Tabernacle of Glory hath been raised.*[ao] *Happy are they that attain thereunto; happy they that set their faces towards it. And likewise He saith: "Our God will come, and He will not be silent."* [178]

Had Joel taken a thought from Amos? These two prophets were separated in time by over two hundred years, but it seems that Joel encountered much the same social conditions that Amos had, and the Lord was

---

[ao] The tent that was erected for Bahá'u'lláh during His four visits to Mount Carmel was referred to by His followers as the Tabernacle of Glory.

getting impatient. However, said Joel, there will be a future when the Lord will be a refuge and a stronghold for His people.

> *"Then you will know that I, the LORD your God,*
> *dwell in Zion, my holy hill.*
> *Jerusalem will be holy;*
> *never again will foreigners invade her.*
>
> *"In that day the mountains will drip **new wine**,*
> *and the hills will flow with **milk**;*
> *all the ravines of Judah will run with water.*
> *A **fountain** will flow out of the LORD's house*
> *and will water the valley of acacias."*
> (Joel 3:17-18, emphasis added)

The *new wine* refers to a new dispensation from God, one that cannot be contained within the old one. *Milk* is mild as nature's first nourishment for infants; humanity will not be overwhelmed by the new teachings but carefully nurtured. A *fountain* is often used as a metaphor for a font of spiritual knowledge. For example, Bahá'u'lláh wrote about His Dispensation, *"This is the Fountain of living water for all that dwell in the realm of being."* [179]

And Joel's final words? *"The LORD dwells in Zion!"* (Joel 3:21)

Chapter 16

MALACHI – THE RETURN
OF ELIJAH

---

*"Above all, you must understand that no prophecy
of Scripture came about by the prophet's own interpretation
of things. For prophecy never had its origin in the human will,
but prophets, though human, spoke from God as they were
carried along by the Holy Spirit."*

2 Peter 1:20–21

H ebrew biblical history after Moses can be divided into six phases—
the era of the judges; the united kingdom of Saul, David, and Solomon; the northern kingdom of Israel and its fall to the Assyrians; the
southern kingdom of Judah and its fall to the Babylonians; the Babylonian Exile; and the Restoration and succeeding years through the end of
the 400s BCE. In Hebrew prophetic history, prophets such as Samuel,
Nathan, and Elijah were driving forces for obedience to God and His
Covenant. The classical prophets followed, first appearing in the eighth
century after the division of the kingdom and continuing through the
fifth century. The era of the classical prophets ended with either Malachi
or Joel.

The identity of Malachi is a mystery. His book starts with *"A prophecy: The word of the* L<small>ORD</small> *to Israel through Malachi"* (Malachi 1:1). The name Malachi is a title that translates from Hebrew as "my messenger." Although no direct references are given to the time of Malachi, there are hints such as a governor being mentioned, which would indicate the time of the Persian occupation. Malachi does not directly mention the Second Temple, but it appears that the Second Temple had been long completed by Malachi's time because half of his book is a condemnation of the corrupt priesthood and dubious religious practices. The socioeconomic and religious problems Malachi addressed were distressingly similar to those of preexilic times.

Why had the joy of the Restoration not been sustained? The religious and social divide between the returnees who settled in Jerusalem and the rest of the people seems to have defeated the sense of unity probably envisioned on the trek back to Jerusalem. Maybe there was an undercurrent of feeling among the returnees about having been misled by leaders of the return. Despite the supposed promises of Haggai as popularly understood, the Davidic dynasty was not restored, and prophetic promises of a bucolic countryside of peace and tranquility had not literally come true. The land with its poor topsoil and unreliable rainfall was still impoverished. People faced with an everyday struggle for survival would not have been interested in the fine points of temple sacrifices or the symbolism of a signet ring or any lamb lying down with a wolf.

Malachi speaks tersely in his four short chapters. For two chapters and a few verses of the third, Malachi echoes the voices of the preexilic prophets by addressing the sins of Judah and the sorrow of God. This will sound familiar. The last two chapters are devoted to the coming of the day of the Lord and the messengers who will prepare the way.

A RANT AGAINST THE SINS OF JUDAH

The book of Malachi begins with the familiar lament of God's love and His peoples' rejection of Him, using a question-and-answer format. *"I have loved you," says the* LORD. *"But you ask, 'How have you loved us?'"* (Malachi 1:2) Malachi presents the Lord's rebukes to the priests' arrogance:

> *"A son honors his father, and a slave his master. If I am a father, where is the honor due me? If I am a master, where is the respect due me?" says the* LORD *Almighty. "It is you priests who show contempt for my name.*
>
> > *"But you ask, 'How have we shown contempt for your name?'*
> >
> > *"By offering defiled food on my altar.*
> >
> > *"But you ask, 'How have we defiled you?'*
> >
> > *"By saying that the* LORD'S *table is contemptible. When you offer blind animals for sacrifice, is that not wrong? When you sacrifice lame or diseased animals, is that not wrong? Try offering them to your governor! Would he be pleased with you? Would he accept you?" says the Lord Almighty.* (Malachi 1:6-7)

Malachi's wrath fell hard on a priesthood that had not honored its responsibilities. The Levitical priesthood had been charged by Moses to educate the people in the Covenant and the law. More recently in Jewish history, the Persian king Artaxerxes I had directed Ezra: *"And you, Ezra, administer justice to all the people of Trans-Euphrates—all who know the laws of your God. And you are to teach any who do not know them"* (Ezra 7:25). Malachi warned the priests that if they did not honor the Lord's name, He would send a curse on them and on their blessings, rebuke their descendants, and smear their faces with the dung from their festival sacrifices.

> *"For the lips of a priest ought to preserve knowledge, because he is the messenger of the* LORD *Almighty and people seek instruction from his mouth. But you have turned from the way and by your teaching have caused many to stumble; you have violated the covenant with Levi," says the* LORD *Almighty. "So I have caused*

*you to be despised and humiliated before all the people, because you
have not followed my ways but have shown partiality in matters
of the law."* (Malachi 2:7-9)

Malachi railed against the custom of men marrying women who
worshipped foreign gods. This intermarriage persisted even though it
had been forbidden since the days of Moses. Malachi also trod into an
area where I don't recall any of the other prophets treading. He sought
to protect women's status and security as wives when he tackled the
subject of serial wives.

*Another thing you do: You flood the Lord's altar with tears. You
weep and wail because he no longer looks with favor on your
offerings or accepts them with pleasure from your hands. You ask,
"Why?" It is because the LORD is the witness between you and the
wife of your youth. You have been unfaithful to her, though she is
your partner, the wife of your marriage covenant.*

*Has not the one God made you? You belong to him in body
and spirit. And what does the one God seek? Godly offspring.
So be on your guard, and do not be unfaithful to the wife of
your youth.*

*"The man who hates and divorces his wife," says the LORD, the
God of Israel, "does violence to the one he should protect," says the
LORD Almighty.*

So be on your guard, and do not be unfaithful. (Malachi
2:13-16)

Malachi described how social injustice, the overwhelming concern
of all the prophets, wearied the Lord.

You have wearied the LORD with your words.

"How have we wearied him?" you ask

By saying, "All who do evil are good in the eyes of the LORD,
and he is pleased with them" or "Where is the God of justice?"
(Malachi 2:17)

Malachi addressed the law of tithing[ap] to the Levite priesthood that
was being sorely neglected.

> *"Ever since the time of your ancestors you have turned away from
> my decrees and have not kept them. Return to me, and I will
> return to you," says the* LORD *Almighty.*
>
> *"But you ask, 'How are we to return?'*
>
> *"Will a mere mortal rob God? Yet you rob me.*
>
> *"But you ask, 'How are we robbing you?'*
>
> *"In tithes and offerings. You are under a curse—your whole
> nation—because you are robbing me. Bring the whole tithe into
> the storehouse, that there may be food in my house. Test me in this,"*
> says the LORD *Almighty, "and see if I will not throw open the
> floodgates of heaven and pour out so much blessing that there will
> not be room enough to store it."* (Malachi 3:7-10)

THE RETURN OF ELIJAH

Malachi is best known for his penultimate verse: *"See, I will send the
prophet Elijah to you before that great and dreadful day of the* LORD *comes"*
(Malachi 4:5).

The ninth-century prophet Elijah had heard the voice of God on an
inner, private level. This had been a major departure from the Middle
Eastern tradition of storm gods and miracle workers. Here was the
demarcation between the old and a new understanding of God and

---

[ap] "A tithe of everything from the land, whether grain from the soil or fruit from the trees,
belongs to the LORD; it is holy to the LORD" (Leviticus 27:30).

how He communicated with His people.[180] It was reported that Elijah was taken from earth by a celestial chariot, which led to speculation as to whether and how he would return. Malachi proclaimed a momentous event:

> *"I will send my **messenger**, who will prepare the way before me. Then suddenly the LORD you are seeking will come to his temple; the **messenger of the covenant**, whom you desire, will come," says the LORD Almighty.* (Malachi 3:1, emphasis added)

According to the Gospel of Matthew, Jesus identified the *messenger* as John the Baptist when He answered His own question to a crowd of people: What had they gone into the wilderness to see?

> *"What did you go out into the wilderness to see? A reed swayed by the wind? If not, what did you go out to see? A man dressed in fine clothes? No, those who wear fine clothes are in kings' palaces. Then what did you go out to see? A prophet? Yes, I tell you, and more than a prophet. This is the one about whom it is written:*
>
> > *'I will send my **messenger** ahead of you,*
> > *who will prepare your way before you.'* [aq]
>
> *Truly I tell you, among those born of women there has not risen anyone greater than John the Baptist; yet whoever is least in the kingdom of heaven is greater than he. From the days of John the Baptist until now, the kingdom of heaven has been subjected to violence, and violent people have been raiding it. For all the Prophets and the Law prophesied until John. And if you are willing to accept it, he is the Elijah who was to come. Whoever has ears, let them hear."* (Matthew 11:7-15, emphasis added)

[aq] Malachi 3:1

After Peter, James, and John witnessed the Transfiguration of Jesus with Moses and Elijah, Jesus explained to them that Elijah had indeed appeared but had not been recognized They understood that He meant John the Baptist. Yet, John the Baptist had denied being Elijah. 'Abdu'l-Bahá explained this mystery. Although John the Baptist was the promised Elijah, he was not the actual man but his essence.

> *The reason is that we consider here not the individuality of the person but the reality of his perfections—that is to say, the very same perfections that Elias possessed were realized in John the Baptist as well. Thus, John the Baptist was the promised Elias. What is being considered here is not the essence but the attributes.*[181]

The Jews had expected a literal return of Elijah before the Messiah appeared; his apparent nonappearance was a major reason they would not accept Jesus as their messiah.

The verse Malachi 3:1 could also have foretold the coming of the Báb. Although a Manifestation of God in His own right (with the shortest length of a religious dispensation in religious history, nineteen years), the Báb was the Messenger who prepared the way for Bahá'u'lláh. Shoghi Effendi referred to the Báb as symbolizing the return of Elijah in the following portion of His intriguing description of the nine concentric circles.

> *The outermost circle in this vast system, the visible counterpart of the pivotal position conferred on the Herald of our Faith, is none other than the entire planet. Within the heart of this planet lies the "Most Holy Land," acclaimed by 'Abdu'l-Bahá as "the Nest of the Prophets" and which must be regarded as the center of the world and the Qiblih of the nations. Within this Most Holy Land rises the Mountain of God of immemorial sanctity, the Vineyard of the Lord, the Retreat of Elijah, Whose return the Báb Himself symbolizes.*[182]

(See Appendix D for the complete presentation of the nine concentric circles.)

Shoghi Effendi also spoke of the Báb as the return of Elijah when he wrote about the deeply significant occasion of the interment of the Báb's mortal remains on Mount Carmel in 1909 CE.

> With the transference of the remains of the Báb—Whose advent marks the return of the prophet Elijah—to Mt. Carmel, and their interment in that holy mountain, not far from the cave of that Prophet Himself, the Plan so glorious envisaged by Bahá'u'lláh, in the evening of His life, had been at last executed, and the arduous labors associated with the early and tumultuous years of the ministry of the appointed Center of His Covenant ['Abdu'l-Bahá] crowned with immortal success." [183]

THE DAY OF HIS COMING

After promising that a messenger would prepare the way for the Lord, the messenger of the covenant, Malachi asked: *"But who can endure the day of his coming? Who can stand when he appears? For he will be like a refiner's fire or a launderer's soap"* (Malachi 3:2).

This was a warning. Who can endure the day of His coming? This would seem especially applicable to the increasing global chaos, strife, and travails as the early stages of the Cycle of Fulfillment replace the Adamic Cycle, which the Báb's appearance closed. Malachi spoke of that day, the day of God, as a time of great testing.

> *For, behold, the day cometh, that shall burn as an oven; and all the proud, yea, and all that do wickedly, shall be stubble: and the day that cometh shall burn them up, saith the LORD of hosts, that it shall leave them neither root nor branch.*

> *But unto you that fear my name shall the **Sun of righteousness arise with healing in his wings;** and ye shall go forth, and*

grow up as calves of the stall. And ye shall tread down the wicked;
for they shall be ashes under the soles of your feet in the day that
I shall do this, saith the LORD of hosts. (Malachi 4:1-3, KJV,
emphasis added)

The *sun of righteousness* is another reference to Bahá'u'lláh. Shoghi
Effendi commented on the day of the Lord as follows: "His Day Ezekiel
and Daniel had, moreover, both acclaimed as the 'day of the Lord,' and
Malachi described as 'the great and dreadful day of the Lord'[ar] when 'the
Sun of Righteousness' will 'arise, with healing in His wings,'[as] whilst
Daniel had pronounced His advent as signalizing the end of the "abom-
ination that maketh desolate." [184]

Bahá'u'lláh was called the Divine Physician because He brought the
healing for our times that are gravely ill with warfare, ignorance, racism,
corruption, greed, and other maladies. As Shoghi Effendi commented:

We have no indication of exactly what nature the apocalyptic
upheaval will be; it might be another war…but as students
of our Bahá'í Writings, it is clear that the longer the 'Divine
Physician' (i.e. Bahá'u'lláh) is withheld from healing the ills
of the world, the more severe will be the crisis, and the more
terrible the sufferings of the patient.[185]

With Malachi we come to the end of the Hebrew prophets except
for Daniel. Why have we not covered Daniel in chronological order with
the other exilic prophets Ezekiel and Second Isaiah? The answer is that
all of the canonical prophets foretold the coming of Bahá'u'lláh and the
Bahá'í Era, but none of them, except Daniel, told *when.* Daniel gave five
time-explicit, accurate-to-the-year prophecies for Jesus, Muḥammad,
the Báb, and Bahá'u'lláh. The Major Plan of God was exquisitely foretold in Daniel's visions about Christianity, Islam, and the Bahá'í Faith.

[ar] Malachi 4:5
[as] Malachi 4:2

Chapter 17

DANIEL – KINGDOMS AND FULFILLMENT

*"The mysteries of the Holy Books have become explained
in the manifestation of Bahá'u'lláh. Before He appeared,
these mysteries were not understood. Bahá'u'lláh opened
and unsealed these mysteries."*

'Abdu'l-Bahá[186]

Which prophet was the most enigmatic, apocalyptic, and escha-tological—Ezekiel or Daniel? We've explored Ezekiel's visions and prophecies. Now let's examine Daniel's. Then readers can decide for themselves.

The book of Daniel states that in the third year of the reign of the Judean king Jehoiakim (608-597 BCE), which would have been 605 BCE, promising young men of Judah's royal house and nobility were taken to Babylon to be trained to serve the royal court. One of those young men was Daniel (Daniel 1:6), who was devoutly religious and faithful to God. Daniel lived in Babylon before and during the Exile, throughout the reigns of the Babylonian kings Nebuchadnezzar II

(605-562) and Belshazzar (556-539), and at least the first three years of the Persian king Cyrus II (539-529).

Scholars have differed as to when this book was written, whether in Babylon shortly before and during the Exile, or during the third or second century BCE. Roughly half of it, from chapter 2, verse 4, through the end of the seventh chapter, is believed to have been written in late Aramaic, and chapters 8 through 12 in Hebrew. The first vision of Daniel, which was received in a dream (Daniel 7:1-28), is believed to have been written in Aramaic but his other visions in Hebrew. Aramaic was the lingua franca of the Middle East from Babylonian and Persian times through the Hellenistic and Roman, and beyond. It's possible that Daniel's original writings and notes were used to translate and organize the book two or three centuries after his time. It's also possible that earlier portions of Daniel's book that extol his upright character and observance of Jewish law were added in the third or second century as a model for Jewish life. His steadfastness in the stories of the lion's den and the fiery furnace would have provided comfort and inspiration at a time when the Jews were challenged by the pagan influences of their overlords.

The second century BCE was perilous for the Jewish people. In 168, their Greek overlords launched a campaign of repression against the Jewish religion. The Second Temple was defiled with statues of Greek gods and goddesses. Attendance was mandated at festivals celebrating pagan cults. This outrage led to the Maccabean revolt, which mainly lasted from 167 to 160. These tumultuous years were not only times of war against the Greeks but also cultural war within the Jewish community. Conflict smoldered until in 141 the Greeks were expelled from the Jerusalem citadel, a core defensive fortress. An ensuing compromise led to the establishment of the semi-autonomous Hasmonean dynasty, with a measure of Jewish independence, that ruled from 140 to 116 under the Greeks and to 37 under the Romans.

Regardless of when the book of Daniel was assembled, in whole or in part, or who its original author was, its inherent value lies in the fact that this prophet called Daniel was the first and only Hebrew prophet who gave *time-specific prophesies that were accurate to the year.* These five time-specific prophecies could not be understood when they were given. Indeed, at least one of them was sealed until *the end of time,* and none of them could have been understood until in hindsight. This raises the question of why these prophecies were given. I think one reason was to give us today additional insight into the Major Plan of God, the systematic process whereby God has sent successive Messengers to educate humankind. Another reason might be to provide the "proof" that some individuals may require.

My purpose is to present Daniel's prophecies from a Bahá'í perspective with the understanding that *the time of the end* means the end of the Adamic Cycle and the beginning of the Cycle of Fulfillment. In this light, Daniel's visions can be well understood. Of course, it helps that all of his prophesied events have come to pass!

The book of Daniel cannot be fully covered unless done so in conjunction with the books of Ezekiel, Isaiah, Zechariah, and Revelation, some of whose recorded visions share imagery and seemed to reinforce each other. However, the herculean task of presenting this aspect is far beyond the parameters of this volume. Such a study would be a book by itself.

Before discussing the five time-specific prophecies in the last chapter, we'll review two dreams—one received by King Nebuchadnezzar and interpreted by Daniel, and the other one that was Daniel's own dream.

FOUR KINGDOMS AND A FIFTH

Nebuchadnezzar II had a worrisome dream and demanded that his astrologers and soothsayers not only interpret the dream, but first describe the dream to him on pain of death if they could not. Panic ensued. Only Daniel was able to do this. He explained to Nebuchadnezzar that no wise man, enchanter, magician, or diviner could reveal the secret the king demanded, *"But there is a God in heaven that revealeth secrets, and maketh known to the king Nebuchadnezzar what shall be in the latter days"* (Daniel 2:28, KJV).

Daniel described the king's dream to him, that it showed an enormous, dazzling statue, awesome in appearance. The head was made of pure gold, its chest and arms of silver, its belly and thighs of bronze, and its legs of iron, with its feet partly of iron and partly of baked clay. Daniel explained that God has shown the King what will happen in the days to come.

> *While you were watching, a rock was cut out, but not by human hands. It struck the statue on its feet of iron and clay and smashed them. Then the iron, the clay, the bronze, the silver and the gold were all broken to pieces and became like chaff on a threshing floor in the summer. The wind swept them away without leaving a trace. But the rock that struck the statue became a huge mountain and filled the whole earth.* (Daniel 2:34-35)

Daniel interpreted the dream. Nebuchadnezzar was a king of dominion, power, might, and glory. His was the head of gold. After him, another kingdom, inferior to his, will arise. And a third kingdom will arise and rule over the whole earth. The fourth kingdom, that of iron, will crush and break the others. However, the feet and toes made of baked clay and iron represent a kingdom both strong and brittle, and the people a mixture that will not remain united.

> *"In the time of those kings, the God of heaven will set up a kingdom that will never be destroyed, nor will it be left to another people. It will crush all those kingdoms and bring them to an end, but it will itself endure forever. This is the meaning of the vision of the rock cut out of a mountain, but not by human hands—a rock that broke the iron, the bronze, the clay, the silver and the gold to pieces. The great God has shown the king what will take place in the future.* (Daniel 2:44-45)

The traditional interpretation of the four kingdoms is that Babylonia was the first, the Persians the second, the Greeks the third, and the Romans the fourth. The Roman empire was the most successful in terms of longevity and the immense areas it governed. However, it crumbled slowly because of the uprisings of its vassals and a factor that is mostly overlooked—the social and spiritual influence of Christianity. The Roman empire was divided by the end of the fourth century CE into the Eastern empire ruled from Byzantium (Constantinople), and the Western empire ruled from Rome. Western Christian civilization emerged from the Roman empire and was plagued for many centuries by religious warfare.

The scholar Robert Riggs studied this dream and offered his interpretation. Instead of four kingdoms, he focused on four eras of civilization as experienced in Babylon, which now lies partially buried under Baghdad, Iraq. Gold represented the Babylonian empire, silver the Persian empire, bronze both the Greek and Roman empires, and iron the Islamic empire and the centuries of various empires that followed to present day. He described the iron era and the fifth era as follows:

> During the reign of the "fourth kingdom" and as the iron era draws to a close in Daniel's interpretation, the final "kingdom" of divine origin is represented by a "stone hewn from a mountain." A mountain has often represented a religion in sacred literature, while a stone may represent Truth. In ancient times, and even in some areas of today's world, "stones from heaven" (meteorites) have become objects of reverence. The Ka'bih at Mecca still contains such a stone that was revered even before Muḥammad's time.
>
> The symbol is appropriate and describes the Bahá'í Revelation (stone) that was hewn from the Faith (mountain) of the Báb. The stone struck the weakest foot of the Muslim world – the iron mixed with clay – that symbolizes the Shi'ih tradition centered in modern Iran. Daniel goes on to prophesy that this stone will, itself, become a great mountain that will shatter all the other "kingdoms" and will endure "forever."

The meaning is clear: the Bahá'í Faith will inevitably become a great religion that will transcend all others, both in spiritual power and in duration.[187]

Daniel told Nebuchadnezzar that God made known *what shall be in the latter days*. We are living in *the latter days*, the transition from the Adamic Cycle to the Cycle of Fulfillment. Our news cycle reports constantly on forces that crush and smash. Yes, these traumatic forces are alarming, frightening, terrifying. A positive response to these traumas is remembering that old beliefs, attitudes, and mindsets are being destroyed so that the new can fill the earth and humankind can live in peace and unity. Reform of the old is not an option. This fifth era would be the Kingdom of God, as mentioned many times by Jesus, a kingdom that can never be destroyed and will endure forever.

ANOTHER FOUR KINGDOMS AND A FIFTH

In the first year of the regency of Crown Prince Belshazzar (553-542 BCE), Daniel saw in a dream the four winds of heaven upon the sea and four great beasts coming out of the sea. The first beast was like a *lion* and had eagle wings that were plucked, so the beast was lifted upon the earth and made to stand like a man and a human mind was given to it. The second beast was like a *bear* and had three ribs between his teeth. It was told to arise and devour much flesh. The third was like a *leopard* but had upon its back four wings of a bird. Hosea used these three animal symbols when he told of God's punishment for the people He had served but who had forgotten Him. His retribution would be to Israel like the lion, the bear, and the leopard:

*"So I will be like a **lion** to them,*
*like a **leopard** I will lurk by the path.*
*Like a **bear** robbed of her cubs,*
I will attack them and rip them open;

like a lion I will devour them—
  a wild animal will tear them apart.
"You are destroyed, Israel,
  because you are against me, against your helper."
(Hosea 13:7-9, emphasis added)

After the leopard, the bear, and the lion, Daniel saw another beast that was terrifying. It had iron teeth and ten horns and had been given authority to rule.

*"After that, in my vision at night I looked, and there before me was a fourth beast—terrifying and frightening and very powerful. It had large iron teeth; it crushed and devoured its victims and trampled underfoot whatever was left. It was different from all the former beasts, and it had **ten horns.***

*"While I was thinking about the horns, there before me was **another horn, a little one,** which came up among them; and three of the first horns were uprooted before it. This horn had eyes like the eyes of a human being and a mouth that spoke boastfully."*

*I beheld till the thrones were cast down, and the Ancient of days did sit, whose garment was white as snow, and the hair of his head like the pure wool: his throne was like **the fiery flame,** and his wheels **as burning fire.***

A fiery stream issued and came forth from before him: thousand upon thousands ministered unto him, and ten thousand times ten thousand stood before him: the judgment was set, and the books were opened. (Daniel 7:8-10, KJV, emphasis added)

The foremost Bahá'í scholar in the Bahá'í Faith's early years, Mírzá Muḥammad Gulpáygání, better known by the title Mírzá Abu'l Faḍl, identified the various places where Isaiah, Ezekiel, and Zechariah had spoken of the coming of Bahá'u'lláh. He wrote concerning Daniel's identification of Bahá'u'lláh: "Likewise, consider the 7th chapter of Daniel. First, in the 9th and 10th verses, God hath announced the Manifestation of the Great Lord, the Ancient King, the Most Holy Beauty of ABHA (Glorified is His Supreme Name!) and hath spoken of the founding of the sound religion and manifest law and of the rise of the hosts of chosen ones and holy ones." [188]

Daniel's vision was similar to Ezekiel's vision of a throne flaming with fire with wheels all ablaze. Ezekiel had seen a vault over which was a throne of lapis lazuli, and on the throne was a figure like that of a man. *"I saw that from what appeared to be his waist up he looked like glowing metal, as if full of fire, and that from there down he looked like fire; and brilliant light surrounded him. Like the appearance of a rainbow in the clouds on a rainy day, so was the radiance around him. This was the appearance of the likeness of the glory of the LORD"* (Ezekiel 1:27-28, emphasis added).

In his dream, Daniel heard the boastful words of the little horn and saw the beast slain, its body destroyed and thrown into the blazing fire. The other beasts had been stripped of their authority but they had been allowed to live for a time.

> *I saw in the night visions, and, behold, one like the Son of man came with the clouds of heaven, and came to the Ancient of days, and they brought him near before him. And there was given him dominion, and glory, and a kingdom, that all people, nations, and languages, should serve him: his dominion is an everlasting dominion, which shall not pass away, and his kingdom that which shall not be destroyed.* (Daniel 7:13-14, KJV)

Mírzá Abu'l Faḍl continued his commentary as follows:

> Then He [Daniel] hath said in the 13th and 14th verses of the same chapter that the Excellent Branch shall be extended from that Ancient Root, and the Spirit of God descended from Heaven shall shine forth from His Beaming Face, and Glory and Kingdom shall be conferred upon Him from God;

His command shall influence all nations and multitudes, and
His Kingdom shall continue forever.[189]

Daniel was understandably *"troubled in spirit"* and he asked *"one of
those standing there"* the meaning of what he had seen. *"So he told me
and gave me the interpretation of these things: The four great beasts are four
kings that will rise from the earth. But the holy people of the Most High
will receive the kingdom and will possess it forever—yes, for ever and ever'"*
(Daniel 7:16-18).

But Daniel wanted to know more about the terrifying fourth beast
with iron teeth and bronze claws. He asked the meaning of the ten
horns on its head and the other horn that came up, the eyes, and the
mouth that spoke boastfully, that had displaced three of the horns. Daniel could see this horn waging war against the holy people and defeating
them. *"As I watched, this horn was waging war against the holy people and
defeating them, until the Ancient of Days came and pronounced judgment in
favor of the holy people of the Most High, and the time came when they pos-
sessed the kingdom"* (Daniel 7:21-22). Daniel's questions were answered
as follows:

> *"He gave me this explanation: 'The fourth beast is a **fourth
> kingdom** that will appear on earth. It will be different from
> all the other kingdoms and will devour the whole earth, tram-
> pling it down and crushing it. The ten horns are ten kings
> who will come from this kingdom. After them another king
> will arise, different from the earlier ones; he will subdue three
> kings. He will speak against the Most High and oppress his
> holy people and try to change the set times and the laws. The
> holy people will be delivered into his hands for **a time, times
> and half a time.***
>
> *"'But the court will sit, and his power will be taken away
> and completely destroyed forever. Then the sovereignty, power and
> greatness of all the kingdoms under heaven will be handed over to*

the holy people of the Most High. His kingdom will be an everlasting kingdom, and all rulers will worship and obey him.'

"This is the end of the matter. I, Daniel, was deeply troubled by my thoughts, and my face turned pale, but I kept the matter to myself." (Daniel 7:23-28, emphasis added)

The phrase *a time, times and half a time* is the time frame that gives the exact year of fulfillment. In biblical counting, a time is a year (360 days), times is two years (720 days), and half a time is half a year (180 days). The resulting date is explained in the next, last chapter, in conjunction with another of Daniel's prophecies that cites *a time, times and half a time.*

For further commentary on the *fourth beast*, see Appendix E.

Chapter 18

DANIEL – SEALED AND UNSEALED

*"I have, moreover, with the hand of divine power, unsealed
the choice wine of My Revelation, and have wafted its holy, its
hidden, and musk-laden fragrance upon all created things."*

Bahá'u'lláh[120]

Prophecies of the Hebrew prophets were usually vague as to when
they would be fulfilled. The predictions of conquests by the Assyrians and the Babylonians could be reasonably foreseen to within a few
years. However, no time frames accompanied the many prophetic assurances of better days such as *when* God's people would be restored to
their homeland forever and live in peace and prosperity. This pattern was
broken by the five time-specific prophecies of Daniel. Although they
would not be understood for many centuries, they are evidence that the
Plan of God had indeed been mapped out within our comprehension
of time, within the calendar of years by which humanity calculates time.

The biblical numerical codes for time are essential for deciphering the days and years in Daniel's time prophecies. First, a year equals
a day. This is indicated from two sources: *"For forty years—one year for*

each of the forty days you explored the land—you will suffer for your sins and know what it is like to have me against you" (Numbers 14:34), and *"I have assigned you the same number of days as the years of their sin. So for 390 days you will bear the sin of the people of Israel. After you have finished this, lie down again, this time on your right side, and bear the sin of the people of Judah. I have assigned you 40 days, a day for each year"* (Ezekiel 4:5-6). Second, a time equals a year (360 days).

Daniel's five time-specific prophecies are given below in the chronological order of their fulfillment. They were unerring markers for the time of the end—the end of the Prophetic Cycle and the beginning of the Cycle of Fulfillment.

THE SEVENTY 'SEVENS'

70 'sevens' (weeks) = 490 years, subtract from 457 BCE = 33 CE

Daniel was in emotional distress while contemplating the word of the Lord as given to Jeremiah the prophet that the desolation of Jerusalem would last seventy years. *"So I turned to the Lord God and pleaded with him in prayer and petition, in fasting, and in sackcloth and ashes."* (Daniel 9:3). He abjectly confessed his peoples' sins and rebellion, that they had not listened to the Lord's servants the prophets, who had spoken in His name to the kings, princes, and all the people of the land. Now the people had been scattered because of their unfaithfulness to the Lord. Daniel implored the Lord in His righteousness to turn away His anger and wrath from Jerusalem and to hear the prayers and petitions of his servant. *"LORD, listen! LORD, forgive! LORD, hear and act! For your sake, my God, do not delay, because your city and your people bear your Name* (Daniel 9:19). While Daniel was praying, the angel Gabriel[at] came to him.

[at] The angel Gabriel is mentioned in four episodes in the Bible. He appeared in two of Daniel's visions as an intermediary and an interpreter. He appeared to Zechariah, the husband of Elizabeth, to announce that she would give birth to a man to be named John. Gabriel also appeared to the Virgin Mary in Nazareth in the Annunciation. The Word of God was revealed to Muḥammad through Gabriel.

He instructed me and said to me, "Daniel, I have now come to give you insight and understanding. As soon as you began to pray, a word went out, which I have come to tell you, for you are highly esteemed. Therefore, consider the word and understand the vision:

"Seventy 'sevens' are decreed for your people and your holy city to finish transgression, to put an end to sin, to atone for wickedness, to bring in everlasting righteousness, to seal up vision and prophecy and to anoint the Most Holy Place.

*"Know and understand this: From the time the word goes out to restore and rebuild Jerusalem until the Anointed One, the ruler, comes, there will be **seven 'sevens,' and sixty-two 'sevens.'** It will be rebuilt with streets and a trench, but in times of trouble. After the sixty-two 'sevens,' the Anointed One will be put to death and will have nothing. The people of the ruler who will come will destroy the city and the sanctuary. The end will come like a flood: War will continue until the end, and desolations have been decreed. He will **confirm a covenant** with many for **one 'seven.'** In the middle of the 'seven' he will put an end to sacrifice and offering. And at the temple he will set up an **abomination that causes desolation,** until the end that is decreed is poured out on him."*
(Daniel 9:22-27, emphasis added)

Because a day equals a year in biblical timekeeping, seven days are seven years, and *seventy 'sevens'* equal 490 years. But from what date does the counting for the 490 years begin? From the year 457 BCE. Why? This was the year that Artaxerxes I issued the decree authorizing the rebuilding of Jerusalem. 'Abdu'l-Bahá confirmed this beginning date and explained the vision.

What Daniel intended is the third edict, which was issued in 457 BC. Seventy weeks makes 490 days. Each day, according to the text of the Bible, is one year, for in the Torah it is said: "The day of the Lord is one year." Therefore, 490 days is 490 years. The third edict of Artaxerxes was issued 457 years before the birth of Christ, and Christ was thirty-three years old at the time of His martyrdom and ascension. Thirty-three added to 457 is 490, which is the time announced by Daniel for the advent of Christ.[191]

Daniel was also told that the *seventy 'sevens'* could be broken down into *sixty-two 'sevens', 'seven sevens',* and *'one seven'.* 'Abdu'l-Bahá explained that seventy 'sevens' started with the edict of Artaxerxes for the rebuilding of Jerusalem but that the sixty-two 'sevens' started with the completion of the building of Jerusalem, which was believed to have taken forty-nine years, or seven weeks.

But in Daniel 9:25 this is expressed in another manner, that is, as seven weeks and sixty-two weeks, which outwardly differs from the first statement. Many have been at a loss to reconcile these two statements. How can reference be made to seventy weeks in one place and to sixty-two weeks and seven weeks in another? These two statements do not accord.

In reality, Daniel is referring to two different dates. One begins with the edict Artaxerxes issued to Ezra to rebuild Jerusalem, and corresponds to the seventy weeks which came to an end with the ascension of Christ, when sacrifice and oblation were ended through His martyrdom. The second begins after the completion of the rebuilding of Jerusalem, which is sixty-two weeks until the ascension of Christ. The rebuilding of Jerusalem took seven weeks, which is the equivalent of forty-nine years. Seven weeks added to sixty-two weeks makes sixty-nine weeks, and in the last week the ascension of Christ took place. This completes the seventy weeks, and no contradiction remains.[192]

The statement that *He will confirm a covenant with many for one 'seven'* means the final confirmation of Jesus's covenant during the last week of His life. The *abomination that causes desolation* is mentioned in more than one of Daniel's visions but it is not defined. Possible definitions could include religious fanaticism and militarism on one hand, and on the other, irreligion and hostility toward religion and the sacred word of any religious tradition. This abomination could also refer to the corruption of religions whose time has passed, whose worship has degenerated into form and ritual and has entered its spiritual winter.

Daniel was the only Hebrew prophet who had nesting prophecies, that is, one prophecy placed inside another. The first two of Daniel's five time-specific prophecies are based on counting from the year 457 BCE. The counting was based on an event that occurred long after Daniel's death—the letter that Artaxerxes I issued to Ezra authorizing the rebuilding of Jerusalem. This letter, or edict, was a nesting prophecy.

THE 2,300 YEARS

457 BCE plus 2,300 solar years = 1844 CE

In the third year of Crown Prince Belshazzar's regency (c. 553 to 543 BCE), Daniel saw himself in the citadel of Susa in the province of Elam, Persia. Jeremiah had prophesied that God would set His throne in Elam, destroy her authorities, and then restore her fortunes.[193] Susa was once the capital of Elam but it is now a mound for archeologists. In the nineteenth century, Shiraz was the birthplace of the Báb and the major city of Elam.

Daniel saw a ram with two long horns. This powerful ram charged west, north, and south. Then a goat with one horn between its eyes came from the west, crossing the whole earth without touching the ground. It charged the ram in great rage and shattered its two horns. The goat trampled the defeated ram and none could rescue it. *"The goat became very great, but at the height of its power the large horn was broken off, and in its place four prominent horns grew up toward the four winds of heaven"* (Daniel 8:8). Out of one of the goat's horns came another that grew in power to the south and to the east, toward the *Beautiful Land* (the Holy Land). Daniel's vision continued about this last horn as follows:

> *It grew until it reached the host of the heavens, and it threw some of the starry host down to the earth and trampled on them. It set itself up to be as great as the commander of the army of the Lord; it took away the daily sacrifice from the Lord, and his **sanctuary** was thrown down. Because of rebellion, the Lord's people and the daily sacrifice were given over to it. It prospered in everything it did, and truth was thrown to the ground.*
>
> *Then I heard a holy one speaking, and another holy one said to him, "How long will it take for the vision to be fulfilled—the vision concerning the daily sacrifice, **the rebellion that causes desolation,** the surrender of the **sanctuary** and the trampling underfoot of the* LORD's *people?"*
>
> *He said to me, "It will take **2,300 evenings and mornings;** then the **sanctuary** will be reconsecrated."* (Daniel 8:10-14, emphasis added)

It was verse 8:14 that captivated Protestant biblical scholars in the early nineteenth century and fueled the Millerite movement with the expectation of the imminent return of Jesus Christ.[194] Referring to Daniel 8:14, 'Abdu'l-Bahá gave an account of the end of the 2,300 years when the sanctuary would be reconsecrated, as follows:

> *That is to say, how long shall this misfortune, this ruin, this abasement and degradation endure? Or, when will the morn of Revelation dawn? Then he [Gabriel] said, "Two thousand and three hundred days; then shall the sanctuary be cleansed." Briefly, the point is that he fixes a period of 2,300 years, for according to the*

text of the Torah each day is one year. Therefore, from the date of the edict of Artaxerxes to rebuild Jerusalem until the day of the birth of Christ there are 456 years, and from the birth of Christ until the day of the advent of the Báb there are 1,844 years, and if 456 years are added to this number it makes 2,300 years. That is to say, the fulfilment of the vision of Daniel took place in A.D. 1844, and this is the year of the advent of the Báb. Examine the text of the Book of Daniel and observe how clearly he fixes the year of His advent! There could indeed be no clearer prophecy for a Manifestation than this.[195]

The Báb declared His identity to Mullá Husayn on May 22, 1844, in Shiraz, his place of birth in the province of Elam. Within a few months, eighteen persons recognized Him one by one. These disciples were called the Letters of the Living. The Báb then went on pilgrimage to Mecca in 1844 where He proclaimed His identity and mission to the highest authority in Mecca, the holiest place in Islam. The appearance of the Báb in 1844 catalyzed the cleansing of the sanctuary of the abomination of desolation.

'Abdu'l-Bahá referred to the Olivet discourse in Matthew 24 and Jesus's reference to the eighth chapter of Daniel.

In Matthew 24:3 Christ clearly says that what Daniel meant by this prophecy was the date of the advent, and this is the verse: "As He sat upon the mount of Olives, the disciples came unto Him privately, saying, Tell us, when shall these things be? and what shall be the sign of Thy coming, and of the end of the world?" Among the words He uttered in reply were the following: "When ye therefore shall see **the abomination of desolation,** *spoken of by Daniel the prophet, stand in the holy place, (whoso readeth, let him understand)." Thus He referred them to the eighth chapter of the Book of Daniel, implying that whoever reads it should grasp when that time shall be. Consider how clearly the advent of the Báb has been specified in the Torah and the Gospel!* [196]

Daniel's choice of words, *the abomination of desolation* in the *sanctuary*, was dire. Perhaps he was referring not only to the corruption that had crept into Judaism that the Hebrew prophets had railed against, but also the corruption that would creep into Christianity and Islam. If Daniel meant the condition of the sanctuary of religion and worship, he might have been seeing the extreme division within the major religions today. Judaism has many sects within the traditional Orthodox movements (including the ultra-traditionalist and modern Orthodox branches), and the modernist movement such as Conservative, Reform, and Reconstructionist Judaism. Islam has split into five major sects—Sunni, Shia, Sufi, Ahmadiyya, and Ibadi—as well many smaller ones. Christianity is the most extreme example of divisiveness with about 4,500 denominations globally with membership as of 2019 ranging from a few dozen to over a billion.[197] The messages of Moses, Jesus, and Muḥammad have been fractured. The eastern dharmic religions such as Buddhism and Hinduism have also separated into innumerable splinter groups.

The scholar Elena Maria Marsella gave her understanding of the meaning of the sanctuary as the heart of mankind.

> Here we encounter a "desolation" of the sanctuary which is to endure 2300 years, each day again being a year, and it is obvious that the sanctuary here denoted cannot be an earthly one because no Jewish Tabernacle or Temple endured that long and the Jews themselves have been scattered during the major portion of the 2300 years. The sanctuary must then be the "heart" of mankind which will not truly become the abode of the word of God until the end of time.[198]

The vision continued with Daniel hearing a man's voice calling from the Ulai Canal, a river near the city of Susa: *"Gabriel, tell this man the meaning of the vision"* (Daniel 8:16). A petrified Daniel prostrated himself as Gabriel approached and raised Daniel to his feet. Gabriel explained that the two-horned ram represented the kings of Media and Persia, the goat the king of Greece, and the large horn between its eyes its first king. The four horns that replaced the one broken horn represented the four kingdoms that would emerge but would not have the same power.

"In the latter part of their reign, when rebels have become completely wicked, a fierce-looking king, a master of intrigue, will arise. He will become very strong, but not by his own power. He will cause astounding devastation and will succeed in whatever he does. He will destroy those who are mighty, the holy people. He will cause deceit to prosper, and he will consider himself superior. When they feel secure, he will destroy many and take his stand against the Prince of princes. Yet he will be destroyed, but not by human power.

"The vision of the evenings and mornings that has been given you is true, but seal up the vision, for it concerns the distant future."
(Daniel 8:23-26)

The kingdoms listed might be symbolic since Gabriel also mentioned the stand against the Prince of princes, and that the vision concerned the distant future. In the third prophecy, which presents this second prophecy in different terms, the phrase *time of the end* is used.

Daniel took to his bed! *"I, Daniel, was worn out. I lay exhausted for several days. Then I got up and went about the king's business. I was appalled by the vision; it was beyond understanding"* (Daniel 8:27).

A TIME, TIMES, AND HALF A TIME – THE 1,260 YEARS

360 + 720 + 180 **lunar** years[au] = 1,260, add to 622 CE = 1844

In the third year of the reign of King Cyrus over Babylon (539-530 BCE), Daniel had been praying and mourning for three weeks when

---

[au] In the Hijri calendar, a lunar year is 354 or 355 days. https://en.wikipedia.org/wiki/Islamic_calendar.

a man clothed in linen with fine gold appeared. *"His body also was like the beryl, and his face as the appearance of lightning, and his eyes as lamps of fire, and his arms and his feet like in colour to polished brass, and the voice of his words like the voice of a multitude"* (Daniel 10:6). Daniel trembled as he was told that he was a man greatly beloved and his words were heard. *"But the prince of the Persian kingdom resisted me twenty-one days. Then Michael, one of the chief princes, came to help me, because I was detained there with the king of Persia. Now I have come to explain to you what will happen to your people in the future, for the vision concerns a time yet to come"* (Daniel 10:13-14).

Daniel was told at length of the kings of the North and the South, of their times of alliance, betrayal, and warfare. Eventually the king of the North, described as *contemptible,* prevails over the king of the South *through intrigue* and *a prince of the covenant will be destroyed* (Daniel 11:21-22). After much fighting, *"The two kings, with their hearts bent on evil, will sit at the same table and lie to each other, but to no avail, because an end will still come at the appointed time* (Daniel 11:27). Then at the *appointed time,* the North will unsuccessfully invade the South because ships of the western coastlands will oppose him. The king of the North turns back to vent his fury against the holy covenant and his army desecrates the temple fortress and will abolish the daily sacrifice and then set up the abomination that causes desolation. Some of the wise will instruct the people, but for a time they will be killed, burned, or captured. *"Some of the wise will stumble, so that they may be refined, purified and made spotless until* **the time of the end,** *for it will still come at the appointed time"* (Daniel 11:35, emphasis added).

The king will do as he wishes and magnify himself *above every good, and shall speak* marvelous *things against the God of gods* (Daniel 11:36). He will honor a strange god with gold and silver and will divide the land for gain. *"And at* **the time of the end** *shall the king of the south push at him: and the king of the north shall come against him like a whirlwind, with chariots, and with horsemen, and with many ships; and he shall enter into the countries, and shall overflow and pass over, He will also invade* *the Beautiful Land"* (Daniel 11:40, emphasis added). There's been war brought by two kings, but then will come Michael.

> *"At that time **Michael**, the great prince who protects your people, will arise. There will be a **time of distress** such as has not happened from the beginning of nations until then. But at that time your people—everyone whose name is found written in the book—will be delivered. Multitudes who sleep in the dust of the earth will awake: some to everlasting life, others to shame and everlasting contempt. Those who are wise will shine like the brightness of the heavens, and those who lead many to righteousness, like the stars for ever and ever. But you, Daniel, **roll up and seal the words of the scroll until the time of the end.** Many will go here and there to increase knowledge."* (Daniel 12:1-4, emphasis added)

In Jewish tradition, there are seven archangels—Gabriel, Jeremiel, Michael, Raguel, Raphael, Sariel, and Uriel. Marsella gave her thoughts on Daniel 12:1:

> This is obviously that same "time of trouble" such as has never been seen, which was foretold by Jesus as written in Matthew, chapter 24. Revelation further describes this chaotic era, and mentions Michael:
>
> > "And there was war in heaven: Michael and his angels fought against the dragon: and the dragon fought and his angels" (Revelation 12:7, KJV).
>
> Michael, one of the seven great archangels of Semitic theology is one of the "seven eyes" and seven "spirits of God" mentioned in the first chapters of Revelation. This is not to suggest that there are only seven angels in the ministry of God's plan for earth, but these are seven phases of particular importance in the prophetic time-span covered by the

Old and New Testaments, each of these periods approximately a thousand years in length and presumably under the dominion of one or another of these angelic messengers, or "sons of God." According to angelology, the greatest of these celestial leaders is appropriately titled "one like God," or *Michael*.

Michael's position at the head of the heavenly hierarchy, his association with events of the last of the Lord's Days, and his name, all point to him as symbolic of the Lord of Hosts, the Messiah of the Last Days who shall by his power vanquish the tyrannical forces of the modern era and usher in a reign of peace.[199]

Bahá'u'lláh was born into a Persian noble family descended from Yazdigird III, the thirty-eighth and last monarch of the Sasanian empire of Persia (224–651 CE). Hence, Bahá'u'lláh was a prince of Persia (for further discussion of Michael, see William Sears's thoughts in Appendix F).

Daniel had been warned of a *time of distress* more severe than any since the beginning of nations, marked by suffering more tremendous than any ever seen. Daniel asked the anguished, eternal question—*when*—and the answer was received in biblical counting.

> *Then I, Daniel, looked, and there before me stood two others, one on this bank of the river and one on the opposite bank. One of them said to the man clothed in linen, who was above the waters of the river, "How long will it be before these astonishing things are fulfilled?"*
>
> *The man clothed in linen, who was above the waters of the river, lifted his right hand and his left hand toward heaven, and I heard him swear by him who lives forever, saying, "It will be for* **a time, times and half a time**. *When the power of the holy people has been finally broken, all these things will be completed."*

I heard, but I did not understand. So I asked, "My lord, what will the outcome of all this be?"

*He replied, "Go your way, Daniel, because the words are rolled up and **sealed until the time of the end**. Many will be purified, made spotless and refined, but the wicked will continue to be wicked. None of the wicked will understand, but those who are wise will understand."* (Daniel 12:5-10, emphasis added)

Twice now, Daniel had been told that the meanings of two of his visions were *sealed until the time of the end*, until 1844. And with that the case, it seems only logical that the Messengers of God for this age would unseal them.

A time, times, and half a time translates to three and a half years because a time is 360 days, times is two years, or 720 days, and half a time is half a year, or 180 days. The total is 1,260 years. 'Abdu'l-Bahá elaborated on the 1,260 years.

As I have already explained the meaning of "day", no further explanation is needed, but let me briefly say that each day of the Father is equivalent to one year, and each year consists of twelve months. Thus three and a half years makes forty-two months, and forty-two months is 1,260 days, and each day in the Bible is equivalent to one year. And it is in the very year 1260 from the emigration of Muhammad, according to the Muslim calendar, that the Báb, the Herald of Bahá'u'lláh, revealed His mission.[200]

In this vision, *lunar* years are being used. The counting of the 1,260 lunar years begins in the year 622 CE, the year of the *Hijrah* (Arabic for Hegira), the flight of Muḥammad and His followers from Mecca to Medina. This year was designated the first year of the Islamic calendar (1 AH). Freed from persecution and threats of assassination in Mecca, Muḥammad and His faith prospered in Medina. Muḥammad assumed temporal leadership of Medina in addition to His spiritual leadership, thus reminding us of the utterance of Moses: *"The LORD your God will raise up for you a prophet like me from among you, from your fellow Israelites. You must listen to him"* (Deuteronomy 18:15).

Adding 1,260 lunar years to the year 622 CE, the year that Muḥammad and His followers left Mecca for Medina, reaches the year 1844—the advent of the Báb. This math is calculated by using the lunar years upon which the Islamic calendar is based.

Here is another example of how Daniel put a nesting prophecy within a prophecy. He lived over a thousand years before Muḥammad and the inauguration of Islam, yet Islam was foreseen and a momentous year in Islamic history was identified. Perhaps Daniel's use of an Islamic date to launch the 1,260 years was to validate Islam to Christians.

It's easy to miss the biblical references to Muḥammad and Islam in the Bible, but they are there. Shoghi Effendi wrote: "References in the Bible to 'Mt. Paran' and 'Paraclete' refer to Muḥammad's Revelation. Deuteronomy 33.2; Genesis 21.21.; Numbers 12.16; Numbers 13.3. Genesis 17.20 refer to the twelve Imams and in the Revelation of St. John, Chap. 11, where it mentions two witnesses, it refers to Muḥammad and 'Alí." [201] The verses are given chronologically as follows:

He [Ishmael] *will be the father of twelve rulers, and I will make him into a great nation.* (Genesis 17:20)

He lived in the desert and became an archer. While he was living in the Desert of Paran, his mother got a wife for him from Egypt. (Genesis 21:21)

After that, the people left Hazeroth and encamped in the Desert of Paran. (Numbers 12:16)

So at the Lord's command Moses sent them out from the Desert of Paran. All of them were leaders of the Israelites. (Numbers 13:3)

This is the blessing that Moses the man of God pronounced on the Israelites before his death. He said:

"The Lord came from Sinai
and dawned over them from Seir;
he shone forth from Mount Paran.
He came with myriads of holy ones
from the south, from his mountain slopes."
(Deuteronomy 33:1-2)

The word *paraclete* can mean advocate, comforter, or counselor.[av]
Bahá'u'lláh used paraclete in reference to Muḥammad when He wrote:
"His Holiness Abraham, on Him be peace, made a covenant concerning His
Holiness Moses and gave the glad-tidings of His coming. His Holiness Moses
made a covenant concerning the Promised One, i.e. His Holiness Christ, and
announced the good news of His Manifestation to the world. His Holiness
Christ made a covenant concerning the Paraclete and gave the tidings of His
coming." [202]

THE 1,290 YEARS

613 plus 1,290 **lunar** years = 1863 CE

Daniel's third prophecy of the 1,260 years took three chapters to relate.
His fourth and fifth prophecies each took only one sentence!

The fourth prophecy is: *"From the time that the daily sacrifice is abol-*
ished and the abomination that causes desolation is set up, there will be 1,290
days" (Daniel 12:11). The counting is in lunar years from 613 CE, the
date of Muḥammad's public declaration of His station as a Prophet of
God, to 1863, the date of Bahá'u'lláh's declaration of His station as a
Prophet of God. Again Muḥammad and the Islamic Faith are implicitly

---

[av] "John is the only author in the NT to use the term parákletos (tr. counselor in RSV; comforter in KJV). In 1 John 2:1, he applies it to the exalted Lord; in the gospel he employs it
four times (John 14:16, 26; 15:26; 16:7) to denote Jesus' description of the Holy Spirit who
should continue His ministry to the disciples." Encyclopedia of the Bible–Paraclete, Bible
Gateway, https://www.biblegateway.com/resources/encyclopedia-of-the-bible/Paraclete.

recognized. 'Abdu'l-Bahá remarked on the meaning of the 1,290 years as follows:

> *The commencement of this lunar reckoning is from the day of the proclamation of the prophethood of Muḥammad in the land of Ḥijáz; and that was three years after the revelation of His mission, because in the beginning the prophethood of Muḥammad was concealed, and no one knew of it save ***Kh**adíjih* and Ibn-i-Nawfal,*[aw]* until it was publicly announced three years later. And it was in the year 1290 from the proclamation of the mission of Muḥammad that Bahá'u'lláh announced His Revelation.*[203]

An endnote to the above states, "As Muḥammad began His public ministry ten years before the Hijrah, this date corresponds to A.H. 1280, or A.D. 1863."

THE 1,335 YEARS

628 plus 1,335 **solar** years = 1963 CE

Daniel gave his fifth and final time-specific prophecy in the penultimate verse of chapter 12 and was told that his mission on earth was finished.

> *"Blessed is the one who waits for and reaches the end of the 1,335 days.*
>
> *"As for you, go your way till the end. You will rest, and then at the end of the days you will rise to receive your allotted inheritance."* (Daniel 12:12-13)

The prophecies of the 1,290 years and the 1,335 years were given in two adjacent verses, Daniel 12:11-12. The 1,335 solar years start with the year 628 CE, the year Muhammad signed a treaty with His enemies

---

[aw] That is, Muḥammad's wife and her cousin Varaqih-Ibn-i-Nawfal.

in Mecca that signified that the Muslim community in Medina was recognized not only as a legitimate force but also one to be respected and accorded contractual or diplomatic status. This agreement also gave Muslims the freedom to move unmolested throughout Arabia. Muḥammad's declaration, His flight to Medina, and His treaty with Mecca were all nested prophecies.

The 1,335 solar years added to 628 equals 1,963 years, or the year 1963, which was momentous in Bahá'í history. That was the year when members of the fifty-six National Spiritual Assemblies cast ballots to elect members of the first Universal House of Justice—the global administrative body of the Bahá'í Faith, the nucleus and pattern of Bahá'u'lláh's World Order.

The declaration of Bahá'u'lláh in 1863 (the 1,290 years) was followed in 1963 (the 1,335 years) by completion of the three-tier Administrative Order that Bahá'u'lláh had devised for the internal governance of the Bahá'í Faith.

The year 1963 was also momentous for Bahá'ís because it concluded the Ten Year Plan (1953-1963), also called the Ten Year Crusade,[ax] launched by Shoghi Effendi, whose successful conclusion had made possible the first election of the Universal House of Justice. The Ten Year Plan had been launched to facilitate an organized, global expansion of the Faith. Shoghi Effendi mentioned Daniel's prophecies when addressing the pioneering needs of the Ten Year Crusade when he wrote:

Sometimes people strive all their lives to render outstanding service. Here is the time and opportunity to render historic services; in fact the most unique in history, aiding in the

---

[ax] The Ten Year Crusade launched by Shoghi Effendi was a global effort to facilitate an organized expansion of the Bahá'í Faith. It had 27 objectives, the four most important of which were the development of the institutions at the Bahá'í World Centre, the consolidation of the Faith in the twelve countries where it was well established, the consolidation of the Faith in other countries and territories where only a few Bahá'ís resided, and the opening of the Faith in countries and territories where no Bahá'ís resided by having Bahá'ís settle there.

fulfillment of Daniel's Prophecies of the Last Day, and the 1335 days, when men are to be blessed by the Glory of the Lord, covering the entire globe—which is the real goal of the Ten Year Crusade. In other words, when we fulfill the Ten Year Crusade we will have brought into fulfillment Daniel's great prophecy of 'Blessed is he who waits and comes to the 1335 days.' What could be more wonderful than taking part in the fulfillment of religious prophecy of over 3,000 years!" [204]

'Abdu'l-Bahá elaborated upon Daniel's prophecy of the 1,335 years in a tablet he wrote to a Kurdish friend:

> *Now concerning the verse in Daniel, the interpretation thereof thou didst ask, namely, "Blessed is he who cometh unto the thousand three hundred and thirty-five days." These days must be reckoned as solar and not lunar years. For according to this calculation a century will have elapsed from the dawn of the Sun of Truth, then will the teachings of God be firmly established upon the earth, and the Divine Light shall flood the world from the East even unto the West. Then, on this day, will the faithful rejoice.* [205]

Let us rejoice for the days we are in regardless of its challenges. There is indeed light at the end of the tunnel—and it's not a train!

Appendix A

NOAH AND HIS NUMBERS

Mathematics is a timeless and universal language. It has no dialects. Its rules are fixed. A mathematical law or formula has the same meaning everywhere, regardless of what human language is used to explain it. Therefore, mathematics can transcend time and communication barriers. What better way to communicate from preliterate to literate times?

Numerology is the study of the symbolic meanings of numbers. Don Dainty, a Canadian Bahá'í and retired engineer, was interested in the possibility of a numerological interpretation of the days of Noah's flood. He used the biblical method of counting whereby one day equals a year. This method draws upon two biblical verses: *"For forty years—one year for each of the forty days you explored the land—you will suffer for your sins and know what it is like to have me against you"* (Numbers 14:34) and, *"After you have finished this* [lying on his left side for 390 days], *lie down again, this time on your right side, and bear the sin of the people of Judah. I have assigned you 40 days, a day for each year"* (Ezekiel 4:6). In biblical counting, one year equals 360 days.

The following is a summary of the highlights of Dainty's personal interpretation of the Noah saga as he wrote in his booklet *As It Was in the Days of Noah: So Unfolds the Surprising Fulfilment of Biblical Foresights of the 'Return.'* Dainty uses the year 1844 as the starting point for counting. This was the year pinpointed by Daniel's famous prophecy of the 2,300 days/years: *"It will take 2,300 evenings and mornings; then the sanctuary will be reconsecrated"* (Daniel 8:14). This was the year that the Báb declared His station to His first disciple, thus closing the Adamic Cycle and opening the Bahá'í cycle.

To read the following easily and efficiently, please note that the time frames are shown on the left in **bold,** and that they are followed by the appropriate passage(s) from Genesis in *italics* with the specific numbers of years mentioned shown in **bold.** Quotations from Dainty's book and other sources are block indented and have endnotes. Commentary added by Maddocks starts at the left margin and uses the regular format.

1844–1963/64 CE

Then the Lord said, "My Spirit will not contend with humans forever, for they are mortal,[ay] *their days will be a **hundred and twenty years"*** (Genesis 6:3).

The starting date of 1844 *plus* **120 years** bring us to the year 1964. Dainty wrote:

> The reference to 120 years in Genesis brings into focus the element of time related to the period needed for the construction of the 'Ark' and the 'warning of the people'. Notice that 'days' is spoken of as 'years'. That respite period for humankind provided Noah, the ancient Saviour, and those close to Him with time to construct the ark of salvation for the believers, the means of security from the ravages to come. Failure to become heedful of the warnings and guidance within that time (and thus miss becoming dwellers within the Ark) meant that dramatic human suffering would inevitably result.

[ay] A footnote to the biblical text states that *mortal* also means *corrupt*.

Bahá'u'lláh, as the modern Noah, confirmed this process both in general and for our time:

We have fixed a time for you, O peoples. If ye fail, at the appointed hour, to turn towards God, He, verily, will lay violent hold upon you, and will cause grievous afflictions to assail you from every direction. Know, verily, that an unforeseen calamity followeth you and grievous retribution awaiteth you. Think not that which ye have committed hath been effaced in My sight.[az]

The flood analogy gains additional metaphorical strength when one realizes that Bahá'u'lláh, by revealing the spiritual truths and principles for the new age of the Kingdom, and defining its administrative structures (symbolized as the new 'ark of salvation'), started a building process that took 120 years from its initiation on May 23, 1844, when the Báb announced that the new Day of God had begun, and heralded the Advent of Bahá'u'lláh, the Promised Return of the Christ, only 19 years from the date of His own declaration.

The advents of these two Manifestations of the Spirit signaled the beginning of that agonizing period called the 'time of the end' or 'end of the world' trials as biblically foreseen. The Revised Standard Version of the Bible translates such phrases as the 'end of the age' (Matthew 24:3), thus casting a rather different, non-literal meaning on these amazing historical processes. Further, Revelation 20:2-7 mentions that the famous period called 'the millennium' follows the 'Return of the Son of Man'. So the 'end' was not really the end, but rather, the end of one Age, and the beginning of a new Age of fulfillment for all humanity.[206]

[az] Bahá'u'lláh, cited by Shoghi Effendi, *The World Order of Bahá'u'lláh*, 201.

Dainty clarified the dating system as follows:

In order to carefully define the dating system, it bears repeating that, in the birthplace of the Bahá'í Faith, the beginning of the New Year, called Naw Rúz, has been celebrated on the first day of Spring, March 21, for thousands of years. From March 21, 1844, AD, the beginning of the Bahá'í calendar, to March 21, 1963 AD, represented the passage of 119 complete years. Thus, one month into the 120th year of the 'Bahá'í Era' (April 21, 1963 AD)

> ...the momentous first International Bahá'í Convention yielded the long-awaited crown of the Bahá'í Administrative Order: the Universal House of Justice.[ba]

The confirmed Universal House of Justice formulated its first systematic plan for the development of the 'Kingdom' near the end of 120 BE [Bahá'í Era] (1963/64 AD). This Nine-Year Plan was communicated to the Bahá'í World. Thus, in accord with the 120-year biblical time prophesy, the process of building 'the Ark' was complete, the 'Mariner' had taken its helm according to the Will of Bahá'u'lláh, and a plan had been formulated to direct the 'Ark' through the tempestuous years ahead.[207]

Make a roof for it, leaving below the roof an opening one cubit high all around. Put a door in the side of the ark and make lower, middle and upper decks (Genesis 6:16).

Dainty wrote that the Administrative Order of Bahá'u'lláh was thus anticipated to have three levels—the Local Spiritual Assemblies, the National Spiritual Assemblies, and the Universal House of Justice. Shoghi Effendi noted the uniqueness and importance of the Administrative Order as follows:

[ba] Universal House of Justice, *Wellspring of Guidance*, p. v.

It should be noted in this connection that this Administrative Order is fundamentally different from anything that any Prophet has previously established, inasmuch as Bahá'u'lláh has Himself revealed its principles, established its institutions, appointed the person to interpret His Word and conferred the necessary authority on the body designed to supplement and apply His legislative ordinances. Therein lies the secret of its strength, its fundamental distinction, and the guarantee against disintegration and schism. Nowhere in the sacred scriptures of any of the world's religious systems, nor even in the writings of the Inaugurator of the Bábí Dispensation, do we find any provisions establishing a covenant or providing for an administrative order that can compare in scope and authority with those that lie at the very basis of the Bahá'í Dispensation.[208]

1963/64–1971 CE

After inviting Noah and his family into the ark and giving instructions for animals and birds to be brought aboard, the Lord then said to Noah: *"Seven days from now I will send rain on the earth for forty days and forty nights, and I will wipe from the face of the earth every living creature I have made"* (Genesis 7:4).

The 120 days of mankind *plus* the 7 days of grace equal **127 years** and bring us to the year 1971. Noah used the additional time to continue teaching and warning the people. Dainty commented:

Although the Genesis narrative is not specific with respect to the purpose of this extra period of respite, Noah's mission in general was to inform and warn the people, and this additional period provided further opportunity to do so. But Noah's call went unheeded.

To ensure that the call of Bahá'u'lláh would not suffer the same ultimate fate, the Universal House of Justice wrote:

The foundation of the Kingdom has been securely laid, the framework has been raised. The friends must now consolidate their achievements, safeguard their institutions, and gather the peoples and kindreds of the world into the ark which the Hand of God has built. [Letter dated October 1963 from the Universal House of Justice, *Wellspring of Guidance*, 14] [209]

The global Nine Year Plan was inaugurated in 1964 and was a global effort to further the accomplishments of the Ten Year Crusade (1953-1963) with systematic teaching and consolidation of the Faith. By 1971, the seven years from 1964 to 1971 had seen an unprecedented world-wide proclamation of the Faith with a corresponding growth in the number of adherents and Bahá'í institutions. Then a plateau was experienced from 1971 to 1973. Dainty correlates the seven-year respite given by God to Noah, an opportunity for further teaching and warning, with the seven-year spurt of growth in the Bahá'í international community. Dainty commented:

Toward the mid-point of this seven-year period of respite (BE 124, October 1967), the Message from the Universal House of Justice to six Bahá'í International Conferences...affirmed that difficult times were ahead for the world (emphasis added).

As humanity enters the dark heart of the age of transition, our course is clear – the achievement of the assigned goals and the proclamation of Bahá'u'lláh's healing Message. It is our ardent hope that from these conferences radiant souls may arise with noble resolve and in loving service to ensure the successful and early accomplishment of the sacred tasks that lie ahead.[210]

Closely in line with the time-frame 1964-1971, a think tank called the Club of Rome, whose members were scientists, economists, businessmen, international high civil servants, present and former heads of state, presented a report in 1972 titled *The Limits to Growth: A Report for the Club of Rome's Project on the Predicament of Mankind* to various international gatherings. This report, first published on 2 March 1972, was the first to model our planet's interconnected systems and to make clear that if growth trends in population, industrialization, resource use, and pollution continued unchanged, we would reach and then over-shoot the carrying capacity of the Earth at some point in the next one hundred years.[211]

1971–2011 CE

For forty days the flood kept coming on the earth, and as the waters increased they lifted the ark high above the earth. The waters rose and increased greatly on the earth, and the ark floated on the surface of the water (Genesis 7:17-18).

The **120 days** of mankind *plus* the 7 days of grace *plus* the 40 days of rain equal **167 years** since 1844, which bring us to the year 2011.

Humanity had continued blithely on its morally downward course. In the West, these forty years were a period of swift decline of ethics and moral standards. Some persons blame this situation on the loss of "traditional values" and others point to the negative values pressed upon society by an entertainment industry that pushed beyond the limits of decency towards depravity with the prostitution of the arts. The general strength of families decreased, religious belief declined, and consumer materialism was pushed incessantly by the creation of false needs regardless of resulting waste of the earth's resources. Also of note were the increasing levels of greed, mendacity, political and corporate corruption, drug addiction, and growing irreligion and amorality, along with extreme individualism.

Shoghi Effendi quoted Bahá'u'lláh as follows concerning the essential role of religion and the dire results to society when religion is forgotten:

"The face of the world," Bahá'u'lláh laments, "hath altered. The way of God and the religion of God have ceased to be of any worth in the eyes of men." "The vitality of men's belief in God," He also has written, "is dying out in every land. ... The corrosion of ungodliness is eating into the vitals of human society." "Religion," He affirms, "is verily the chief instrument for the establishment of order in the world, and of tranquility amongst its peoples. ... The greater the decline of religion, the more grievous the waywardness of the ungodly. This cannot but lead in the end to chaos and confusion." And again: "Religion is a radiant light and an impregnable stronghold for the protection and welfare of the peoples of the world." [212]

These forty years also saw an unprecedented decline in the health of the earth and its ecological systems, upon which all life depends. The phenomenon called climate change was starting to cause calamities hitherto unknown and was projected to cause catastrophes such as had not been seen on earth in historical times.

In 1988, almost midway through these forty years, the Intergovernmental Panel on Climate Change (IPCC), a body of the United Nations, was formed for assessing the science related to climate change.

In addition to literal floods, the actions of humanity, the result of spiritual darkness and irreligion, can bring a flood of tribulations, as Dainty suggested:

> The flood-like tribulation of the modern world is the subject of the following comment by the Guardian of the Bahá'í Faith [Shoghi Effendi]:

> > The judgment of God, as viewed by those who have recognized Bahá'u'lláh as His mouthpiece and His greatest messenger on earth, is both a retributory calamity and an act of holy and supreme discipline. It is at once a visitation from God and a cleansing process for all mankind. [Shoghi Effendi, *The Promised Day Is Come*, 2] [213]

Dainty also wrote:

Bahá'u'lláh, the modern Noah, pointed out that His Ark is as indestructible as that of the ancient tradition:

> *The world's equilibrium hath been upset through the vibrating influence of this most great, this new World Order. The Hand of Omnipotence hath established His Revelation upon an unassailable, and enduring, foundation. Storms of human strife are powerless to undermine its basis, nor will men's fanciful theories succeed in damaging its structure.* [Baha'u'llah, *The World Order of Bahá'u'lláh*, 109]

> According to the biblical analogy, as the start of the 21st century is already past, the increasing depth of trouble during the 'heart of darkness' is to approach its peak at the end of the 40-plus years of 'rain', that is, in 2011.[214]

Symbolic prophecy is usually best understood in retrospect. Dainty wrote *As It Was in the Days of Noah* in 2009, two years before 2011and during the end of the Great Recession, a period of marked general decline observed in national economies globally that occurred from late 2007 to 2009. The scale and timing of the recession varied from country to country. We have the vantage point of many years later when it does not appear that a peak of the "heart of darkness" was reached in 2011.

2011–2121 CE

*The waters flooded the earth for a **hundred and fifty days** (Genesis 7:24).*

*The water receded steadily from the earth. At the end of the **hundred and fifty** days the water had gone down, and on the **seventeenth day of the seventh month [one hundred and ten days]** the ark came to rest on the mountains of Ararat (Genesis 8:3-4).*

The **120 days** of mankind *plus* the 7 days of grace *plus* the 40 days of rain *plus* 110 days of flood recession equal 277 years and bring us to the year 2121. Dainty remarked:

> The Ark of the Cause of God comes to permanent rest on the Mountain of God (Mount Carmel), suggesting a stability which substantially ends its imperiled existence due to persecution and trouble. It now rests on a secure foundation which suggests a stability.[215]

The early years since 2011 that we have seen so far indicate a sharp escalation of trials and catastrophes. A global pandemic called Covid-19 started in late 2018 and killed almost seven million people worldwide by July 19, 2023.[216] The pandemic triggered a health and fiscal response unprecedented in terms of speed and magnitude, throwing the world economy into its deepest recession since the end of World War II with an impact likely to be long lasting. War returned to Europe on a scale not seen since World War II in 2022 when Russians invaded Ukraine. In addition, the process of climate change reached the point where it constantly commanded news headlines. In August 2021, the IPCC issued its sixth assessment report that had been prepared by 234 scientists from 66 countries, relying on more than 14,000 studies from around the globe. The report called climate change "widespread, rapid, and intensifying" with "some of the changes already set in motion—such as continued sea level rise—irreversible over hundreds to thousands of years." [217] It also stated that carbon dioxide in the atmosphere had risen to levels not seen in two million years, the oceans had turned acidic, sea levels continued to rise, Arctic ice was disintegrating, and weather-related disasters were growing more extreme and affecting every region of the world. The Secretary-General of the United Nations, António Guterres, warned, "The climate crisis is a code red for humanity." [218] In March 2023, an updated report was released by the IPCC that stated, "There is a rapidly closing window of opportunity to secure a liveable and sustainable future for all. The choices and actions implemented in this decade will have impacts now and for thousands of years." [219]

Bahá'u'lláh issued many warnings of what would result if humanity did not reverse the path it was on. One of the most dire stated:

> *"The world is in travail, and its agitation waxeth day by day. Its face is turned towards waywardness and unbelief. Such shall be its plight, that to disclose it now would not be meet and seemly. Its perversity will long continue. And when the appointed hour is come, there shall suddenly appear that which shall cause the limbs of mankind to quake. Then, and only then, will the Divine Standard be unfurled, and the Nightingale of Paradise warble its melody."* [220]

Bahá'u'lláh also encouraged us by writing: *"Soon will the present-day order be rolled up, and a new one spread out in its stead. Verily, thy Lord speaketh the truth, and is the Knower of things unseen."* [221] Looking back, these forty years, and more, have been a time when the activities of humanity greatly accelerated the pace of the rolling up of the old world order. There is no definitive timeline for *"soon,"* only the assurance that *"thy Lord speaketh the truth."*

2121–2195 CE

*The waters continued to recede until the tenth month, and on the **first day of the tenth month** the tops of the mountains became visible* (Genesis 8:5).

There were 14 days left in the seventh month and then 60 days in the eighth and ninth months, and these days total 74. The 120 days of mankind *plus* the 7 days of grace *plus* 40 days of rain *plus* 110 days of the water receding *plus* 74 days of the water continuing to recede equal 351 years since 1844, which brings us to the year 2195. Dainty wrote:

> From its hard-won position of safety, the institutions of the Kingdom of God begin to flourish as the 'end-time of troubles' subsides for humankind, and persecution of the Bahá'í

Faith diminishes. These effects are due to the increasingly leavening effect on global society of its twelve spiritual principles of the Bahá'í revelation.[222]

2195–2249 CE

*After forty days Noah opened a window he had made in the ark and sent out a raven, and it kept flying back and forth until the water had dried up from the earth. Then he sent out a dove to see if the water had receded from the surface of the ground. But the dove could find nowhere to perch because there was water over all the surface of the earth; so it returned to Noah in the ark. He reached out his hand and took the dove and brought it back to himself in the ark. He waited **seven more days** and again sent out the dove from the ark. When the dove returned to him in the evening, there in its beak was a freshly plucked olive leaf! Then Noah knew that the water had receded from the earth. He waited **seven more days** and sent the dove out again, but this time it did not return to him* (Genesis 8:6–12).

Previously we came to the year 2195. Now we add the 40 days on the mountain waiting for the raven *plus* 7 days after the dove's first return *plus* 7 days after the dove's second return to arrive at the **2249**, 405 years since 1844. Dainty commented:

Mention of the 'raven' is fascinating. Ravens fed Elijah in a time of drought (1 Kings 17:2–7) and the birds have symbolic importance in other traditions. Does the raven by moving 'to and fro' foster a return to equilibrium…? Certainly the imagery of the receding waters and the adventures of the dove suggest a gradual recovery of the real world from the ravages of tribulation. This relief leads to a flourishing state of humanity, including implementation of that most cherished universal peace of which the 'dove' and the 'olive branch' are ancient, traditional, enduring and widely accepted symbols. It seems that peace is to envelope the world some 405 years (2249 – 1844) after the start of building the Ark.[223]

2249–2294 CE

By the twenty-seventh day of the second month the earth was completely dry. Then God said to Noah, "Come out of the ark, you and your wife and your sons and their wives. Bring out every kind of living creature that is with you—the birds, the animals, and all the creatures that move along the ground—so they can multiply on the earth and be fruitful and increase in number on it" (Genesis 8:14-17).

The water finished receding and the ground dried, enabling the people and animals to disembark. Dainty emphasizes this heartwarming aspect of the Noah story—the saving of the animals, an endeavor that will be increasingly important as climate change and ecological devastation take their toll.

An interesting modern parallel to Noah's time is that in addition to saving the people, the animals were saved. This might appear as quaint in the Noah story…but it is fraught with foreboding meaning in our time, substantially due to 'global warming.' It can be inferred that a pre-eminent purpose of the modern Noah, Bahá'u'lláh, is not only to 'save' the people as Noah did, but also to save the species in existence at the time of His return. That is, He would establish by grace the structures and spiritual approaches necessary for a serious world-wide attack on the uniquely modern problem of a deteriorating world environment, global warming, and the consequent threatened disappearance of numerous species of life.[224]

After disembarkation, Noah built an altar for sacrifices. *"The Lord smelled the pleasing aroma and said in his heart: "Never again will I curse the ground because of humans, even though every inclination of the human heart is evil from childhood. And never again will I destroy all living creatures, as I have done"* (Genesis 7:21). God then established a covenant with Noah, his sons, and every living creature that was with them. *"Never again will all life be destroyed by the waters of a flood; never again will there be a flood to destroy the earth*" (Genesis 9:11). The sign of this covenant would be the rainbow. *"I have set my rainbow in the clouds, and it will be the sign of the covenant between me and the earth*" (Genesis 9:13). God gave the command *"be fruitful and increase in number; multiply on the earth and increase upon it*" (Genesis 9:7). Humanity obeyed this directive exceedingly well. Future destructions of the earth would be at its hands.

Appendix B

AKKA IN HOLY SCRIPTURES

Note: The following is an excerpt from *God Passes By* written by Shoghi Effendi. None of the endnotes appear in the original but were added by Eileen Maddocks to assist the reader.

'Akká, itself, flanked by the *"glory of Lebanon,"* and lying in full view of the *"splendor of Carmel,"* [225] at the foot of the hills which enclose the home of Jesus Christ Himself, had been described by David as *"the Strong City,"* [226] designated by Hosea as *"a door of hope,"* [227] and alluded to by Ezekiel as *"the gate that looketh toward the East,"* [228] whereunto *"the glory of the God of Israel came from the way of the East,"* [229] His voice *"like a noise of many waters."* [230] To it the Arabian Prophet had referred as *"a city in Syria to which God hath shown His special mercy,"* [231] situated *"betwixt two mountains...in the middle of a meadow,"* [232] *"by the shore of the sea...suspended beneath the Throne,"* [233] *"white, whose whiteness is pleasing unto God."* [234] *"Blessed the man,"* He, moreover, as confirmed by Bahá'u'lláh, had declared, *"that hath visited 'Akká, and blessed he that hath visited the visitor of 'Akká."* [235] Furthermore, *"He that raiseth therein the call to prayer, his voice will be lifted up unto Paradise."* [236] And again: *"The poor of 'Akká are the kings of Paradise and the princes thereof. A month in 'Akká is better than a thousand years elsewhere."*[237] Moreover, in a remarkable tradition, which is contained in Shaykh Ibnu'l-'Arabí's work, entitled "Futúḥát-i-Makkíyyih," and which is recognized as an authentic utterance of Muḥammad, and is quoted by Mírzá Abu'l- Faḍl in his "Fará'd," this significant prediction has been made: *"All of them* (the companions of the Qá'im) *shall be slain except One Who shall reach the plain of 'Akká, the Banquet-Hall of God."*

Bahá'u'lláh Himself, as attested by Nabíl in his narrative,[238] had, as far back as the first years of His banishment to Adrianople, alluded to that same city in His Lawḥ-i-Sáyyaḥ, designating it as the "Vale of Nabíl," the word Nabíl being equal in numerical value to that of 'Akká. *"Upon Our arrival,"* that Tablet had predicted, *"we were welcomed with banners of light, whereupon the Voice of the Spirit cried out saying: 'Soon will all that dwell on earth be enlisted under these banners.'"*[239]

Appendix C

THE BAHÁ'Í
ADMINISTRATIVE ORDER

The following is quoted from The Bahá'í Faith: The Official Website of the Worldwide Bahá'í Community.

The affairs of the Bahá'í community are administered through a system of institutions, each with its defined sphere of action. The origins of this system—known as the Bahá'í Administrative Order—are found in the Writings of Bahá'u'lláh Himself. He revealed principles that guide its operation, established its institutions, appointed 'Abdu'l-Bahá as the sole interpreter of His Word, and conferred authority on the Universal House of Justice. In His Will and Testament, 'Abdu'l-Bahá appointed his grandson, Shoghi Effendi, as the Guardian of the Bahá'í Faith. From the outset of his ministry, Shoghi Effendi dedicated energy to the development of the Administrative Order, bringing it into being in embryonic form and paving the way for the election of the Universal House of Justice.

Today the Universal House of Justice is the central governing body of the Administrative Order. Under its guidance, elected bodies, known as Local Spiritual Assemblies and

National Spiritual Assemblies tend to the affairs of the Bahá'í community at their respective levels, exercising legislative, executive, and judicial authority. An institution of appointed individuals of proven capacity—the institution of the Counsellors—also functions under the guidance of the Universal House of Justice and exerts influence on the life of the Bahá'í community, from the grassroots to the international level. The members of this Institution encourage action, foster individual initiative, and promote learning within the Bahá'í community as a whole, in addition to offering advice to Spiritual Assemblies.

Acting in their respective roles, the institutions of the Counsellors and the Spiritual Assemblies share responsibility for the protection and propagation of the Bahá'í Faith. The harmonious interactions between them ensure the constant provision of guidance, love, and encouragement to members of the Bahá'í community throughout the world. Together, they invigorate individual and collective efforts to contribute to the wellbeing of society.

Bahá'í institutions are not conceived only as a means of administering the internal aspects of Bahá'í community life, essential though this is. Foremost, the Administrative Order is intended to serve as a channel through which the spirit of the Faith is to flow, embodying in its operation the kind of relationships that must come to bind together and sustain society as humanity moves towards collective maturity.[240]

The webpage also includes the following quotations. The endnotes were added to assist readers:

It is the structure of His New World Order, now stirring in the womb of the administrative institutions He Himself has created, that will serve both as a pattern and a nucleus of that world commonwealth which is the sure, the inevitable destiny of the peoples and nations of the earth.[241]

The bedrock on which this Administrative Order is founded is God's immutable Purpose for mankind in this day. The Source from which it derives its inspiration is no one less than Bahá'u'lláh Himself.[242]

Appendix D

THE CENTER OF
NINE CONCENTRIC CIRCLES

The following is an excerpt from *Citadel of Faith* by Shoghi Effendi.

For, just as in the realm of the spirit, the reality of the Báb has been hailed by the Author of the Bahá'í Revelation as "The Point round Whom the realities of the Prophets and Messengers revolve," so, on this visible plane, His sacred remains constitute the heart and center of what may be regarded as nine concentric circles, paralleling thereby, and adding further emphasis to the central position accorded by the Founder of our Faith to One "from Whom God hath caused to proceed the knowledge of all that was and shall be," "the Primal Point from which have been generated all created things."

The outermost circle in this vast system, the visible counterpart of the pivotal position conferred on the Herald of our Faith, is none other than the entire planet. Within the heart of this planet lies the "Most Holy Land," acclaimed by 'Abdu'l-Bahá as "the Nest of the Prophets" and which must be regarded as the center of the world and the Qiblih of the nations. Within this Most Holy Land rises the Mountain of God of immemorial sanctity, the Vineyard of the Lord, the Retreat of Elijah, Whose return the Báb Himself symbolizes. Reposing on the breast of this holy mountain are the extensive properties permanently dedicated to, and constituting the sacred precincts of, the Báb's holy Sepulcher. In the midst of these properties, recognized as the international endowments of the Faith, is situated the most holy court, an enclosure comprising gardens and terraces which at once embellish, and lend a peculiar charm to, these sacred precincts. Embosomed in these lovely and verdant surroundings stands in all its exquisite beauty the mausoleum of the Báb, the shell designed to preserve and adorn the original structure raised by `Abdu'l-Bahá as the tomb of the Martyr-Herald of our Faith. Within this shell is enshrined that Pearl of Great Price, the holy of holies, those chambers which constitute the tomb itself, and which were constructed by `Abdu'l-Bahá. Within the heart of this holy of holies is the tabernacle, the vault wherein reposes the most holy casket. Within this vault rests the alabaster sarcophagus in which is deposited that inestimable jewel, the Báb's holy dust. So precious is this dust that the very earth surrounding the edifice enshrining this dust has been extolled by the Center of Bahá'u'lláh's Covenant, in one of His Tablets in which He named the five doors belonging to the six chambers which He originally erected after five of the believers associated with the construction of the Shrine, as being endowed with such potency as to have inspired Him in bestowing these names, whilst the tomb itself housing this dust He acclaimed as the spot round which the Concourse on high circle in adoration.[243]

Appendix E

THE FOURTH BEAST
WITH TEN HORNS

———————————————————

In order to understand the fourth beast with its ten horns, we must digress to a critically important event in Islamic history, the breaking of the Covenant of Muḥammad immediately after His death. His chosen successor had been his son-in-law, 'Alí ibn Abí Ṭálib. In the last year of His life, Muḥammad announced to His followers that His son-in-law, was to be His successor. H. M. Balyuzi, a preeminent scholar of Islam, wrote:

> Shi'ah tradition has it that…on urgent bidding received from God, Muḥammad made, all of a sudden, a forced halt by the pool of Khum, a most inconvenient place; had a pulpit raised with saddles, and from this announced 'Alí as His successor, requiring the large body of Muslims who were with Him to pledge their loyalty to 'Alí.[244]

Tradition also states that on his deathbed, Muḥammad asked for writing materials, but that wish was ignored.

There seems to be some agreement that one day towards the
end, Muḥammad asked for writing material to be brought, so
that He might dictate His last wishes. What exactly happened
next is obscured by disputation. Obviously the Prophet was in
extremity because the S̲h̲i‘ah tradition holds that 'Umar said:
'The man is delirious, the Book of God sufficeth us.' [245]

His request was not granted and Abú Bakr was chosen to be the
first imam. The Covenant of Muḥammad was thus broken. Twenty-
four years later, 'Alí finally became imam, the fourth and last of the
Rashidun caliphate, but it was too late for him to have the influence
on the development of Islam that Muḥammad had desired. 'Alí was
adamantly and ruthlessly opposed by the powerful Umayyad faction. In
his fifth year, 'Alí and several of his supporters were murdered through
the evil machinations of Mu‘áwiyah, an Umayyad. Balyuzi described the
calamitous succession of Muawiyah and the founding of the Umayyad
dynasty as follows:

On the very day that Muḥammad passed out of this mortal
world and before His body was laid to rest, winds of dissension blew through the edifice of His Faith. Having created a
coherent nation out of an agglomerate of contending, restless
tribes, and having founded a state with a framework of laws, it
is inconceivable that He would not have envisaged who should
succeed Him. Moses had conferred authority upon Joshua,
Christ had put the keys of Heaven and Earth in the hands
of Peter; yet neither of them had in His lifetime established
a realm demanding an administration. But this was exactly
what Muḥammad had done. Of His four immediate successors, ...only the first, Abú-Bakr, died a natural death. 'Umar
and 'Alí were both assassinated and 'Ut̲h̲mán fell before the
murderous onslaught of a demented mob. The appalling circumstances attending the death of 'Ut̲h̲mán opened wide the
way for usurpers. Mu‘áwiyah, the extremely able but totally

unprincipled champion of the House of Umayyah, challenged 'Alí and won in the end. The contest between 'Alí and
Mu'áwiyah was responsible for the rise of the Pietists—the
Khawárij—and the awakening of blind fanaticism. 'Ali fell
victim to the sword of one such fanatic. The stance of the
Khawárij and their repeated depredations, through the ensuing years, could result only in anarchy and harsh suppression.
Syed Ameer Ali writes: 'Had Ali been accepted to the Head-
ship of Islam, the birth of those disastrous pretensions that
led to so much bloodshed in the Moslem world would have
been averted.' [246]

Depriving Islam of the leadership of 'Alí as the intended first imam
during its most early and formative years prepared the way for the
fourth beast. The Covenant-breaking that denied the successorship that
Muḥammad stipulated changed the course of Islam forever. The consequences were severe. Islam was split into two main factions: the Sunnis
who followed the caliphates, and the Shi'as who followed the descendants of 'Alí in the Imamate, which ended in 874 CE with the twelfth
imam. The twelfth imam is believed by Shi'as to have gone into occul-
tation in 872 CE, that is, to have gone into hiding. Messianic Shi'as
expect this twelfth imam to return and head a perfect Islamic world. The
damage done by the Umayyad caliphate is the background for the fourth
beast. The ten horns referred to the ten names of the caliphs of the
Umayyad caliphate. 'Abdu'l-Bahá specified their meaning as follows:

*The ten horns represent the names of the Umayyad rulers, for,
barring repetition, they are ten sovereigns, or ten names of chiefs
and rulers. The first is Abú Sufyán and the last is Marwán. Some
of their names have been repeated, including two Mu'áwíyahs,
three Yazíds, two Walíds, and two Marváns. If, however, these
names are each counted only once, they number ten in total. These
Umayyads—the first of whom was Abú Sufyán, the former chief
of Mecca and founder of the dynasty, and the last of whom was*

Marván—destroyed a third of the holy and sanctified souls who descended from the pure lineage of Muḥammad and who were even as the stars of heaven.[bb]

One of the least understood aspects of the book of Revelation is that it's primarily a history of past events that were given as prophecies two thousand years ago, and these prophecies were about three Prophets of God to come—Muḥammad, the Báb, and Bahá'u'lláh. I recommend two particular books for the study of Revelation: *The Logic of the Revelation of St. John* by Stephen Beebe, and *Apocalypse Secrets* by John Able, who give their personal interpretations.

'Abdu'l-Bahá gave several explanations of events in chapter 12 of the book of Revelation that pertain to Umayyad dynasty.

"A woman clothed with the sun, with the moon under her feet and a crown of twelve stars on her head was pregnant and about to give birth. A red dragon appeared with seven heads and ten horns and seven crowns upon their heads" (Revelation 12:1-3).

'Abdu'l-Bahá explained: *"This dragon represents the Umayyads, who seized the reigns of the religion of Muḥammad; and the seven heads and seven crowns represent the seven dominions and kingdoms over which they came to rule: the Roman dominion in Syria; the Persian, the Arabian, and the Egyptian dominions; the dominion of Africa—that is, Tunisia, Morocco, and Algeria; the dominion of Andalusia, which is now Spain; and the dominion of the Turkish tribes of Transoxania."* [247]

"The dragon stood in front of the woman who was about to give birth, so that it might devour her child the moment he was born." (Revelation 12:4)

[bb] The stars of heaven is a reference to Rev. 12:4, *"And his tail drew the third part of the stars of heaven, and did cast them to the earth."* The tail belonged to the dragon, which in the book of Revelation represents the Ummayad.

'Abdu'l-Bahá explained: *"This child was the promised Manifestation, Who is the offspring of the religion of Muhammad. The Umayyads were ever anxious to lay hold on the Promised One who was to appear from the lineage of Muhammad, that they might destroy and annihilate him, for they greatly feared his ascent. And so whenever they found a descendant of Muhammad who was respected in the eyes of the people, they killed him."* [248]

"She gave birth to a son, a male child, who "will rule all the nations with an iron scepter." And her child was snatched up to God and to his throne" (Revelation 12:5).

'Abdu'l-Bahá explained: *"'And she brought forth a man child who was to rule all nations with a rod of iron.' This glorious son is the promised Manifestation, Who was born of the religion of God and reared in the bosom of the divine teachings. The iron rod is a symbol of might and power—it is not a sword—and means that He will shepherd all the nations of the earth by virtue of His divine might and power. And by this son is meant the Báb."* [249]

"And the woman fled into the wilderness, where she hath a place prepared of God, that they should feed her there a thousand two hundred and threescore days." (Revelation 12:6, KJV)

'Abdu'l-Bahá tied this verse with Daniel 12:6, which explains that the 1,260 years start in 622 AD, the year of Muhammad's migration to Medina, which enabled the Islamic Faith to establish itself, and end in 1844, the year of the declaration of the Báb. *"Thus for 1,260 years the religion of God was fostered in the vast desert of Arabia, until the Promised One appeared. After these 1,260 years that religion ceased to be in effect, for the fruit of that tree had been manifested and its result had been produced."* [250]

'Abdu'l-Bahá also commented on the Law of God that would be brought:

As to the woman in the Revelation of Saint John, chapter 12, who fled into the wilderness, and the great wonder appearing in the heavens—that woman clothed with the sun, with the moon under her feet: what is meant by the woman is the Law of God. For according to the terminology of the Holy Books, this reference is to the Law, the woman being its symbol here. And the two luminaries, the sun and the moon, are the two thrones, the Turkish and the Persian, these two being under the rule of the Law of God. The sun is the symbol of the Persian Empire, and the moon, that is, the crescent, of the Turkish. The twelve-fold crown is the Imams, who, even as the Apostles, supported the Faith of God. The newborn Child is the beauty of the Adored One [the Báb], come forth out of the Law of God. He then saith that the woman fled into the wilderness, that is, the Law of God was carried out of Palestine to the desert of Hijaz, where is remained for 1,260 years—that is, until the advent of the promised Child.[251]

Appendix F

EXCERPT FROM
THIEF IN THE NIGHT

Villiam Sears commented in his book *Thief in the Night* on the chief prince or archangel Michael as follows:

This vision of the 'Glory of God' promised by Christ and seen by St. John and Isaiah, is identical with the vision which came to Ezekiel. He saw the 'Glory of God' on more than one occasion, and associated it with a Promised One who would come into His House in a latter day. His coming, Ezekiel said, was: "...the appearance of...the Glory of the Lord. And when I saw it, I fell upon my face." (Ezekiel 1:28)

It was this same 'Glory of God' that appeared to Daniel as well. When Daniel had his vision of the last days, he spoke movingly of the Prince, Michael, who came to help him, Michael who would stand up for the children of God at the time of the end.

When Daniel had his vision, he was unable to bear the glory of it. In his own words: "...I set my face toward the ground, and I became dumb" (Daniel 10:15).

The meaning of the word MICHAEL when translated into English is: One who looks like God. Thus, it appeared, that Daniel, too, had seen the 'Glory of God'.

I uncovered another important clue that seemed to confirm the belief that this Figure seen by Daniel was identical with the one promised by Christ Himself for the time of His return. Christ clearly explained the conditions of His second coming. He foretold that in that day everyone would see "... the Son of man coming in the clouds of heaven..." (Matthew 24:30, Luke 21:27).

This exact same picture was given by Daniel as the vision he saw of the 'latter days'. In fact, in almost the exact same words Daniel said: "...one like the Son of man came with the clouds of heaven..." (Daniel 7:13).

Furthermore, in that same chapter, for the second time, I found that Daniel foretold the hour when this would take place. This wondrous event, the coming of the Messiah, Daniel promised, will come to pass after "...a time and times and the dividing of time" (Daniel 7:25).

There seemed to be no end to the references that brought me back to the year 1844. Here once again I had found that same prophecy of 1,260 days, forty and two months, three and a half years, and now, 'a time and times and the dividing of time'. Students of Scripture agreed that all these phrases referred to one period of time, namely 1,260 years. This meant that I had found another reference to when the Messiah would come. According to Daniel, He would appear in the year 1260, and I knew already that in the calendar of the land in which Daniel saw his vision (Persia), the year 1260 coincided with the year 1844 of the West.

Daniel and Christ both had promised the coming of the 'Son of man'. Daniel had been overwhelmed and had fallen to the ground because of the glory of his vision.

In other places too numerous to detail, I found this same prophecy of the coming of the 'Glory of God'. Isaiah promised the faithful that: "...the Glory of the Lord shall be thy reward" (Isaiah 58:8). And again: "Arise, shine; for thy light is come, and the Glory of the Lord is risen upon thee...I the Lord am thy Savoir and thy Redeemer..." (Isaiah 60:1, 16).

I was satisfied that I had uncovered sufficient evidence to indicate that the title by which the Messiah would be known when He appeared would be: 'the Glory of the Lord'. This would be the new name, just as Christ, 'the Anointed One', had been the old name. In making the investigation into His name, I had also discovered additional information pointing to His coming with this new name in the year 1844. I felt I was making progress. [252]

NOTES

Introduction

1   Eileen Maddocks, "The Coming of Adam," *The Coming of the Glory: How the Hebrew Scriptures Reveal the Plan of God, Vol. I* (Brooklyn, WI: Something or Other Publishing, 2022), 31-33. The Bahá'í Writings indicate that the Adamic Cycle lasted six thousand years, starting with the advent of the Prophet Adam. Shoghi Effendi wrote: *"Then, and only then, will the vast, the majestic process, set in motion at the dawn of the Adamic cycle, attain its consummation—a process which commenced six thousand years ago, with the planting, in the soil of the divine will, of the tree of divine revelation, and which has already passed through certain stages and must needs pass through still others ere it attains its final consummation. The first part of this process was the slow and steady growth of this tree of divine revelation, successively putting forth its branches, shoots and offshoots, and revealing its leaves, buds and blossoms, as a direct consequence of the light and warmth imparted to it by a series of progressive dispensations."* Shoghi Effendi, *Messages to the Bahá'í World: 1950-1957* (Wilmette, IL: Bahá'í Publishing Trust, 1971), 153-54.

2   'Abdu'l-Bahá, *'Abdu'l-Bahá in London* (London: Bahá'í Publishing Trust, 1982), 18.

3   *Star of the West*, vol. 14, no. 1 (April 1923-March 1924), 55. file:///C:/Users/emadd/OneDrive/Documents/Revelation%20of%20St.%20John/Revelation%20of%20John%20Wilmette%20Course/Star%20of%20the%20West%20all%20issues/SW_Volume14-SW_Volume14.pdf.

4   'Abdu'l-Bahá, *The Promulgation of Universal Peace* (Wilmette, IL: Bahá'í Publishing Trust, 1982, 201.

5   The Báb, Bahá'u'lláh, et al., *The Bible: Extracts on the Old and New Testament* (compiled by the Research Department of the Universal House of Justice), https://bahai-library.com/uhj_old_new_testaments.

6   'Abdu'l-Bahá, *The Promulgation of Universal Peace*, compiled by Harold Mc-Nutt. (Wilmette, IL: Bahá'í Publishing Trust, 2007), 212.

7   'Abdu'l-Bahá, *Promulgation*, 155.

8   *The Bible: Extracts*. Cited in a letter dated January 31, 1955, written on behalf of Shoghi Effendi to an individual. https://bahai-library.com/uhj_old_new_testaments.

9   *The Bible: Extracts*, Cited in a letter dated August 9, 1984, written on behalf of the Universal House of Justice to an individual.

10   Michael Sours, *Without Syllable or Sound: The World's Sacred Scriptures in the Bahá'í Faith* (Los Angeles: Kalamát Press, 2000), 49-50. The quotation is from *The Kitáb-i-Íqán*, 84. Sours is a Bahá'í author who has written seven books about Christian subjects.

11   'Abdu'l-Bahá, *Some Answered Questions* (Haifa: Bahá'í World Centre, 2014), no. 39:7, 178.

12   'Abdu'l-Bahá, *Some Answered Questions*, 47:1, 207.

13   'Abdu'l-Bahá, *Some Answered Questions*, 38:4, 172–73.

14   'Abdu'l-Bahá, *Some Answered Questions*, 35:2–4, 156.

15   Bahá'u'lláh, *Gleanings from the Writings of Bahá'u'lláh* (Wilmette, IL: Bahá'í Publishing Trust, 1988), *LXXIX*, 153.

16   'Abdu'l-Bahá, *Some Answered Questions*, 61:2, 262.

Chapter 1: Biblical Criticism and Archaeology

17   "Biblical Criticism," *Theopedia: An Encyclopedia of Biblical Christianity*, accessed July 21, 2023, https://www.theopedia.com/biblical-criticism. *Theopedia* is a growing online evangelical encyclopedia of biblical Christianity, a network of interconnected pages, constantly being refined and updated.

18   "Biblical Criticism," *Theopedia*.

19   R. A. Torrey, A. C. Dixon, et al., eds. *The Fundamentals: A Testimony to the Truth* (Chicago, IL: Testimony Publishing Company, 1910-1915; Los Angeles: Bible Institute of Los Angeles, 1971; Peabody, MA: Baker Books, 2003). This set of ninety essays in four volumes reflects concern with certain theological innovations related to liberal Christianity, especially biblical higher criticism. It is widely considered to be the foundation of modern Christian fundamentalism.

20   Maddocks, "The Decalogues and Codes," *The Coming of the Glory, Vol. I*, 114-121.

21   William G. Dever, *Did God Have a Wife? Archaeology and Folk Religion in Ancient Israel* (Grand Rapids, MI: Wm. B. Eerdmans Publishing Co., 2008), 79-80. Dever is an American archaeologist, Hebrew Bible scholar, and historian who specializes in the history of the Ancient Near East and the ancient kingdoms of Israel and Judah. He was Professor of Near Eastern Archaeology and Anthropology at the University of Arizona in Tucson from 1975 to 2002 and is a Distinguished Professor of Near Eastern Archaeology at Lycoming College, Pennsylvania. He was Director of the Harvard Semitic Museum-Hebrew Union College Excavations at Gezer 1966-71, 1984, and 1990; Director of the dig at Khirbet el-Kôm and Jebel Qacaqir (West Bank) from 1967-71; Principal Investigator at Tell el-Hayyat excavations (Jordan) 1981-85, and Assistant Director, the University of Arizona Expedition to Idalion, Cyprus, 1991, among other excavations. In his retirement, he became a documentary filmmaker on biblical issues.

22   Dever, *Did God Have a Wife?* 81.

23   Shalom Yerushalmi, "Israeli official: Turkey agrees to return ancient Hebrew inscription to Jerusalem," *The Times of Israel,* March 11, 2022. https://www. timesofisrael.com/israeli-official-turkey-agrees-to-return-ancient-hebrew-inscription-to-jerusalem/.

24   Dever, *Did God Have a Wife?* 76.

25   *Madain Project: Encyclopedia of Abrahamic History & Archaeology*, "Tel Dan Stele." https://madainproject.com/tel_dan_stele#overview.

26   Lawrence E. Stager, "Forging an Identity: The Emergence of Ancient Israel," *The Oxford History of the Biblical World* (Oxford, UK: Oxford University Press, 1998), 94. Dr. Stager (1943–2017) was a graduate of Harvard Divinity School, and then discovered archaeology and obtained a PhD from Harvard

University in Near Eastern Languages and Civilizations. He taught Syro-Palestinian and biblical archaeology at the Oriental Institute of the University of Chicago from 1973 to 1985, and returned to an endowed chair at Harvard as the inaugural Dorot Professor of the Archaeology of Israel and as Director of the Semitic Museum from 1985 to 2012. In 2016, he received the Percia Schimmel Prize from the Israel Museum for his contributions to archaeology in Israel, an honor rarely given to a non-Israeli.

27   Stager, "Forging an Identity," 94.

28   Stager, "Forging an Identity," 95-96.

29   Stager, "Forging an Identity," 96-97.

30   Stager, "Forging an Identity," 97.

31   Stager, "Forging an Identity," 97.

32   Stager, "Forging an Identity," 102.

33   Christopher Rollston, Joseph Garfinkel, et al., "The Jerubbaʻal Inscription from Khirbet al-Raʾi: A Proto-Canaanite (Early Alphabetic) Inscription," (*Jerusalem Journal of Archaeology*, 2, 2021-2022), 1-15. https://jjar.huji.ac.il/sites/default/files/jjar/files/rollston_et_al._2021_jjar_2_1-15.pdf.

34   Rollston, et al., "The Jerubbaʻal Inscription from Khirbet al-Raʾi," 9.

35   Rollston, et al., "The Jerubbaʻal Inscription from Khirbet al-Raʾi," 9.

36   Abduʾl-Bahá, *Some Answered Questions*, 30:3-4, 138.

37   Abduʾl-Bahá, *Some Answered Questions*, 30:13, 142.

38   Letter dated March 3, 1957, written on behalf of the Guardian in answer to a question raised by an individual, *Lights of Guidance*, no. 1659, 494.

39   Sohrab Kourosh, *Self Study Notes for the Kitáb-i-Íqán: The Book of Certitude, Vol 1* (Southlake, TX: Koroush Publishing, 2021), 48-49. Kourosh has a PhD in medical and biomedical engineering and a JD with a concentration in environmental law. Fluent in Persian and Arabic, Kourosh is the author of *Self Study Notes for The Seven Valleys of Baháʾuʾlláh* and *Self Study Notes for The Kitáb-i-Íqán: The Book of Certitude, Volumes I and II.*

40   From a letter written on behalf of the Guardian to an individual believer, October 28, 1949, *Baháʾí News*, No. 228, February 1950, 4. https://bahai.works/Bah%C3%A1%E2%80%99%C3%AD_News/Issue_228/Text.

Chapter 2: Canaan and the Canaanites

41   Maddocks, "A Collapse," *The Coming of the Glory, Vol. I,* 100-03.

42   Marc Haber, Claude Doumet-Serhal, et al., "Continuity and Admixture in the Last Five Millennia of Levantine History from Ancient Canaanite and Present-Day Lebanese Genome Sequences," *The American Journal of Human Genetics,* Vol. 101:2 (August 3, 2017), 274-82. https://www.cell.com/ajhg/fulltext/S0002-9297(17)30276-8.

43   Haber, et al., "Continuity and Admixture."

44   Jonathan Laden, "Jews and Arabs Descended from Canaanites," *Biblical Archaeology Review,* Biblical Archaeological Society (Nov. 24, 2022). https://www.biblicalarchaeology.org/daily/ancient-cultures/ancient-near-eastern-world/jews-and-arabs-descended-from-canaanites/. This article is a summary of "The Genomic History of Southern Levant Bronze Age," Lily Agranat-Tamir, Shamam Waldman, et. al., in the research journal *Cell,* 181:5, May 18, 2021. https://www.cell.com/cell/fulltext/S0092-8674(20)30487-6.

45   Michal Feldman, Daniel M. Master, et. al., "Ancient DNA sheds light on the ancient origins of early Iron Age Philistines," *Science,* Vol. 5:7, July 3, 2019, https://www.science.org/doi/10.1126/sciadv.aax0061.

46   Mary Ellen Buck, *The Canaanites* (Eugene, OR: Cascade Books, 2019), 10.

47   Buck, *The Canaanites,* 44-45, 92.

48   Schniedewind, *How the Bible Became a Book: The Textualization of Ancient Israel* (Cambridge, UK: Cambridge University Press, 2004), 56.

49   Israel Finkelstein and Neil Asher Silberman, *The Bible Unearthed: Archaeology's New Vision of Ancient Israel and the Origin of Sacred Text*s (New York: Simon and Schuster, 2002), 62-63.

50   Carol A. Redmount, "Bitter Lives: Israel In and Out of Egypt," *The Oxford History of the Biblical World,* ed. Michael D. Coogan (Oxford, UK: Oxford University Press, 1998), 87.

51   "A Spiritual Exodus," *The Coming of the Glory, Vol. I,* 109-123.

52   John Bottéro, *Religion in Ancient Mesopotamia* (Chicago, IL: University of Chicago Press, 2004),106-96.

53   Ira Spar, "The Gods and Goddesses of Canaan," The Metropolitan Museum of Art: Heilbrunn Timeline of Art History (April 2009), https://www.metmuseum.org/toah/hd/cana/hd_cana.htm.

54   David Penchansky, *Twilight of the Gods: Polytheism in the Hebrew Bible* (Louisville, KY: Westminster John Knox Press, 2005), 83.

55   James L. Kugel, *The Great Shift: Encountering God in Biblical Times* (Boston and New York: Mariner Books, Houghton Mifflin Harcourt, 2017), 75.

Chapter 3: Monolatry and Monotheism

56   Abdu'l-Bahá, *Selections from the Writings of Abdu'l-Bahá* (Haifa: Bahá'í World Centre, 1978), no. 25, 59.

57   Shoghi Effendi, *The Advent of Divine Justice* (Wilmette, IL: Bahá'í Publishing Trust, 1971), 17. The quotation continues: "…the barbarous cruelty, the gross idolatry and immorality, which had for so long been the most distressing features of the tribes of Arabia and brought such shame upon them when Muḥammad arose to proclaim His Message in their midst; the indescribable state of decadence, with its attendant corruption, confusion, intolerance, and oppression, in both the civil and religious life of Persia, so graphically portrayed by the pen of a considerable number of scholars, diplomats, and travelers, at the hour of the Revelation of Bahá'u'lláh—all demonstrate this basic and inescapable fact."

58   Shoghi Effendi, *Advent*, 17-18.

59   "Ancient Jewish History: The Birth and Evolution of Judaism, No. 2," *Jewish Virtual Library*, https://www.jewishvirtuallibrary.org/the-birth-and-evolution-of-judaism#2.

60   "Ancient Jewish History," *Jewish Virtual Library*.

61   "Ancient Jewish History," *Jewish Virtual Library*.

62   Peter Enns, *Inspiration and Incarnation: Evangelicals and the Problem of the Old Testament*, 1st ed. (Ada, MI: Baker Academic, Baker Publishing Group, 2005), 159. A second edition was published in 2015 by Baker Academic. Dr. Enns obtained a PhD from Harvard University in Near Eastern Languages and Civilizations. He was a professor of Old Testament and biblical hermeneutics at Westminster Theological Seminary from 1994-2005. Enns has been a senior fellow of biblical studies with the BioLogos Foundation, a Christian organization that explores, promotes, and celebrates an integration of science and Christian faith. As of 2023, he is the Abram S. Clemens professor of biblical studies at Eastern University, St. Davids, Pennsylvania.

63   Bahá'u'lláh, *The Kitáb-i-Íqán: The Book of Certitude* (Wilmette, IL: Bahá'í Publishing Trust, 2003), no. 161, 140, emphasis added. *The Kitáb-i-Íqán* was written before Bahá'u'lláh declared His station as a Prophet of God.

64   Bahá'u'lláh, *The Kitáb-i-Íqán*, no. 191, 162-63.

65   Bahá'u'lláh, *Gleanings*, XXXVIII, 87.

66   Bahá'u'lláh, *Gleanings*, XXXIV, 80.

67   Bahá'u'lláh, "Lawḥ-i-Aqdas" (Most Holy Tablet), *Tablets of Bahá'u'lláh Revealed after the Kitáb-i-Íqan* (Wilmette, IL: Bahá'í Publishing Trust, 1988), No. 10, 12. Otherwise known as the Tablet to the Christians, this tablet was addressed to a believer of Christian background.

68   Maddocks, "The Decalogues and Codes," *The Coming of the Glory, Vol. I*, 114-121.

Chapter 4: Ezekiel – A Spectacular Call

69   *Merriam-Webster Dictionary*, https://www.merriam-webster.com/dictionary/eschatology.

70   Shoghi Effendi, *God Passes By* (Wilmette, IL: Bahá'í Publishing Trust, 1971), 95.

71   Donald E. Gowan, *Eschatology in the Old Testament* (Edinburgh, UK: T&T Clark; 2nd edition, 2000), 122. Gowan was ordained in the Presbyterian Church (U.S.A.) and served churches in the Midwest. He has been the Professor Emeritus Robert of Old Testament at Pittsburgh Theological Seminary (a Presbyterian graduate seminary).

72   Gowan, *Eschatology*, 123.

73   Maddocks, "Jeremiah—If You Do Not Listen" and "The End of the Davidic Kingdom," *The Coming of the Glory: How the Hebrew Bible Reveals the Plan of God, Vol. II*, (Brooklyn, WI: Something Or Other Publishing, 2022), 173-207. These pages give a full account of Jeremiah's ministry and warnings.

74   Hushidar Motlagh, *The Lord of Lords* (Mt. Pleasant, MI: Global Perspective, 2000), 318. Motlagh taught courses in psychology of human development, educational psychology, mental health, and creativity for 33 years at SUNY Fredonia and Central Michigan University, where he became professor emeritus. He authored about fifty books relating to the knowledge

of God, the relationship between the Bahá'í Faith and Christian prophecy, understanding the Qur'án, and life after death.

75   Bahá'u'lláh, *The Kitáb-i-Aqdas: The Most Holy Book* (Haifa: Bahá'í World Centre, 1992), no. 103, 57.

76   Lady Sara Louise Blomfield, *The Chosen Highway* (Wilmette, IL: Bahá'í Publishing Trust, 1967), 53. Lady Blomfield (named Sitárih Khánum by 'Abdu'l-Bahá) was a distinguished early Bahá'í. She declared her Faith in Bahá'u'lláh in 1907 and was the first native of Ireland to do so, although she spent most of her life in England. She became a close friend of Shoghi Effendi while he was pursuing his studies at Balliol College, Oxford, and after 'Abdu'l-Bahá's death she accompanied him to Haifa to assist him in his new role of Guardian. She remained in Haifa for several years and performed the invaluable service of obtaining extensive verbal memoirs from Bahíyyih Khánum and other members of the holy family and persons who were close to them.

77   Blomfield, *The Chosen Highway*, 242.

78   Blomfield, *The Chosen Highway*, 242.

Chapter 5: Ezekiel – Judgement and Redemption

79   Maddocks, "Prophetic Immunity Tested," *The Coming of the Glory, Vol. II*, 181-82.

80   'Abdu'l-Bahá, *Selections from the Writings of 'Abdu'l-Bahá*, no. 201.1, 257–58, emphasis added.

81   Bahá'u'lláh, *Gleanings*, CXVII, 250.

82   Bahá'u'lláh, *Tablets of Bahá'u'lláh Revealed After the Kitáb-i-Aqdas*, 66-67.

83   'Abdu'l-Bahá, *Some Answered Questions*, no. 11:34, 64, emphasis added.

84   Bahá'u'lláh, *The Proclamation of Bahá'u'lláh* (Wilmette, IL: Bahá'í Publishing Trust, 1978), 89.

Chapter 6: Ezekiel – Gog and Magog

85   'Abdu'l-Bahá, *Promulgation*, 212.

86   Paul Thigpen and Marcus Grodi, "The Rapture Trap: A Catholic View," BeliefNet (accessed October 2, 2023). Reprinted from *The Rapture Trap: A*

Catholic Response to 'End Times' Fever by Paul Thigpen, PhD with permission of Ascension Press, West Chester, PA. https://www.beliefnet.com/faiths/catholic/2001/08/the-rapture-trap-a-catholic-view.aspx. Thigpen earned a PhD in Historical Theology from Emory University, where he was awarded the George W. Woodruff Fellowship. He was appointed by the United States Conference of Catholic Bishops as a lay representative on its National Advisory Council. He also serves the Church as an historian, apologist, evangelist, and catechist. Grodi is a former Presbyterian minister who converted to Catholicism. He is the founding president of Coming Home Network International, whose mission is to help non-Catholic clergy come home to the Church.

87   Thigpen and Grodi, "The Rapture Trap: A Catholic View."

88   Roger Barrier, "Gog and Magog: Who Are They and What Do They Have To Do with the Last Days?" Crosswalk (March 13, 2023), https://www.crosswalk.com/church/pastors-or-leadership/ask-roger/gog-and-magog-who-are-they-and-what-do-they-have-to-do-with-the-last-days.html. Dr. Barrier holds degrees from Baylor University, Southwestern Baptist Theological Seminary, and Golden Gate Baptist Theological Seminary (a graduate school affiliated with the Southern Baptist Convention), where he studied Greek, religion, theology, and pastoral care. He is retired as senior teaching pastor for Casas Church, a megachurch in Tucson, Arizona.

89   Maddocks, Introduction, *The Coming of the Glory, Vol. I*, xxvi-xxvii.

90   John Able, *Apocalypse Secrets: Bahá'í Interpretation of the Book of Revelation* (John Able Books Ltd, 2nd ed., 2021), 132. Able is a retired intensive-care physician. His biblical research interprets the book of Revelation as a global tale of three millennia of religious history that is now culminating into what is sometimes called the end times. It is a tale of the struggles of seven Empires and seven Faiths, of their materialism and militarism, and the resulting chaos and confusion into which the world is now fast descending.

91   Able, *Apocalypse Secrets*, 132.

92   Jean Masson, "The Bahá'í Movement—Is it the coming Universal Religion?" *Star of the West*, Vol. 10, no. 3, (April 28, 1919), https://bahai-library.com/pdf/sw/SW_Volume10.pdf. J. E. Esslemont, *Bahá'u'lláh and the New Era*, 243-44. Masson quoted from notes taken during 'Abdu'l-Bahá's talk at Leland Stanford Junior University in Palo Alto, California, in October, 1912. Following the quotation as reported by Esslemont, it is stated: "Reported by

Mrs. Corinne True in *The North Shore Review*, September 26, 1914, Chicago, U.S.A." This quotation is in the nature of pilgrims' notes.

93   Shoghi Effendi, *God Passes By*, 305.

94   'Abdu'l-Bahá, *Tablets of 'Abdu'l-Bahá Abbas, Vol. III* (Chicago, IL: Bahá'í Publishing Society, 1915/1919), 659.

95   Bahá'u'lláh, *The Kitáb-i-Aqdas*, no. 37, 32.

96   Shoghi Effendi, *God Passes By*, 100.

97   Gary L. Matthews, *He Cometh with the Clouds* (Welwyn, UK: George Ronald Publisher, 2000).

98   Bahá'u'lláh, *Gleanings*, XVII, 42.

Chapter 7: Ezekiel – A New Temple for Humanity

99   Bahá'u'lláh, *The Summons of the Lord of Hosts: Tablets of Bahá'u'lláh* (Haifa: Bahá'í World Centre, 2002), no. 13, 8. Bahá'u'lláh continues: "Beneath the shadow of every letter of this Temple We shall raise up a people whose number none can reckon save God, the Help in Peril, the Self-Subsisting. Erelong shall God bring forth from His Temple such souls as will remain unswayed by the insinuations of the rebellious, and who will quaff at all times of the cup that is life indeed. These, truly, are of the blissful."

100   'Abdu'l-Bahá, cited by Shoghi Effendi, *World Order of Bahá'u'lláh* (Wilmette, IL: Bahá'í Publishing Trust, 1991), 74-75.

101   Bahá'u'lláh, *Epistle to the Son of the Wolf* (Wilmette, IL: Bahá'í Publishing Trust, 1979), 79.

102   Bahá'u'lláh, *Epistle*, 178-79.

103   Thomas Tai-Seale, *Thy Kingdom Come: A Biblical Introduction to the Bahá'í Faith* (Los Angeles, CA: Kalamát Press, 1991), 65-66. Tai-Seale is an Associate Professor at Texas A&M University in the School of Public Health and a lifelong student of religion.

104   'Abdu'l-Bahá, *Some Answered Questions*, 11:7, 54-55.

105   Able, *Apocalypse Secrets*, 83, citing Louis Ginzberg, "Moses Meets the Messiah in Heaven," *The Legends of the Jews*, 3, chapter 7, Sacred Texts-Judaism, https://sacred-texts.com/jud/loj/loj309.htm.

106   Able, *Apocalypse Secrets*, 83. He quotes Bahá'u'lláh, *The Summons of the Lord of Hosts*, no. 276, 137. The complete quotation is: "Thus have We built the Temple with the hands of power and might, could ye but know it. This is the Temple promised unto you in the Book. Draw ye nigh unto it. This is that which profiteth you, could ye but comprehend it. Be fair, O peoples of the earth! Which is preferable, this, or a temple which is built of clay? Set your faces towards it. Thus have ye been commanded by God, the Help in Peril, the Self-Subsisting. Follow ye His bidding, and praise ye God, your Lord, for that which He hath bestowed upon you. He, verily, is the Truth. No God is there but He. He revealeth what He pleaseth, through His words 'Be and it is'."

107   Shoghi Effendi, *Directives from the Guardian* (Wilmette: Bahá'í Publishing Trust, 1973), 51-52.

108   *Issues Related to Study of the Bahá'í Faith* (Wilmette, IL: Bahá'í Publishing Trust of the United States, 1998-2005), Initially published in Bahá'í Canada, May 1998. Compilation by and on behalf of the Universal House of Justice, letter dated March 14, 1996, https://www.bahai.org/library/authoritative-texts/compilations/issues-related-study-bahai-faith/.

Chapter 8: Obadiah – Deliverance on Mount Zion

109   Bahá'u'lláh, *Gleanings*, X, 12-13.

Chapter 9: Second Isaiah – Comfort Ye, Comfort Ye My People

110   Bahá'u'lláh, "Súrih of the Temple," *Summons*, no. 164, 86.

111   H. M. Balyuzi, *'Abdu'l-Bahá: The Centre of the Covenant of Bahá'u'lláh* (London: George Ronald Publishers, 1971), 499.

112   Bahá'u'lláh, *Epistle*, 144-45.

113   Mírzá Abu'l-Faḍl, "In Praise of the Greatest Branch," read in Washington, D.C., on November 22, 1912, at the celebration of the anniversary of The Feast of the Appointment of The Center of the Covenant. *Star of the West*, Vol. 3:14,1912, 13. https://bahai.works/Star_of_the_West/Volume_3/Is-

sue 14. *Star of the West* was a newsletter of the American Bahá'í community that was published from 1910 to 1935.

114   Abraham J. Heschel, *The Prophets* (New York: Harper Collins Publishers; Harper Perennial Modern Classics; 1st Perennial classics edition, 2001), 190.

115   Shoghi Effendi, *God Passes By*, 53.

116   Shoghi Effendi, *God Passes By*, 166.

117   Maddocks, "Appendix A – Noah and His Numbers," *The Coming of the Glory, Vol. II.*

118   The complete story of the retrieval of the Báb's body, with that of Anís's, and their eventual journey to Mount Carmel can by read in the book *Journey to a Mountain: The Story of the Shrine of the Báb, Vol. 1: 1850-1921I,* (Oxford, UK: George Ronald Publisher, 2017), by Michael V. Day.

119   Maddocks, "Psalm 45," *The Coming of the Glory, Vol. I,* 152-56.

120   'Abdu'l-Bahá, *Tablets of 'Abdu'l Bahá, Vol. I* (Chicago, IL: Bahá'í Publishing Society, 1915/1919), 107-08.

Chapter 10: The Restoration

121   Mary Joan Winn Leith, "Israel Among the Nations," *The Oxford History of the Biblical World*, Michael D. Coogan, ed. (New York: The Oxford University Press), 289. Leith is professor of religious studies and theology at Stonehill College. She trained as an archaeologist and obtained a PhD from Harvard University. One of her areas of expertise is the archaeology and history of Israel in the Persian period.

122   Maddocks, "Prophet to the Early Exiles," *The Coming of the Glory, Vol. II,* 194-95.

123   Israel Finkelstein, "The Territorial Extent and Demography of Yehud/Judea in the Persian and Early Hellenistic Periods," *Biblical Review*, vol. 117, no. 1 (January 2010), 39-54, https://israelfinkelstein.files.wordpress.com/2013/07/yehud-judea-rb.pdf. Dr. Finkelstein is professor emeritus of archaeology at the University of Tel Aviv, Israel, and the head of the School of Archaeology and Maritime Cultures at the University of Haifa. He is noted for applying archaeological data life sciences and to reconstructing biblical history.

124   Israel Finkelstein, "Jerusalem in the Persian (and Early Hellenistic) Period and the Wall of Nehemiah," *Journal for the Study of the Old Testament,* Vol. 32, no. 4 (2008). https://archive.org/details/sim_journal-for-the-study-of-the-old-testament_2008-06_32_4/page/n1/mode/2up.

125   Leith, "Israel Among the Nations," 298.

126   Finkelstein, "Jerusalem in the Persian (and Early Hellenistic) Period and the Wall of Nehemiah," 509.

127   Finkelstein, "Jerusalem in the Persian (and Early Hellenistic) Period," 514.

Chapter 11: Haggai – Build That Temple

128   Jay C. Williams, *Understanding the Old Testament* (Hauppauge, NY: B.E.S. Publishing, 1972), 256. Williams received his PhD from Columbia University and is the Walcott-Bartlett Professor of Religious Studies Emeritus at Hamilton College, Clinton, New York.

129   Hushimar Motlagh, *Lord of Lords: Vol. II, Prophecies of the Second Coming* (Mt. Pleasant, MI: Global Perspective, 2000), 458.

130   Motlagh, *Lord of Lords,* 459.

131   Thomas Wolfe, *You Can't Go Home Again* (New York and London: Harper & Row, 1940). This book tells the story of a fledgling author who makes many references to his home town, not always positive, that show how it had changed with time to the point where the book's protagonist could not "go home again."

132   Bahá'u'lláh, *Gleanings,* CXLIII, 313.

133   Bahá'u'lláh, *Gleanings,* LXX, 136.

134   Shoghi Effendi, *God Passes By,* 94.

135   Bahá'u'lláh, *Summons,* no. 55, 208, emphasis added.

136   'Abdu'l-Bahá, *Tablets of 'Abdu'l-Bahá Abbas,* Vol. III, 93.

137   William Sears, *Thief in the Night: The Case of the Missing Millennium* (Oxford: George Ronald Publishing, 1961), 116, https://bahai-library.com/pdf/s/sears_thief_night.pdf. Sears (1911–1992) was a popular radio sportscaster and television and radio personality in various shows. He left media popularity for lifelong service to the Bahá'í Faith.

138   'Abdu'l-Bahá, *A Traveler's Narrative: Written to Illustrate the Episode of the Báb* (Wilmette, IL: Bahá'í Publishing Trust, 1982), 82.

139   Bahá'u'lláh, *The Proclamation of Bahá'u'lláh*, 89, emphasis added.

140   Maddocks, "Appendix F – The Titles of Bahá'u'lláh," *The Coming of the Glory, Vol. II.*

Chapter 12: Zechariah – Let Your Hands Be Strong

141   'Abdu'l-Bahá, *Paris Talks*, 119.

142   'Abdu'l-Bahá, *Selections from the Writings of 'Abdu'l-Bahá*, no. 39, 81, emphasis added.

143   Bahá'u'lláh, *Prayers and Meditations*, , section LIII, 76.

144   Bahá'u'lláh, *The Proclamation of Bahá'u'lláh*, 111.

145   'Abdul-Bahá, trans. by Shoghi Effendi. *Star of the West*, June 4, 1919, vol. 10, no. 12, 232.

146   Shoghi Effendi, *Directives from the Guardian*, no. 141, 52.

147   'Abdu'l-Bahá, *Some Answered Questions*, no. 12-13, 56-57, emphasis added.

148   Maddocks, "A Rod and a Branch," *The Coming of the Glory, Vol. II*, 111-116.

149   Bahá'u'lláh, "Súrih of the Temple," *Summons*, no. 44, 23-24.

150   Bahá'u'lláh, *Summons*, ii, emphasis added.

151   Bahá'u'lláh, "Súrih of the Temple," Tablet to Násiri'd-Dín Sháh, *Summons*, no. 276, 137.

Chapter 13: Second and Third Zechariah – Flickers of the Future

152   *The Báb, Selections from the Writings of the Báb*, 161, emphasis added.

153   Leith, "Israel Among the Nations," 300.

154   Leith, "Israel Among the Nations," 301.

155   Rex Mason, "The Book of Zechariah," *The Oxford Companion to the Bible*, Bruce M. Metzger and Michael D. Coogan, eds. (New York: Oxford Uni-

versity Press, 1993), 828. Rex Mason is one of six authors of the four-volume series *Studies on Zechariah* issued by Sheffield Academic Press.

156   Shoghi Effendi, *The World Order of Bahá'u'lláh*, 125.

157   Shoghi Effendi, *The World Order of Bahá'u'lláh*, 125.

158   Shoghi Effendi, *The Promised Day Is Come*, 71.

159   Maddocks, "The New Cycle," *The Coming of the Glory, Vol. II*, 135.

160   Bahá'u'lláh, *The Kitáb-i-Aqdas*, no. 82, 49.

161   Bahá'u'lláh, "Súriy-i-Haykah," *Summons*, no. 102, 54, emphasis added.

Chapter 14: Third Isaiah – The Day That Shall Not Be Followed by Night

162   'Abdu'l-Bahá, *Promulgation*, 27.

163   Bahá'u'lláh, *Tablets of Bahá'u'lláh Revealed after the Kitáb-i-Aqdas*, 171-72.

164   Bahá'u'lláh, "Súrih of the Temple," *Summons*, no. 63, 34.

165   Shoghi Effendi, *God Passes By*, 244.

166   Shoghi Effendi, *God Passes By*, 244-45.

167   Shoghi Effendi, *God Passes By*, 245.

168   Maddocks, "Appendix H – 'Abdu'l-Bahá, Shoghi Effendi, and the Bahá'í Covenant," *The Coming of the Glory, Vol. II*, 233-236.

169   Bahá'u'lláh, *The Kitáb-i-Íqán*, no. 46, 41.

170   Bahá'u'lláh, *The Kitáb-i-Íqán*, no. 48, 42-43.

171   'Abdu'l-Bahá, *Some Answered Questions*, 13:2, 76-77.

Chapter 15: Joel – Blow the Trumpet

172   Bahá'u'lláh, *Tablets of Bahá'u'lláh Revealed After the Kitáb-i-Aqdas*, 244. Hájí Mírzá Haydar-'Ali was a hero of the Bahá'í Faith who served Bahá'u'lláh and 'Abdu'l-Bahá steadfastly until his passing in 1920.

173   Maddocks, *The Coming of the Glory, Vol. II*, 141-43.

174   Bahá'u'lláh, *Epistle to the Son of the Wolf*, 143-44.

175   Bahá'u'lláh, *The Kitáb-i-Íqán*, no. 31, 33-34.

176   Bahá'u'lláh, *The Kitáb-i-Íqán*, no. 38, 36.

177   Bahá'u'lláh, *The Kitáb-i-Íqán*, no. 123, 107, emphasis added.

178   Bahá'u'lláh, *Epistle*, 145. See Maddocks, "The Symbology of Carmel," *The Coming of the Glory, Vol. II*, 44-47.

179   Bahá'u'lláh, *Tablets of Bahá'u'lláh Revealed After the Kitáb-i-Aqdas*, 195.

Chapter 16: Malachi – The Return of Elijah

180   Maddocks, "The Prophet Elijah," *The Coming of the Glory, Vol. I*, 161-64.

181   'Abdu'l-Bahá, *Some Answered Questions*, no. 33.6, 150.

182   Shoghi Effendi, *Citadel of Faith: Messages to America 1947-1957* (Wilmette, IL: Bahá'í Publishing Trust, 1980), 95, emphasis added.

183   Shoghi Effendi, *God Passes By*, 276-77.

184   Shoghi Effendi, *God Passes By*, 95.

185   Shoghi Effendi, *Directives from the Guardian*, no. 35, 12-13.

Chapter 17: Daniel – Kingdoms and Fulfillment

186   'Abdu'l-Bahá, *The Promulgation of Universal Peace*, 197. He made this statement in Brooklyn, New York, on June 16, 1912, when addressing a gathering in a private home.

187   Robert Riggs, "I Daniel," Bahá'í Library Online (1998), https://bahai-library.com/riggs_i_Daniel.

188   Mírzá Abu'l Faḍl, "In Praise of The Greatest Branch," *Star of the West*, Vol. 3, Issue 14, November 23, 1912, 13-14. https://bahai.works/Star_of_the_West/Volume_3/Issue_14.

189   Mírzá Abu'l Faḍl, "In Praise of The Greatest Branch," *Star of the West*.

Chapter 18: Daniel – Sealed and Unsealed

190   Bahá'u'lláh, *Gleanings*, CLIII, 328.

191   'Abdu'l-Bahá, *Some Answered Questions*, no. 10:12, 47.

192 'Abdu'l-Bahá, *Some Answered Questions*, no. 10:13-14, 47-48.

193 Maddocks, "An Oracle for Elam," *The Coming of the Glory, Vol. II*, 190-91.

194 Maddocks, *1844: Convergence in Prophecy for Judaism, Christianity, Islam, and the Bahá'í Faith* (Burlington, VT: Jewel Press, 2018).

195 'Abdu'l-Bahá, *Some Answered Questions*, no. 10:16, 48-49.

196 'Abdu'l-Bahá, *Some Answered Questions*, no. 17, 49, emphasis added.

197 Donavin Coffey, "Why does Christianity have so many denominations?" *Live Science*, July 29, 2022. https://www.livescience.com/christianity-de-nominations.html. Also, the Center for the Study of Global Christianity reports 41,000 denominations. https://www.gordonconwell.edu/center-for-global-christianity/research/quick-facts/.

198 Elena Maria Marsella, *The Quest for Eden* (New York: Philosophical Library, 1966), 134. Marsella (1913-2002) was an American Bahá'í who pursued careers as a pianist, a member of the Foreign Service, and a teacher. She was a Knight of Baha'u'llah to the Gilbert and Ellis Islands (now Kiribati and Tuvalu) and a member of the first National Spiritual Assembly of the Bahá'ís of the Hawaiian Islands and the National Spiritual Assembly of Central America and the Antilles. She served on the Board of Counsellors for Northeastern Asia. Marsella was known for her encyclopedic knowledge of the Faith.

199 Marsella, *The Quest for Eden*, 208.

200 'Abdu'l-Bahá, *Some Answered Questions*, no. 10:20, 50.

201 Letter dated December 26, 1941, written on behalf of Shoghi Effendi to an individual, *Letters to Australia and New Zealand* (Australia: Australian Bahá'í Publishing, 1971), 41. https://bahai-library.com/shoghi-effendi_let-ters_australia_new-zealand.

202 'Abdu'l-Bahá, *Bahá'í World Faith: Selected Writings of Bahá'u'lláh and 'Abdu'l-Bahá* (Wilmette: Bahá'í Publishing Trust, 1943/1976), 358. The quotation continues: "His Holiness the Prophet Muḥammad made a covenant concerning His Holiness the Báb and the Báb was the One promised by Muḥammad, for Muḥammad gave the tidings of His coming. The Báb made a Covenant concerning the Blessed Beauty of Bahá'u'lláh and gave the glad-tidings of His coming for the Blessed Beauty was the One promised by His Holiness the Báb. Bahá'u'lláh

made a covenant concerning a promised One who will become manifest after one thousand or thousands of years."

203   'Abdu'l-Bahá, *Some Answered Questions*, no. 10:22, 50-51.

204   Shoghi Effendi, *Directives from the Guardian*, 54-55.

205   Abdu'l-Bahá, cited by Shoghi Effendi and Lady Blomfeld, "Tablet to a Kurdish Friend," *The Passing of 'Abdu'l-Bahá* (Haifa: Rosenfeld Bros., 1922), 24. Also cited in Helen Hornby, compiler, *Lights of Guidance: A Bahá'í Reference File* (New Delhi, India: Bahá'í Publishing Trust, 2nd edition 1988), no. 1414, 431-32. Also partially cited in *Century of Light*, commissioned by the Universal House of Justice (Haifa: Bahá'í World Centre, 2001), 94-45.

Appendix A: Noah and His Numbers

206   Don Dainty, *As It Was in the Days of Noah: So Unfolds the Surprising Fulfilment of Biblical Foresights of the 'Return'* (Ottawa: E. Don Dainty, 2009), 20-21.

207   Dainty, *As It Was in the Days of Noah*, 24.

208   Shoghi Effendi, *World Order of Bahá'u'lláh*, 145.

209   Dainty, *As It Was in the Days of Noah*, 25.

210   Dainty, *As It Was in the Days of Noah*, 26-27.

211   Donella H. Meadows, Dennis L. Meadows, et al. *The Limits to Growth: A Report for the Club of Rome's Project on the Predicament of Mankind* (Washington, D.C.: Potomac Associates Books, 1971; New York: Universe Books, 1972). Also, The Club of Rome, https://www.clubofrome.org/history/. *The Limits to Growth* sold 12 million copies, was translated into 37 languages, and remains the top-selling environmental book ever published. The Club of Rome was founded in Europe in the late 1960s to advance global and long-term perspectives, and to explore intertwined global problems, be they economic, environmental, political or social. An international team of researchers at the Massachusetts Institute of Technology began a study of the implications of unbridled exponential growth and the five major factors of population, agricultural production, nonrenewable resource depletion, industrial output, and pollution. In 1972, the Club's first major Report, *The Limits to Growth*, was published. This call for objective, scientific assessment

of the impact of humanity's behavior and use of resources still defines the Club of Rome today.

212 Shoghi Effendi, *The Promised Day Is Come*, 112-13.

213 Dainty, *As It Was in the Days of Noah*, 28.

214 Dainty, *As It Was in the Days of Noah*, 30-31.

215 Dainty, *As It Was in the Days of Noah*, commentary with Figure 5, unnumbered.

216 "WHO Coronavirus (C-19) Dashboard," World Health Organization, accessed July 21, 2023, https://covid19.who.int/.

217 International Panel on Climate Change, "Climate change widespread, rapid, and intensifying," IPCC, August 9, 2021, https://www.ipcc.ch/2021/08/09/ar6-wg1-20210809-pr/.

218 United Nations, *UN News*, "UN climate report: It's 'now or never' to limit global warming to 1.5 degrees" (April 4, 2022), https://news.un.org/en/story/2022/04/1115452, https://www.ipcc.ch/report/sixth-assessment-report-cycle/.

219 Hoesung Lee, ed., "Summary for Policy Makers in 'Climate Change 2023: Synthesis Report,'" Intergovernmental Panel on Climate Change IPCC, 23, https://www.ipcc.ch/report/ar6/syr/downloads/report/IPCC_AR6_SYR_SPM.pdf, DOI: 10.59327/IPCC/AR6-9789291691647.

220 Bahá'u'lláh, *Gleanings*, LXI, 118-19.

221 Bahá'u'lláh, *Gleanings*, IV, 7.

222 Dainty, *As It Was in the Days of Noah*, commentary with Figure 5, unnumbered insert at back of book.

223 Dainty, *As It Was in the Days of Noah*, 34.

224 Dainty, *As It Was in the Days of Noah*, 19.

Appendix B: Akka in Holy Scriptures

225 Bahá'u'lláh, *Epistle*, 146. "And in another connection He [Isaiah] saith: 'The wilderness and the solitary place shall be glad for them; and the desert shall rejoice, and blossom as the rose. It shall blossom abundantly, and rejoice

even with joy and singing: the glory of Lebanon shall be given unto it, the splendor of Carmel and Sharon, they shall see the glory of the Lord, and the splendor of our God.'"

226   Psalm 60:9 KJV. "Who will bring me into the strong city? who will lead me into Edom?"

227   Hosea 2:15. "There I will give her back her vineyards, and will make the Valley of Achor a door of hope. There she will respond as in the days of her youth, as in the day she came up out of Egypt."

228   Ezekiel 40:6, KVJ. "Then came he unto the gate which looketh toward the east, and went up the stairs thereof, and measured the threshold of the gate, which was one reed broad; and the other threshold of the gate, which was one reed broad."

229   Ezekiel 43:2, KJV. "And, behold, the glory of the God of Israel came from the way of the east: and his voice was like a noise of many waters: and the earth shined with his glory."

230   Ezekiel 43:2, KJV.

231   Bahá'u'lláh, *Epistle*, 178.

232   Bahá'u'lláh, *Epistle*, 178.

233   Bahá'u'lláh, *Epistle*, 178-79.

234   Bahá'u'lláh, *Epistle*, 179.

235   Bahá'u'lláh, *Epistle*, 179.

236   Bahá'u'lláh, *Epistle*, 179.

237   Bahá'u'lláh, *Epistle*, 179.

238   Nabil-i-Azám, *The Dawn-breakers: Nabíl's Narrative of the Early Days of the Bahá'í Revelation*, trans. by Shoghi Effendi (Wilmette, IL: Bahá'í Publishing Trust, 1932).

239   Shoghi Effendi, *God Passes By*, 184.

Appendix C: The Bahá'í Administrative Order

240   The Bahá'í Faith: The Official Website of the Worldwide Bahá'í Community. "The Bahá'í Administrative Order: Introduction." https://www.bahai.org/beliefs/essential-relationships/administrative-order.

241   Shoghi Effendi, *The Promised Day Is Come*, no. 290, 118.

242   Shoghi Effendi, *World Order*, 156.

Appendix D: The Center of Nine Concentric Circles

243   Shoghi Effendi, *Citadel of Faith*, 95-96.

Appendix E: The Fourth Beast with Ten Horns

244   H. M. Balyuzi, *Muḥammad and the Course of Islám*, (Oxford, UK: George Ronald Publisher, 1976),149-50.

245   Balyuzi, *Muḥammad*, 153.

246   Balyuzi, *Muḥammad*, 188.

247   'Abdu'l-Bahá, *Some Answered Questions*, no. 13.6, p. 78-79.

248   'Abdu'l-Bahá, *Some Answered Questions*, no. 13.7, 79.

249   'Abdu'l-Bahá, *Some Answered Questions*, no. 13.8, 80.

250   'Abdu'l-Bahá, *Some Answered Questions*, no. 13:9-12, 80.

251   'Abdu'l-Bahá, *Selections from the Writings of 'Abdu'l-Bahá*, no. 145.7, 180-81.

Appendix F: Excerpt from *Thief in the Night*

252   William Sears, *Thief in the Night*, 40-43.

BIBLIOGRAPHY

THE BÁB

Selections from the Writings of the Báb. Wilmette, IL: Bahá'í Publishing Trust, 1982. https://www.bahai.org/library/authoritative-texts/the-bab/selections-writings-bab/1#103864442.

WORKS OF BAHÁ'U'LLÁH

Bahá'í World Faith: Selected Writings of Bahá'u'lláh and 'Abdu'l-Bahá. Wilmette, IL: Bahá'í Publishing Trust, 1943/1976. https://bahai-library.org/compilation_bahai_world_faith.

Epistle to the Son of the Wolf. Wilmette, IL: Bahá'í Publishing Trust, 1979. https://www.bahai.org/library/authoritative-texts/bahaullah/epistle-son-wolf/. *Gems of Divine Mysteries.* Haifa: Bahá'í World Center, 2002. https://www.bahai.org/library/authoritative-texts/bahaullah/gems-divine-mysteries/.

Gleanings from the Writings of Bahá'u'lláh. Translated by Shoghi Effendi. Wilmette, IL: Bahá'í Publishing Trust, 1988. https://www.bahai.org/library/authoritative-texts/bahaullah/gleanings-writings-bahaullah/.

The Kitáb-i-Aqdas: The Most Holy Book. Haifa: Bahá'í World Centre, 1992. https://www.bahai.org/library/authoritative-texts/bahaullah/kitab-i-aqdas/.

The Kitáb-i-Íqán: The Book of Certitude. Translated by Shoghi Effendi. New pocket-sized edition with paragraph numbers. Wilmette, IL: Bahá'í Publishing Trust, 2003. https://www.bahai.org/library/authoritative-texts/bahaullah/kitab-i-iqan/.

Prayers and Meditations. Wilmette, IL: Bahá'í Publishing Company, 1988. https://www.bahai.org/library/authoritative-texts/bahaullah/prayers-meditations/.

Tablets of Bahá'u'lláh Revealed After the Kitáb-i-Aqdas. Wilmette, IL: Bahá'í Publishing Trust, 1988. https://bahai-library.org/bahaullah_tablets_bahaullah.

The Proclamation of Bahá'u'lláh. Wilmette, IL: Bahá'í Publishing Trust, 1978. https://bahai-library.org/bahaullah_proclamation_bahaullah.

The Summons of the Lord of Hosts: Tablets of Bahá'u'lláh. Haifa: Bahá'í World Centre, 2002. https://www.bahai.org/library/authoritative-texts/bahaulla.

WORKS OF 'ABDU'L-BAHÁ

A Traveler's Narrative: Written to Illustrate the Episode of the Báb. Wilmette, IL: Bahá'í Publishing Trust, 1982. https://www.bahai.org/library/authoritative-texts/abdul-baha/travelers-narrative/.

'Abdu'l-Bahá in London. London: Bahá'í Publishing Trust, 1982. https://bahai-library.com/abdul-baha_abdul-baha_london/.

Selections from the Writings of Abdu'l-Bahá. Haifa: Bahá'í World Centre, 1978. https://www.bahai.org/library/authoritative-texts/abdul-baha/selections-writings-abdul-baha/.

Some Answered Questions. Compiled and translated from the Persian language by Laura Clifford Barney. Newly revised by a committee at the Bahá'í World Centre. Haifa, Israel: Bahá'í World Centre, 2014. https://www.bahai.org/library/authoritative-texts/abdul-baha/some-answered-questions/.

Tablets of 'Abdu'l-Bahá, Vol. I. Chicago, IL: Bahá'í Publishing Society, 1915/1919. https://bahai-library.com/abdul-baha_tablets_abdul-baha/.

Tablets of 'Abdu'l-Bahá Abbas, Vol. III. Chicago, IL: Bahá'í Publishing Society, 1915/1919. https://bahai-library.com/abdul-baha_tablets_abdul-baha/.

The Promulgation of Universal Peace: Talks Delivered by 'Abdu'l-Bahá during His Visit to The United States and Canada in 1912. Compiled by Harold McNutt. Wilmette, IL: Bahá'í Publishing Trust, 2007. https://bahai-library.com/abdul-baha_promulgation_universal_peace/.

WORKS OF SHOGHI EFFENDI

Citadel of Faith: Messages to America 1947-1957. Wilmette, IL: Bahá'í Publishing Trust, 1980. https://www.bahai.org/library/authoritative-texts/shoghi-effendi/citadel-faith/.

Directives from the Guardian. Wilmette, IL: Bahá'í Publishing Trust, 1973. https:// bahai-library.com/shoghi-effendi_directives_guardian/.

God Passes By. Wilmette, IL: Bahá'í Publishing Trust, 1971. https://www.bahai.org/ library/authoritative-texts/shoghi-effendi/god-passes-by/.

Letters to Australia and New Zealand. Australia: Australian Bahá'í Publishing, 1971. https://bahai-library.com/shoghi-effendi_letters_australia_new-zealand/.

Messages to the Bahá'í World: 1950-1957. Wilmette, IL: Bahá'í Publishing Trust, 1971. https://bahai-library.com/shoghi-effendi_messages_bahai_world/.

The Advent of Divine Justice. Wilmette, IL: Bahá'í Publishing Trust, 1971. https://www.bahai.org/library/authoritative-texts/shoghi-effendi/ advent-divine-justice/.

The Promised Day Is Come. Wilmette, IL: Bahá'í Publishing Trust, 1980. https:// bahai-library.org/shoghi-effendi_promised_day_come.

The World Order of Bahá'u'lláh. Wilmette, IL: Bahá'í Publishing Trust, 1991. https://www.bahai.org/library/authoritative-texts/shoghi-effendi/ world-order-bahaullah/.

WORKS COMMISSIONED BY THE UNIVERSAL HOUSE OF JUSTICE

Century of Light. Haifa: Bahá'í World Centre, 2001. https://bahai-library.com/ uhj_century_light/.

One Common Faith. Haifa: Bahá'í World Centre, 2005. https://bahai-library.com/ one_common_faith/.

COMPILATIONS

Bahá'u'lláh, et al. *The Bible: Extracts on the Old and New Testaments.* Research Department of the Universal House of Justice, (publication date not given). https://bahai-library.com/uhj_old_new_testaments.

Hornby, Helen, compiler. *Lights of Guidance: A Bahá'í Reference File.* New Delhi, India: Bahá'í Publishing Trust, 1st ed. 1983, 2nd revised ed. 1988, 3rd revised ed., 1994.

Universal House of Justice, compiler. *Issues Related to Study of the Bahá'í Faith.* Wilmette, IL: Bahá'í Publishing Trust, 1998-2005. https://www.bahai.org/library/authoritative-texts/compilations/issues-related-study-bahai-faith/.

OTHER HOLY SCRIPTURES

The Bible, King James Version (KJV)

The Bible, New International Version (NIV)

OTHER SOURCES

Able, John. *Apocalypse Secrets: Bahá'í Interpretation of the Book of Revelation.* John Able Books Ltd, 2nd ed., 2021.

Agramat-Tamir, Lilly, et al. "The Genomic History of the Bronze Age Southern Levant." *Cell,* Vol. 181, Issue 5, (May 28, 2020): 1146-1157. https://www.cell.com/cell/fulltext/S0092-8674(20)30487-6, DOI: https://doi.org/10.1016/j.cell.2020.04.024.

Bahá'í News, No. 103, October 1936, 1. http://www.bahai-news.info/viewer.erb?vol=01&page=1.

Balyuzi, H. M. *'Abdu'l-Bahá: Centre of the Covenant.* Oxford, UK: George Ronald Publisher, 1971.

Balyuzi, H. M. *Muḥammad and the Course of Islám.* Oxford, UK: George Ronald Publisher, 1976.

Barrier, Roger. "Gog and Magog: Who Are They and What Do They Have To Do with the Last Days?" Crosswalk, March 13, 2023. https://www.crosswalk.com/church/pastors-or-leadership/ask-roger/gog-and-magog-who-are-they-and-what-do-they-have-to-do-with-the-last-days.html.

Beebe, Stephen. *The Logic of the Revelation of St. John.* New Delhi, India: Bahá'í Publishing Trust, 1998.

Bishop, James. "Early Jewish Monolatry in the Old Testament." *Bishop's Encyclopedia of Religion, Society and Philosophy,* July 6, 2019. https://jamesbishopblog.com/2019/07/06/early-*jewish-monolatry-in-the-old-testament/.

Blomfield, Lady Sara Louise. *The Chosen Highway.* Wilmette, IL: Bahá'í Publishing Trust, 1967.

Blomfield, Lady Sara Louise and Shoghi Effendi. *The Passing of 'Abdu'l-Bahá*. Haifa: Rosenfeld Bros., 1922. https://bahai-library.com/shoghi-effendi_blomfield_passing_abdul-baha/.

Bottéro, John. Trans. Teresa Lavender Fagan. *Religion in Ancient Mesopotamia*. Chicago, IL: University of Chicago Press, 2004.

Buck, Mary Ellen. *The Canaanites: Their History and Culture from Texts and Artifacts*. Eugene, OR: Cascade Books, 2019.

Center for the Study of Global Christianity. https://www.gordonconwell.edu/center-for-global-christianity/research/quick-facts.

Cline, Eric H. *1177: The Year Civilization Collapsed*. First volume in the series Turning Points in Ancient History. Princeton: Princeton University Press, revised updated edition, 2021.

Coffey, Donavin. "Why does Christianity have so many denominations?" Live Science, July 29, 2022. https://www.livescience.com/christianity-denominations.html.

Dainty, Don. *As It Was in the Days of Noah: So Unfolds the Surprising Fulfilment of Biblical Foresights of the 'Return.'* Ottawa: E. Don Dainty, 2009.

Day, Michael V. *Journey to a Mountain: The Story of the Shrine of the Báb, Vol. 1: 1850-1921*. Oxford, UK: George Ronald Publisher, 2017.

Dever, William G. *Did God Have a Wife? Archaeology and Folk Religion in Ancient Israel*. Grand Rapids, MI: Wm. B. Eerdmans Publishing Co., 2008.

Enns, Peter. *Inspiration and Incarnation: Evangelicals and the Problem of the Old Testament*, 1st ed. Ada, MI: Baker Academic, Baker Publishing Group, 2005.

Feldman, Michal et. al. "Ancient DNA sheds light on the ancient origins of early Iron Age Philistines," *Science*, Vol. 5, Issue 7 (July 3, 2019). https://www.science.org/doi/10.1126/sciadv.aax0061.

Finkelstein, Israel and Neil Asher Silberman. *The Bible Unearthed: Archaeology's New Vision of Ancient Israel and the Origin of Its Sacred Texts*. New York: Simon and Schuster, 2002.

Finkelstein, Israel. "Jerusalem in the Persian Period (and Early Hellenistic Period and the Wall of Nehemiah." *Journal for the Study of the Old Testament*, Vol. 32, no. 4 (2008). https://israelfinkelstein.files.wordpress.com/2013/07/wall-of-nehemiah-jsot-2008.pdf.

Finkelstein, Israel. "The Territorial Extent and Demography of Yehud/Judea in the Persian and Early Hellenistic Periods." *Biblical Review*, Vol. 117, no. 1 (January 2010). https://israelfinkelstein.files.wordpress.com/2013/07/yehud-judea-rb.pdf.

Ginzberg, Louis. "Moses Meets the Messiah in Heaven." *The Legends of the Jews*, Vol. 3. Sacred Texts-Judaism. https://sacred-texts.com/jud/loj/loj309.htm.

Goodall, Helen S. and Ella Goodall Cooper. *Daily Lessons Received at Akka: January 1908*. Wilmette, IL: Bahá'í Publishing Trust, 1979.

Gowan, Donald E. *Eschatology in the Old Testament*. Edinburgh, UK: T&T Clark; 2nd edition, 2000.

Haber, Mark, et al. "Continuity and Admixture in the Last Five Millennia of Levantine History from Ancient Canaanite and Present-Day Lebanese Genome Sequences." *The American Journal of Human Genetics*, Vol. 101, Issue 2, (August 3, 2017): 274-82. https://www.cell.com/ajhg/fulltext/S0002-9297(17)30276-8.

Heschel, Abraham J. *The Prophets*. New York: Harper Collins Publishers; Harper Perennial Modern Classics; 1st Perennial classics edition, 2001.

IPCC, 2021. Intergovernmental Panel on Climate Change. "Climate change widespread, rapid, and intensifying." IPCC (Aug. 9, 2021). https://www.ipcc.ch/2021/08/09/ar6-wg1-20210809-pr/.

IPCC, 2023: Intergovernmental Panel on Climate Change. Summary for Policymakers. In: *Climate Change 2023: Synthesis Report*. Contribution of Working Groups I, II and III to the Sixth Assessment Report of the Intergovernmental Panel on Climate Change [Core Writing Team, H. Lee and J. Romero (eds.)]. IPCC, Geneva, Switzerland, pp. 1-34. https://www.ipcc.ch/report/ar6/syr/downloads/report/IPCC_AR6_SYR_LongerReport.pdf, DOI: 10.59327/IPCC/AR6-9789291691647.

Jewish Virtual Library. "Ancient Jewish History: The Birth and Evolution of Judaism, No. 2." https://www.jewishvirtuallibrary.org/the-birth-and-evolution-of-judaism#2.

Kourosh, Sohrab. *Self Study Notes for the Kitáb-i-Íqán: The Book of Certitude*, Vol 1. Southlake, TX: Koroush Publishing, 2021.

Kugel, James L. *The Great Shift: Encountering God in Biblical Times*. Boston and New York: Mariner Books, Houghton Mifflin Harcourt, 2017.

Laden, Jonathan. "Jews and Arabs Descended from Canaanites: DNA analysis, from bodies found at several sites, explains more than half of ancestry." *Biblical Archaeology Review*, Biblical Archaeological Society (Nov. 24, 2022). https://www.biblicalarchaeology.org/daily/ancient-cultures/ancient-near-eastern-world/jews-and-arabs-descended-from-canaanites/.

LeBoutillier, Paul. "Ezekiel 38-39." *YouTube* video. https://www.youtube.com/watch?v=jYFWbkzn7Nw.

Lee, Hoesung ed. "Summary for Policy Makers in 'Climate Change 2023: Synthesis Report,'" Intergovernmental Panel on Climate Change IPCC. https://www.ipcc.ch/report/ar6/syr/downloads/report/IPCC_AR6_SYR_SPM.pdf, DOI: 10.59327/IPCC/AR6-9789291691647.

Leith, Mary Joan Winn. "Israel Among the Nations." *The Oxford History of the Biblical World*, Michael G. Coogan, ed. New York: Oxford University Press, 1998.

Maddocks, Eileen. *1844: Convergence in Prophecy for Judaism, Christianity, Islam, and the Bahá'í Faith*. Burlington, VT: Jewel Press, 2018.

Maddocks, Eileen. *The Coming of the Glory: How the Hebrew Scriptures Reveal the Plan of God, Volume I. Göbekli Tepe to Elijah*. Brooklyn, WI: Something or Other Publishing, 2020.

Maddocks, Eileen. *The Coming of the Glory: How the Hebrew Scriptures Reveal the Plan of God, Volume II, The Preexilic Years: Amos to Jeremiah*. Brooklyn, WI: Something or Other Publishing, 2022.

Marsella, Maria Elena. *The Quest for Eden*. New York: Philosophical Library, 1966.

Mason, Rex. "The Book of Zechariah." *The Oxford Companion to the Bible*, Bruce M. Metzger and Michael D. Coogan, eds. New York: Oxford University Press, 1993.

Matthews, Gary L. *He Cometh with the Clouds*. Oxford, UK: George Ronald Publisher, 2000.

Matthews, Victor H. *The Hebrew Prophets and Their Social World: An Introduction*. Grand Rapids, MI: Baker Academic, 2nd ed., 2012.

McFall, Leslie. "Has the Chronology of the Hebrew Kings Been Settled?" *Themelios*, vol. 17:1 (Oct. 1991): 6-11. https://www.thegospelcoalition.org/themelios/article/has-the-chronology-of-the-hebrew-kings-been-finally-settled/.

Madain Project: Encyclopedia of Abrahamic History & Archaeology, 2017. "Tel Dan Stele." https://madainproject.com/tel_dan_stele#overview.

Meadows, Donella H., Dennis L. Meadows, Jørgen Randers, William W. Behrens. *The Limits to Growth: A Report for the Club of Rome's Project on the Predicament of Mankind*. Washington, D.C.: Potomac Associates Books, 1971; New York: Universe Books, 1972.

Mírzá Abu'l Faḍl. "In Praise of The Greatest Branch." *Star of the West*, vol. 3, issue 14. November 23, 1912. https://bahai.works/Star_of_the_West/Volume_3/Issue_14.

Mone, Gregory. "Researcher Pinpoints Cause of King Herod's Death," *Scientific American*, Vol. 286, Issue 1 (Jan. 28, 2002). https://www.scientificamerican.com/article/researcher-pinpoints-caus/.

Motlagh, Hushidar. *The Lord of Lords*. Mt. Pleasant, MI: Global Perspective, 2000.

Nabil-i-Azám. *The Dawn-breakers: Nabíl's Narrative of the Early Days of the Bahá'í Revelation*, trans. Shoghi Effendi. Wilmette, IL: Bahá'í Publishing Trust, 1932.

Penchansky, David. *Twilight of the Gods: Polytheism in the Hebrew Bible*. Louisville, KY: Westminster John Knox Press, 2005.

Pope, Alexander. "An Essay on Man: Epistle 1." England: Alexander Pope, 1733.

Redmount, Carol A. "Bitter Lives: Israel In and Out of Egypt." *The Oxford History of the Biblical World*, ed. Michael D. Coogan. Oxford, UK: Oxford University Press, 1998.

Riggs, Robert. "I Daniel." Bahá'í Library Online (1998). https://bahai-library.com/riggs_i_Daniel.

Riggs, Robert. *The Apocalypse: An Exegesis*. 1998-12. https://bahai-library.org/riggs_apocalypse_exegesis.

Rollston, J Christopher, et al. "The Jerubba'al Inscription from Khirbet Al-Ra'i: A Proto-Canaanite (Early Alphabetic) Inscription." *Jerusalem Journal of Archaeology*, vol. 2 (2021-2022): 1-15. https://jjar.huji.ac.il/sites/default/files/jjar/files/rollston_et_al._2021_jjar_2_1-15.pdf.

Schniedewind, William M. *How the Bible Became a Book: The Textualization of Ancient Israel*. Cambridge, UK: Cambridge University Press, 2004.

Sears, William. *Thief in the Night: The Case of the Missing Millennium*. Oxford, UK: George Ronald Publisher, 1961.

Sours, Michael. *Without Syllable or Sound: The World's Sacred Scriptures in the Bahá'í Faith*. Los Angeles: Kalimat Press, 2000.

Spar, Ira. "The Gods and Goddesses of Canaan." The Metropolitan Museum of Art: Heilbrunn Timeline of Art History, (April 2009). https://www.metmuseum. org/toah/hd/cana/hd_cana.htm.

Stager, Lawrence E. "Forging an Identity: The Emergence of Ancient Israel," *The Oxford History of the Biblical World*, Michael G. Coogan, ed. New York: Oxford University Press, 1998.

Star of the West. Chicago, IL: Bahá'í Publishing Trust, 1910-1935. https://bahai-library. com/star_of_the_west.

Tai-Seale, Thomas. *Thy Kingdom Come: A Biblical Introduction to the Bahá'í Faith*. Los Angeles, CA: Kalamát Press, 1991.

The Fundamentals: A Testimony to the Truth. Testimony Publishing Company of Chicago. (1910-1915). Bible Institute of Los Angeles (1927). Reprinted Baker Books (2003).

Theopedia: An Encyclopedia of Biblical Christianity. "Biblical Criticism." https:// www.theopedia.com/biblical-criticism.

Thigpen, Paul and Marcus Grodi. "The Rapture Trap: A Catholic View." *The Rapture Trap: A Catholic Response to 'End Times' Fever*. West Chester, PA: Ascension Press, rev. ed., 2001. https://www.beliefnet.com/faiths/catholic/2001/08/the-rapture-trap-a-catholic-view.aspx.

Torrey, R. A. and A. C. Dixon, eds. *The Fundamentals: A Testimony to the Truth*. Chicago, IL: Testimony Publishing Company, 1910-1915; Los Angeles: Bible Institute of Los Angeles, 1971; Peabody, MA: Baker Books, 2003.

United Nations. UN News. "UN climate report: It's 'now or never' to limit global warming to 1.5 degrees." (April 4, 2022). https://news.un.org/en/story/2022/04/1115452, https://www.ipcc.ch/report/sixth-assessment-report-cycle/.

Yerushalmi, Shalom. "Israeli official: Turkey agrees to return ancient Hebrew inscription to Jerusalem." *The Times of Israel*, March 11, 2022.

Williams, Jay C. *Understanding the Old Testament*. Hauppauge, NY: B.E.S. Publishing, 1972.

Wolfe, Thomas. *You Can't Go Home Again*. New York and London: Harper & Row, 1940.

World Health Organization. "WHO Coronavirus (C-19) Dashboard." https:// covid19.who.int/.

ACKNOWLEDGMENTS

I t's been a long journey and many people have shared segments of the road with me. Where to begin?

Wade Fransson, the owner of Something or Other Publishing (SOOP), in his words "a scrappy little company," stayed the course with this trilogy. It's been a long haul for both of us. When the goal posts get moved on him, Wade seeks new ways to network and share his vision. Publishing is a tough business in a time when only half of American adults read at least one book per year. Wade's diverse background includes writing, international public speaking, executive roles with various corporations, and three technology startups. He currently lives in Brooklyn, Wisconsin, with his wife, two children, and a growing menagerie of pets.

No book will realize its potential without a competent, dedicated editor. That's Beth Rule in SOOP's Editorial Services. She went far beyond making sure that the proverbial "t's" were crossed and the "i's" dotted. Every word of the manuscript got her scrutiny above and beyond the mandate for an editor. Beth is a lifetime student of the Bible, and her service in Christian youth work spans three decades. She holds an MBA and is English/German bilingual with additional studies in Russian, French and Spanish. Her professional experience includes work for a Christian nonprofit publishing firm, private clients, and both Fortune 500 and mid-market industrial service companies, with over 26 years in the international arena.

Maybe a book can't be judged by its cover, but Dragan Bilic, a graphic designer, made my trilogy's cover designs enticing to book browsers.

Finally, a good book won't go far without excellent promotion and marketing. Jesús Bracho, SOOP's Director of Marketing, not only checked all the boxes for prepublication marketing and postpublication publicity, but approached the job with creativity and enthusiasm.

Writing is a lonely endeavor sometimes made joyous by firm team support.

ABOUT THE AUTHOR

Not much in my life had pointed to becoming a writer. I grew up in rural Maine where I climbed trees, made little shelters from ferns, picked berries, rode my bike on country roads, and swam in ponds. At age 16, the family moved to Kansas where I finished high school. During my first semester at the University of Kansas, I marveled at the huge world that was opening up to me. My major was history because I wanted to know what had been happening in that world, and my favorite activity was the weekly current events forum that introduced me to geopolitics.

My world got much smaller when I found myself raising two children by myself and eking out a living as best I could. The 1970s were not kind to single mothers. The need for the village to raise children and teenagers was not yet recognized. My outlet to a wider world was an international folk dance club. In time, I ended up in Connecticut after years spent in Iowa and Texas.

My inner self was a spiritual seeker and searcher. I had been raised in liberal Protestantism and went to various churches but found no solace or answers to my questions there. Many years were spent wandering in the New Age movement, investigating every shining, enticing object I encountered. That part of my journey was interesting but not fruitful.

Finally, at a low point in midlife, I discovered the Bahá'í Faith. I immediately recognized that it had the answers to my questions. I also knew that if I committed myself to this religion, my life would change dramatically. Oddly, after all the years of seeking, I suddenly felt vulnerable. But turning away from the truths I had just discovered was not an option. I committed to the Bahá'í Faith and never looked back. My spirit, mind, and life opened up beyond all expectations. The sixteen years I served at the Bahá'í World Centre in Haifa, Israel, assigned to positions that required research and writing, were a momentous experience.

When it was time to retire, I returned to my New England roots and settled in bucolic Vermont. I had no idea what I would do in retirement, but the *what* fell into place when a writing assignment was abruptly put into my consciousness. I had been wondering why no one had presented the Hebrew prophets and their prophecies in a chronological manner within the context of Israelite history. I wanted to learn about biblical prophecies from a Bahá'í perspective but got most aggravated by how commentaries on them were scattered throughout several books, given out of context or presented unrelated to the prophets' own lives and times. Why hadn't someone written a book that systematically and chronologically presented the prophecies of the Hebrew prophets within the framework of their times and Israelite history?

The directive to embark on such a project was strongly impressed upon my mind by a source I accepted to be from a realm higher than mine. So I started writing the trilogy *The Coming of the Glory: How the Hebrew Bible Reveals the Plan of God*. And persisted. Ignoring the directive I had been given was not an option. Everyone is, I believe, given assignments for his life on earth.

Nothing entrances me quite like a project to tackle, and I certainly had been given one. Despite spells of writer's block, procrastination, and self-doubt, I have enjoyed the rhythm of research and writing. The process was at times a lonely slog but at other times euphoric when new insights clicked in.

These ten years spent writing the trilogy have been precious. When I settle into research, pondering, and writing, I feel comfort and validation. Inspiration comes. Answers to questions come, usually and eventually. Gratitude comes. It's a blessed space that I will miss when my writing days are over.

Or will my writing days ever be over? My two rescue cats hope not. They greatly enjoy editing my work by walking over my keyboard. And their plaintive cries at mealtime—or what they think is mealtime—pull me out of my mental tunnel.

My self-identity is independent researcher and curious student. That leaves the door open to whatever may next come long.

I balance my intellectual life with a serious study of tap and ballet. The music soars. I move past my perceived physical limitations. With leaps and turns, I push past boundaries and do what I thought I never could. Dancing prepares me for writing.

www.ingramcontent.com/pod-product-compliance
Lightning Source LLC
Chambersburg PA
CBHW060248100426
42742CB00011B/1678